The
FIRST WORLD WAR
Galleries

The
FIRST
WORLD WAR
Galleries

PAUL CORNISH

Foreword by
HRH THE DUKE OF CAMBRIDGE

Introduction by
SIR HEW STRACHAN

Published by IWM, Lambeth Road, London SE1 6HZ
iwm.org.uk

ISBN 978-1-904897-83-5

A catalogue record for this book is available from
the British Library.

Printed by Graphicom SrL
Colour reproduction by DL Imaging

10 9 8 7 6 5 4 3 2 1

CONTENTS

Foreword by   6
HRH THE DUKE OF CAMBRIDGE

Introduction by
SIR HEW STRACHAN   8

Chapter One	HOPE AND GLORY	12
Chapter Two	SHOCK	26
Chapter Three	YOUR COUNTRY NEEDS YOU	44
Chapter Four	DEADLOCK	62
Chapter Five	WORLD WAR	78
Chapter Six	FEEDING THE FRONT	102
Chapter Seven	TOTAL WAR	118
Chapter Eight	AT ALL COSTS	140
Chapter Nine	LIFE AT THE FRONT	160
Chapter Ten	MACHINES AGAINST MEN	174
Chapter Eleven	BREAKING DOWN	192
Chapter Twelve	SEIZING VICTORY	212
Chapter Thirteen	WAR WITHOUT END	228

FURTHER READING   246

ACKNOWLEDGEMENTS   247

PICTURE CREDITS   248

INDEX   251

FOREWORD
HRH THE DUKE OF CAMBRIDGE

In 1920 my great-great-grandfather, King George V, opened the Imperial War Museum at its first home in the Crystal Palace. He spoke of the enormous – almost unthinkable – courage and sacrifices which millions of men and women had made in the First World War. And he spoke of how the museum reflected that 'common effort and common sacrifice' by recording 'faithfully and impartially the efforts of all ranks in the field and of all classes at home.' He described it as a place which 'speaks to the heart and to the imagination' and how he believed the museum would be an inspiration for future generations.

Nearly 100 years later, the strength of his words endures. The Imperial War Museum continues to connect us with those who have served our country in times of conflict and have secured the prosperity and freedoms we enjoy. I am therefore delighted to support IWM's First World War Centenary Programme and to help pass on my great-great grandfather's message.

This book, published to accompany the new First World War Galleries at IWM London, aims to explain why the First World War started; why it continued for so long; how it was won and lost; and what happened afterwards. It presents events as they appeared to unfold to people at the time. Every object, every photograph, every letter or diary entry, helps us to understand their reactions to the events going on around them, and the parts they played in shaping them. They also explain why these people – our recent relatives – continued to fight for what they believed was right, despite a cost in human life and suffering barely imaginable to us today.

The centenary of the war prompts us to reflect upon the nature of the catastrophe which enveloped Europe between 1914 and 1918. I hope that this book and the exhibition it accompanies will both put into context and bring to life the experiences of those who lived through it. We have a responsibility to ensure that their stories are not lost by the passing of time. We will remember them.

INTRODUCTION

The First World War was a turning point in world history. It claimed the lives of around 10 million service personnel and untold numbers of civilians across the globe, and had a huge impact on those who experienced it. It was the first real instance of what later generations would call total war, with whole nations pitted against each other as millions of men fought on land, at sea and in the air. Modern weaponry caused mass casualties and civilian populations suffered hardships and came under threat of enemy attack. The war broke the empires of Germany, Russia, Austria-Hungary and Turkey. It triggered the Russian Revolution and provided the bedrock for the Soviet Union. It forced a reluctant United States on to the world stage and revived the ideals of liberalism. On Europe's edge, it provided a temporary solution to the ambitions of the Balkan nations. Outside Europe it laid the seeds for the conflict in the Middle East. In short, the war shaped not just Europe, but the world in the twentieth century.

Most of these outcomes were in the balance until the war's end, and some remained so after it was over. In 1917 many in Britain and the empire were not optimistic. In February of that year, as the Germans declared unrestricted U-boat warfare and Russia stood on the brink of revolution, the Imperial War Museum was born.

The purpose of the museum was not only to commemorate but to collect, to sift through the products, debris and memorabilia of the war, and to do so in a way that reflected not just the roles of the armed forces but the efforts of the entire nation. By 1920, when the museum opened for the first time at the Crystal Palace, the war had been won, but it was still hard to encompass the conflict as a whole. So great was its enormity that all who had fought in it struggled to give it shape and context. The exhibits were less about telling a story that still lacked a clear narrative, and more about evoking a set of experiences that in their entirety were common to all.

Some aspects of the First World War still resonate today. Soldiers severely wounded in Iraq and Afghanistan have survived thanks not only to the most up-to-date surgical techniques but also to procedures pioneered and developed in 1914–1918. The legitimacy of the war was debated then, just as we argue about war's necessity now. But other themes have lost their purchase. Britain went to war in 1914 as the head of an empire which it has now lost. Many of those men who put on uniforms did not have the vote; nor did any of the women who worked in munitions factories or who joined the newly-established female branches of the armed forces. In 1914, Britain alone of the major belligerents had an effective system of income tax, but only about 1.2 million were assessed for it. By the war's end all men in Britain aged over 21 had the right to vote, and all women aged over 30. Those who set up the Imperial War Museum had to recognise that the empire in its title, although in 1919 greater in geographical extent than it had ever been, was no longer an effective model for international organisation; instead the League of Nations and the United States' role within it promised a different form of English-speaking dominance. That particular ambition would not be fully realised until after 1945.

This book provides the narrative which those who visited the museum in the 1920s felt that either they did not need, or they could not grasp. Today our distance from the First World War enables the museum both to give the war a shape and to put it into fresh perspective. In the twenty-first century the museum must spell out themes that were then so self-evident that they did not need expressing, and highlight events that have assumed greater importance in the light of subsequent developments. Above all, the book reflects the ambitions of IWM's splendid new galleries, opened to mark the centenary of the war's outbreak in 1914. They tell the story of the war in chronological fashion. They do so by putting the experience of the British Empire in a global context, and by simultaneously relating the events at the front to the experiences of those at home.

Above: This poster advertises the opening of the Imperial War Museum at the Crystal Palace in June 1920. The museum broke new ground with its innovative collecting policy and its mission of recording the war efforts of ordinary people.

The galleries tell you more than you can absorb and retain in the course of a single visit. This book enables you to recall what you have seen, to understand it better, and to return for a fresh visit with a clearer sense of significant themes. For those unable to make that visit it stands as a history in its own right. It is powerful testimony to the ways in which the museum has so fully met the ambitions of its founders. Illustrated with objects from the IWM collections which fill the new galleries – from artillery pieces to intensely personal items such as diaries and letters, from photographs to works of art – it serves as a compelling, vibrant and emotive narrative of the war which was the founding event of our modern world.

SIR HEW STRACHAN

Chapter One

HOPE AND GLORY

'We are on the eve of horrible things'

Anyone who had suggested, in mid-July 1914, that a world war might be about to break out, would have been met with disbelief. This was particularly the case in Britain, which had not fought a war in Europe since the final defeat of Napoleon on the battlefield of Waterloo ninety-nine years earlier. Rather than any imminent European conflict, the attention of British people was focused on political and industrial strife on their own doorstep, which many feared threatened the whole fabric of their society.

In 1900 Europe dominated the world. In turn the Continent was dominated by a small group of rival 'Great Powers'. The United States of America, although an economic powerhouse, was a distant and uncommitted player on the world stage. The British Empire and the Russian Empire were Great Powers of long-standing. France had been the principal force in Europe from the seventeenth to the nineteenth centuries. The Austro-Hungarian Empire stretched from the Alps to Western Ukraine. Since 1867 its many ethnic groups had been the subjects of two governments – Austrian and Hungarian – united only by their allegiance to the Hapsburg dynasty, in the person of the Emperor Franz Josef. Italy was a relatively new addition; it had become a united country in 1861 but was too weak to threaten the existing balance of power. The same could not be said of the youngest Great Power, Germany. This was a new nation, born in battle. In 1871 the defeat of France by the most powerful German state, Prussia, had culminated in the creation of a united Germany, with the King of Prussia taking the title of Kaiser. Imperial Germany soon began to outstrip its rivals in industrial output and military strength. From 1888 a new element of instability appeared, when the unpredictable Wilhelm II became Kaiser.

Above: Kaiser Wilhelm II of Germany was a grandson of Queen Victoria. Intelligent and open-minded in many ways, he was also restless and insecure. He habitually wore military uniform in public. This reflected Germany itself, where the Army enjoyed huge power and prestige.

The monarchs of Europe were linked by family ties. Tsar Nicholas II of Russia was the Kaiser's cousin, and this **greatcoat worn by the Kaiser** is that of an officer of a Russian cavalry regiment, the 13th Narvski Hussars. The Kaiser had been made Colonel-in-Chief of this regiment.

The British Empire

In terms of its home territory, Britain was the smallest of the European powers, but this island nation ruled the greatest empire the world had ever known. Its possessions included Canada, Australia, huge tracts of Africa, and, most importantly, the whole Indian subcontinent. Lord Curzon, Britain's Viceroy in India at the turn of the century, was of the opinion that 'as long as we rule India, we are the greatest power in the world, if we lose it we shall drop straight away to a third-rate power'.

Although it included great land-masses, Britain's empire was a maritime one, which had been founded on sea-trade. It was protected by the Royal Navy – the world's most powerful. The Navy policed the seaways upon which sailed Britain's huge merchant fleet. Over forty per cent of the world's merchant ships flew the British flag. The novelist Erskine Childers offered a neat summary of this situation in *The Riddle of the Sands*, written in 1903: 'We're a maritime nation – we've grown by the sea and live by it; if we lose command of it we starve. We're unique in that way, just as our huge Empire, only linked by the sea, is unique.' People at the time saw Britain and its empire as a single entity. Hundreds of thousands of British citizens emigrated every year to other parts of the empire. The inhabitants of the so-called 'White Dominions' of Australia, Canada and New Zealand, along with many South Africans saw themselves as British. Politically active Indians were more inclined to demand a greater role in governing and administering their country as part of the empire than to call for its independence.

Below: This model of HMS *Hercules* was made by her builders, Palmers of Jarrow. Launched in 1910, HMS *Hercules* was a 'Dreadnought' battleship. These ships were the ultimate weapon-systems of their day. They took their name from HMS *Dreadnought* which, when launched by Britain in 1906, had made all existing battleships obsolete.

Dreadnoughts combined specific features. They were heavily-armoured and powered by steam turbines. Earlier battleships had used less efficient reciprocating steam engines. Their firepower was concentrated in large long-range guns, which could fire fore and aft as well as in the traditional 'broadside'.

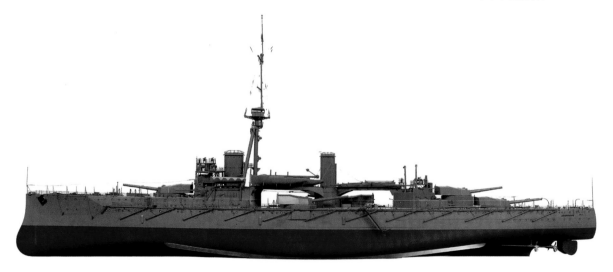

The 'mother country' at the heart of this empire was facing many challenges. Britain had been the first country to undergo an industrial revolution and had already become an urbanised society – only 8 per cent of the population made their living on the land by 1910. Britain was the richest nation on earth. Its cotton and coal industries prospered, and its domination of world trade continued unthreatened. The City of London was the world's leading finance centre; not least because of its control of maritime insurance. By the beginning of the twentieth century, however, Britain was being out-produced by both the USA and Germany. These commercial rivals were also outdoing Britain in the development of new industrial processes and technologies. The Chancellor of Germany noted in 1907 that despite this, Britain 'exudes wealth, comfort, content, and confidence in its own power and future. The people simply cannot believe that things could ever go really wrong, either at home or abroad'.

Above: This photograph of **children on a British city street** before the First World War offers an insight into the inequalities of British society at the time. Britain lagged behind its rival Germany in the field of social welfare. An attempt to address this situation had caused a serious political schism in the years prior to the war. The 1909 budget, which made provision for a national insurance system and old age pensions, caused a constitutional crisis when it was rejected by the House of Lords. Two years of political strife followed, before the Lords were forced to give up their right to vote down financial bills passed by the House of Commons.

To some extent this complacency was reflected in British society. People in the early twentieth century had very different attitudes to their modern descendants. Most were unquestioningly patriotic, and a majority took pride in Britain's imperial status. Organised religion played a major part in people's lives. Class distinctions and a strong sense of what was and what was not 'respectable', governed the way in which society operated. Deference to those regarded as socially superior was the norm. Behind this façade, however, lay the seeds of conflict. The country's wealth was concentrated in the hands of a minority. One per cent of the population owned seventy per cent of the country's wealth. A well-off middle class householder might expect an income up to one hundred times greater than the domestic servants he employed. Industrial strife was common, as trade unions used their growing power to fight for better pay and conditions for their members. In 1912 alone, 40 million working days were lost to strikes. But not all workers were able to improve their lot – over a million farm labourers and an even greater number of domestic servants worked long hours for poor wages, beyond the aid of the industry-based union movement.

Right: With her daughter Christabel, **Emmeline Pankhurst** founded the Women's Social and Political Union (WSPU), the most influential group dedicated to securing the vote for women. This photograph records the moment of her arrest outside Buckingham Palace in May 1914, as she attempted to present a petition to the King.

The coming of war brought a temporary halt to the militant campaign being fought by the suffragettes. Pankhurst pledged the WSPU's support for the war effort and called upon her supporters to be 'worthy of citizenship whether our claim to it be recognised or not.'

Left: Armed members of the **Ulster Volunteer Force** march through Belfast. In the summer of 1914 a civil war in Ireland appeared imminent. The crisis over Irish Home Rule had dominated British politics from 1912 to 1914. Protestants in the north of the country were determined not to accept the rule of the new Irish parliament planned for Dublin, and set up their own militia units. In January 1913 these were amalgamated to form the Ulster Volunteer Force.

Rifles were purchased on the international arms market and clandestinely imported into Ulster. In response, Nationalists now created their own armed force, the Irish Volunteers. But with the coming of war the introduction of Home Rule was postponed, and both sides in Ireland offered their support for the war.

Inequality of wealth was not the only problem threatening the stability of Britain. Only two thirds of men – and no women – were eligible to vote at elections. Supporters of the women's suffrage movement were becoming increasingly forceful in their demands for the right to vote. The issue divided society, especially when women began to take direct action in the form of acts of public protest and vandalism. Further discord was sown by the government's heavy-handed approach to women arrested for these activities – particularly the forced-feeding of some suffragette prisoners who went on hunger-strike.

Yet an even more alarming problem threatened the integrity of the United Kingdom itself. Many people in Ireland, ruled from London since 1801, sought self-rule. In 1912 the Liberal government had introduced an Irish Home Rule bill, aiming to grant Ireland its own parliament. This move was bitterly opposed by many politicians, and especially by the Protestant community in Northern Ireland. The latter saw themselves as British and insisted that they would resist the rule of an Irish parliament. Both sides in Ireland created armed militias to defend their causes. By 1914, as the Home Rule bill was finally passed, there seemed a very real threat of a civil war in Ireland.

The European Situation

The creation of the German Empire in 1871 had destroyed the existing balance of power. Germany tried to keep its bitterest rival, France, isolated, by signing treaties with Austria-Hungary, Italy and Russia. However in 1890 the treaty with Russia was allowed to lapse. Fear of Germany's large Army now stimulated an unlikely friendship between Europe's most democratic nation, France, and its political opposite Russia – ruled by an autocratic Tsar. Both agreed to come to the other's aid if either was attacked by a third power. Germany was the third power they had in mind.

Britain initially stood aloof from these Continental power-blocs. It had an active rivalry with its old enemy France over the acquisition of territory in Africa, and feared a Russian threat to India. By contrast, Germany offered no direct threat to British interests and was admired for its culture and civilisation; particularly its musical heritage. Many influential British families sent their sons to be educated in German universities.

Britain's small army was mainly dispersed around the empire and was not large enough to make a serious impact in a European war. However the country's wealth and the immensely powerful Royal Navy still made it a major player in European politics. France and Russia's fears of Germany encouraged them to establish better relations with Britain by ending their colonial disputes. In 1904 Britain and France signed an Entente. This was aimed at ending Anglo-French rivalry. A similar agreement was reached with Russia in 1907. Germany was alarmed to see Britain moving closer to France and Russia.

Yet Germany itself was responsible for a worsening of its relations with Britain. In 1898 it began building a battle-fleet. This building programme gathered pace due to the enthusiastic backing of Kaiser Wilhelm, who declared, 'our future is on the seas'. The Kaiser was well aware of the prestige of the Royal Navy and saw a large fleet as indispensable if Germany was to be able to act as a 'World Power'. British politicians and admirals believed that Britain's naval supremacy was under threat.

In 1906 Britain changed the game by launching a completely new type of warship, the battleship HMS *Dreadnought*. Fast, heavily-armoured, and with fearsome long-range guns, it made all existing battleships obsolete overnight. All major navies, and many minor ones, now sought to equip themselves with 'Dreadnoughts'. A naval construction race started between Britain and Germany. The British public enthusiastically supported spending on Dreadnoughts. Opinion was led by strident campaigns in many newspapers. In 1909 the *Daily Mail* thundered: 'For England, there is nothing between sea supremacy and ruin [. . .] Our sea supremacy is in peril'.

Left: In the early twentieth century Germany was renowned for its toy manufacture. This **tinplate clockwork battleship** was made by Bing of Nuremberg, the world's largest toy company. German toys of this type were exported all over the world, and this battleship was as likely to have been played with by a British child as a German one.

In this sense it is symbolic of the naval race between Britain and Germany which took place between 1906 and 1910; when each country strove to build as many Dreadnought battleships as it could afford.

Eventually the Kaiser – despite having once referred to himself as 'the Admiral of the Atlantic' – was forced to accept that Germany could not afford to compete with British shipbuilding in addition to keeping its huge army equipped. But the naval race, taken alongside the vainglorious posturing of Wilhelm II himself, did huge damage to relations between the two countries. British people began to view Germany as their most likely enemy. A rash of popular fiction – of which *The Riddle of the Sands* was an early example – appeared, in which Britain was threatened with German invasion. *Spies of the Kaiser* by William le Queux, published in 1909, ends with the words: 'What will happen? When will Germany strike? WHO KNOWS?'

Britain's new stance was made public in 1911 when Germany and France were in dispute about the latter's attempt to bring Morocco under its influence. David Lloyd George, the British Chancellor of the Exchequer, made a speech linking Britain's 'great power' status to its support for France, and as a result the Morocco crisis pushed Britain and France closer together. They reached agreement on naval co-operation and their military staffs began to discuss British military intervention if France was attacked. No formal alliance was made but, by 1914, Britain stood on the side of its former rivals, France and Russia.

The Coming of War

The rival European alliances did not make war inevitable, or even more likely. They were just as likely to act as a deterrent to military action. Diplomatic crises came and went, but even the apparently warlike Kaiser was reluctant to let them lead to war. In the end the event that sparked the war was not part of the Franco-German power struggle or the Anglo-German naval race, but an assassination in an obscure corner of south-eastern Europe.

On 28 June 1914 young Bosnian terrorist Gavrilo Princip murdered the heir to the Austro-Hungarian throne, Archduke Franz Ferdinand, as he made a visit to the town of Sarajevo. The Austrian authorities were quick to blame this outrage on Serbia. In one sense this was true, Princip and

Right: On 28 June 1914, **Archduke Franz Ferdinand** – heir to the throne of the Austro-Hungarian Empire – visited Sarajevo, the capital of Austrian-ruled Bosnia. Members of a nationalist group, Young Bosnia, planned to throw bombs into his open car. Only one of the plotters found the courage to make the attempt, which failed when his bomb bounced off the car.

The state visit continued but, later in the day, the Archduke's car stalled just beside one of the terrorists: nineteen-year-old Gavrilo Princip. He fired a pistol into the car, killing both Franz Ferdinand and his wife Sophie.

Austria-Hungary blamed the Serbian government for backing the assassins. Their weapons had in fact been provided by Serbian military intelligence chief Colonel Dragutin Dimitrijević. Princip – too young to be hanged – died of tuberculosis in prison in 1918.

Hope and Glory | 21

his fellow conspirators had been equipped by a Serbian nationalist secret society called Unification or Death or, more commonly, 'The Black Hand'; which had deep roots in the Serbian Army. Serbia had grown in strength due to its success in the Balkan Wars of 1912–1913 and was regarded as a threat by the Austro-Hungarians – they now seized this opportunity to crush it. Indeed they felt that the Hapsburg Empire would suffer a fatal loss of status if it failed to act strongly.

Serbia could expect to receive the backing of Russia, which saw itself as the protector of all the Slav peoples. Austria-Hungary therefore needed to ensure the support of its German ally before delivering an ultimatum to Serbia. The German leadership agreed to back Austria-Hungary, and encouraged it to adopt a harsh attitude. This was the crucial decision that led to war.

Germany naturally felt bound to support its closest ally, but it was not just motivated by self-defence. Many German policy-makers wanted to see Germany firmly established as a world power. They also believed that their nation, industrially and socially advanced, with a mighty army, was entitled to be the dominant force within Europe. They felt that these ambitions were threatened by France, Russia and Britain. Their world-view was also tinged with fear of 'encirclement' by these adversaries. The Sarajevo crisis appeared to offer an opportunity – their rivals could be forced into a damaging diplomatic climb-down. The alternative was war, yet many in the German armed forces and government saw war as inevitable in the long term. Concerned by Russia's ever-growing military strength, they were happy to risk its outbreak sooner rather than later. Germany's chief military strategist, General Helmuth von Moltke claimed that 'We shall never again strike as well as we do now, with France's and Russia's expansion of their armies incomplete.'

The demands of Austria-Hungary's ultimatum were deliberately made too severe for Serbia to accept in total. The ultimatum was merely a pretext for declaring war, which was done on 28 July after Serbia's failure to comply. Russia decided to stand by Serbia. Its ruler, Tsar Nicholas II, was willing to risk war because he feared that to back down would fatally weaken support for his rule among the Russian people. As recently as 1908, Russia had been duped by Austro-Hungarian diplomatic manoeuvring when Austria had taken possession of Bosnia. The Tsar was determined that there would be no repeat of this humiliation. He ordered his huge army to prepare for the possibility of war against Austria-Hungary. Germany, faced since the creation of the Franco-Russian alliance with a potential war on two fronts, had laid plans to concentrate its forces against France and knock it out of the war quickly. It would then turn on the slower-moving Russian Army. This plan forced it to take the initiative. Russia's preparations were the signal for Germany to mobilise its own army. This in turn prompted full Russian mobilisation.

France was obliged by treaty to support Russia, but there were also those in France who saw a war as an opportunity to avenge their country's defeat by German armies in 1871, and to regain the provinces of Alsace and Lorraine which Germany had taken from them. France would have had little choice but to enter the war anyway, because of Germany's plans to invade it. France too now mobilised its army. On 1 August Germany declared war on Russia. Two days later it declared war on France and its army marched west. Italy refused to join Germany and Austria-Hungary on the grounds that neither had been attacked. Now only the British remained on the sidelines.

A British proposal, made on 29 July, for an international conference to defuse the situation had fallen on deaf ears. Britain was not committed to support France or Russia but the government was desperate to avoid a German-dominated Continent. Such an outcome would threaten Britain's naval supremacy, its trade and, ultimately its empire. Even if Germany failed to win, Britain's status in the world would be ruined if it had been seen to stand aside. When Britain made its position clear, the German Foreign Ministry, with the Kaiser's support, requested British neutrality in exchange for a promise not to invade France or Belgium. This seemed more like a threat than an entreaty and infuriated the British government.

As the Cabinet agonised over what to do, news came that German forces had entered neutral Belgium en route to France. Both the government and the public were outraged. Britain and Germany were both bound by a treaty to maintain Belgium's neutrality. Beyond the moral issues involved, this was a matter of vital national interest. German control of the Belgian coast would be like a dagger aimed at the heart of Britain. The government decided that it must act strongly. An ultimatum was sent to Germany, threatening war if it did not withdraw from Belgium. This expired unanswered and, on 4 August 1914, Britain entered the First World War.

Above: French mobilisation poster. In late July 1914 posters like this went up all over Europe. Their purpose was to mobilise the reservists who comprised an important part of all armies. On the Continent compulsory military service was used to maintain huge armed forces, as military laws compelled young men to serve for two or three years.

Those who had finished their service were still liable to be recalled to serve in reserve formations until their mid-forties. It was these men who were the target of such posters. Their response exceeded the expectations of the generals, with very few failing to report for duty.

Some politicians, including some cabinet ministers and leading members of the fledgling Labour Party, opposed the declaration of war. Bankers in the City of London were horrified by the threat it posed to Britain's financial position. But most people accepted that the government had acted correctly. Soldier Captain James Jack reflected that: 'Apart from sentiments of honour, what would be our position eventually if the Prussian war-lords held the ports just across the English Channel, and we were friendless as well as despised for abandoning our present obligations?'

In towns and cities all over Europe people flocked to read official proclamations or to see the latest editions of newspapers, which were their only source of war news. Sometimes these gatherings developed into demonstrations of patriotic enthusiasm. But there was no universal war-fever. On the Continent military leaders were delighted by the full response to their mobilisation orders. Only a tiny percentage of reservists failed to report for service. But a patriotic sense of duty was more in evidence than extreme enthusiasm. This was especially true in rural areas – the main source of manpower for Continental Europe's armies – where the loss of men from the land was a bitter blow; especially as this was harvest time.

Excitement was also tempered with apprehension. Banks were temporarily closed to stop nervous investors withdrawing their money and causing a banking collapse. Some people even began to hoard food. But in all the warring nations, domestic political quarrels were set aside in this time of crisis. In Britain the trade unions and suffragettes proclaimed their intention to support the government. Even the bitterly opposed parties in Ireland offered their backing for the war, allowing Britain to enter the war in a state of patriotically-inspired national unity. Yet the uneasiness felt by many was expressed by the Prime Minister, Herbert Asquith, who confessed to a fear that 'we are on the eve of horrible things'.

Far left: This **German poster**, dating from the early days of the First World War, shows soldiers from Germany (pink) and Austria-Hungary (yellow) enjoying a successful 'hunt' of animals representing their enemies.

The English are represented by bulldogs, the French by cats and chickens, the Russians by bears and the Serbs by pigs. A monkey representing Japan (Britain's ally) lurks in the East. Belgium, in the form of a dead hare, is already in the hands of a German soldier. Meanwhile, the neutral nations look on with interest.

Chapter Two

SHOCK

'It is murder of troops by machines'

Seven million men marched to war in August 1914. More would follow as the armies completed mobilisation. By the end of the year a million of these men lay dead, millions more had been wounded. This terrible slaughter was never equalled at any other time in the war. It was the price paid for attempting to win swift and decisive victories with huge armies, on a battlefield dominated by new and deadly weapons.

The Central Powers, as Germany and Austria-Hungary were known, faced France, Russia and Britain; soon to become known as the Allied Powers. The armies of Continental Europe relied on conscription – compulsory military service. France, confronted since 1871 with the threat of the huge and populous German Empire, had become the most efficient at exploiting its pool of manpower. Russia's human resources were immense; although it could only field as many soldiers as its underdeveloped industries could equip. Germany's army was reputed to be Europe's most efficient, but would be stretched if it was to carry out its war plan to defeat France, then Russia. Its only ally, Austria-Hungary, was a potential weak link. Its armed forces were divided into three, with each half of the empire fielding an army, alongside a 'common army' recruited from all the Hapsburg territories. This army was also divided by language, with as many as twenty-seven tongues to be heard in its ranks. And military spending in Austria-Hungary had long been kept low.

As they boarded the trains which took them to the front, these armies bore little resemblance to our modern day image of First World War soldiers. They would have been more recognisable to Napoleon or Wellington. Colourful uniforms were still to be seen – especially in the French Army. The French infantry was famed for its red trousers, while exotic uniforms were still sported by many of the professional soldiers raised in France's North African colonies. Cavalry, with lances, crested helmets, and even breastplates were an integral part of every army. Officers carried swords; their men expected to win victory at the point of the bayonet. Few of them anticipated the true character of the war they were about to fight.

Above: This **doll** was one of a series of soldier-dolls sold during the war in France. It wears the uniform of a Zouave, one of a number of exotically-uniformed units originating in the French Empire in North Africa. There were four regiments of Zouaves in the French Army.

Despite their uniform they were not North African Muslims, but were recruited from French settlers in Algeria and Tunisia and even some men from France itself. Their distinctive baggy pantaloons were normally red, but in 1914 they stood out even more in white summer-issue trousers, until less obvious replacements could be issued.

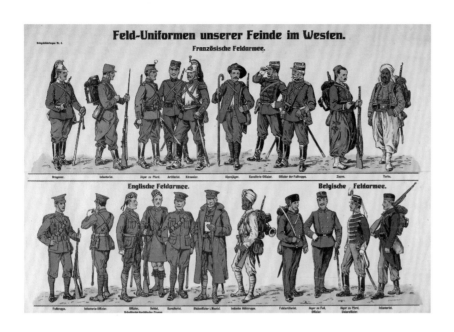

Left: These **posters** from 1914 offer a German view of 'Our Enemies in the West' – the French, British and Belgians, and 'Our Enemies in the East' – the Russians, Serbians and Montenegrins. The 'East' also includes the Far East, as the Japanese, Britain's allies since 1902, are shown. Germany's leaders had taken the gamble of winning a war on two fronts, but they portrayed it to their citizens as a defensive conflict against multiple enemies who were bent on denying Germany its status as a world power.

Deadly Technology

Since the late nineteenth century the nature of warfare had undergone a revolutionary change, due to the introduction of new weapons. The most deadly of these was quick-firing artillery. In 1897 the French introduced a new 75mm field gun, which made all existing guns of its type obsolete overnight. It used a new mechanism to absorb the recoil of the gun and return the barrel to firing position after every shot. Previously gunners had had to re-aim each time the gun was fired. Now they could fire fifteen or more aimed shots per minute. By 1914, all major armies had equipped themselves with quick-firing artillery.

The shells fired by these guns also became more effective. Advances in the manufacture of explosives and propellants had greatly increased their range, accuracy and power since the last major European war in 1870–1871. In 1914 armies relied chiefly upon the shrapnel shell. This contained hundreds of lead balls and was timed to burst in flight, over the heads of enemy troops. It then acted like a giant shotgun cartridge, showering them with its deadly contents.

The cartridges fired by machine guns and rifles had also become more powerful and accurate. New, smokeless, propellants increased the accuracy of small arms fire and enabled it to kill at ranges up to two miles. A new generation of bullets was capable of causing wounds so terrible that, in the early months of the war, they were frequently thought to have been caused by hollow-nosed 'dum dum' bullets, which had been outlawed by international agreement.

Military men were of course aware of these new dangers – but they had never seen them in use in a major European conflict. Their war plans and battlefield tactics were all based on achieving a decisive result by attacking. They hoped that if troops had high enough morale, and if battlefield movements were carried out quickly, they would be able to be able to win victory.

Above and left: When it was first shown to the world in 1897, the **French 75mm field gun** was a technological wonder. It could fire a shell with accuracy every four seconds. At this rate of fire, a battery of four French field guns could saturate an area of 100 x 400 metres with over 10,000 shrapnel balls per minute. **This particular gun** was used by 61st Field Artillery Regiment on the Marne and around Ypres. By 1914 all major armies had been equipped with similar guns.

Flawed Plans

The armies of Germany, Austria-Hungary, Russia and France were all determined to achieve a swift and victorious end to the war by seizing the initiative and attacking their enemies.

The Austro-Hungarian Commander-in-Chief, General Franz Conrad von Hötzendorf, had spent most of his career calling for war against Serbia. Yet he now faced an additional foe – the massive Russian Army. Austria-Hungary's reason for going to war was to crush Serbia, and Conrad was determined to invade it; but he also planned to take the war to the Russians on their own territory.

As part of its alliance with France, Russia had agreed to launch an early attack on Germany. Its military Commander, Grand Duke Nikolai, also intended to attack Austria's easternmost province of Galicia (now in Southern Poland and Western Ukraine). Many of Russia's predominantly peasant soldiers had been called reluctantly away from their harvests, but they faced battle stoically. As one of them wrote, 'I am ready to die for faith, Tsar and fatherland, and for our brothers of the same faith.'

The Germans had long anticipated fighting a war on two fronts. They concentrated their forces against France, hoping to defeat it before turning east to fight the Russian Army, which was slower to deploy. As Kaiser Wilhelm himself put it: 'In order to be able to march against Moscow, Paris must be taken first.' The main German striking force would attempt to outflank and encircle the bulk of the French Army by advancing through neutral Belgium. This plan has become known as the Schlieffen Plan, after the German Chief of Staff who first outlined it; although by 1914 it had been much adapted. The French Army could match German manpower in the West, and its leader Joseph Joffre had no intention of fighting a defensive battle. He planned to find the German's weakest spot and attack it. Many Frenchmen saw an opportunity to avenge their defeat by German forces in 1870. One infantryman, Vincent Martin, heard civilians shouting 'To Berlin – To Berlin! It can't last long!' Britain's decision to act upon its guarantee of Belgium's neutrality ensured that France would have the support of a small British Army.

Below: **Shrapnel shells** like this British 4.5-inch shell were the most widely-issued artillery munition in 1914. They were designed to kill troops moving in the open and could be devastatingly effective. They were time-fused to burst over the heads of the enemy. When this happened the nose of the shell was blown-off, and hundreds of lead shrapnel balls were projected at the men below.

As one British officer wrote, 'it means sure massacre to advance over open ground in face of a most deadly fire'. These shells were the chief reason that men began to seek the shelter of trenches – setting the pattern for much of the remainder of the war.

All of these plans proved far too ambitious. The initial deployment by rail had been meticulously planned; especially in Germany and France. In the former, 2,150 troop trains crossed a single bridge at Cologne between 2 and 8 August. During the same period in France, only 20 of 4,278 troop trains were late. But trains could not carry soldiers directly into action. Men were forced to make arduous marches both before and after facing their enemies. Seemingly endless columns of men filled the roads. An American journalist who witnessed the German advance through Belgium wrote of the 'smell of a half-million unbathed men [. . .] That smell lay for days over every town'.

These marches asked too much of men and horses, and of the supply systems which supported them. Furthermore, the generals found it difficult to control their armies with the limited communications technology available to them. This meant, for instance, that Germany's military chief Moltke, was forced to direct an army of 2.5 million men with a single long-range wireless transmitter. To make matters worse, all armies suffered from poor battlefield intelligence. Their cavalry was supposed to find the enemy and report back on his numbers, movements and positions. But constant riding exhausted its horses, and cavalry officers proved more interested in fighting than reconnaissance. Almost immediately aircraft began to replace the cavalry as the eyes of the battlefield. This was the birth of air warfare, but aeroplanes were few in number in 1914.

Above all, soldiers faced the terrible firepower of modern weapons. To advance across open ground was to invite slaughter. The situation was worsened by the fact that the armies had called up their reserves to fight in the forefront of battle. Officers believed that these men, who lacked up-to-date training, would be hard to control unless they fought in dense formations. Such clumps of men though only increased the already devastating effects of the firepower aimed at them. Medical services were overwhelmed with the quantity and nature of the wounds inflicted. As one German officer lamented: 'The merry, fresh war we were all looking forward to for years has turned out to be quite different from what we thought! It is murder of troops by machines.'

Below: All armies had cavalry units. Their role was to scout out the movement and disposition of hostile troops, force them to deploy by attacking them and, if all went well, to pursue defeated enemies.

They failed in this task. Cavalry officers of both sides were too eager to fight each other. Constant riding exhausted their horses. Their reconnaissance role was almost immediately usurped by a new technology, the aeroplane.

Of all the cavalry of 1914, the most colourful were the French Cuirassiers. Their uniform had scarcely changed in over 100 years. In addition to this **crested helmet**, they wore a cuirass or breast-plate. Both of these gleaming items were provided with drab cloth covers in 1914, but neither offered any protection against modern shells or bullets.

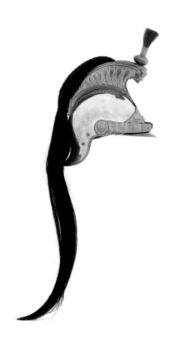

Inconclusive Results

Against all expectation, Serbia fought off Austro-Hungarian attempts to invade, despite temporarily losing its capital Belgrade. Its troops were even able to push into Austrian-ruled Bosnia. Still worse was to befall the Austro-Hungarian Army in Galicia. Its troops advanced into a much larger Russian force and were crushed. By the end of 1914 Austria-Hungary had suffered a devastating 957,000 casualties. Russian troops occupied most of Galicia, depriving Austria of vital oil wells and grain-fields.

In the West the German Army won a succession of victories against the French. Joffre launched his attacks in the wrong places, and suffered bloody defeats. But he refused to panic, continuing with a personal regime of ample sleep and plentiful meals. Meanwhile he mercilessly sacked commanders who had failed in battle. Using the railways to move troops, he concentrated his forces against the German armies which had advanced through Belgium and were threatening Paris. It was now do or die for the French. Joffre's order of the day for 6 September made this the literal truth: 'Soldiers who can advance no more must hold the conquered ground at all costs, or get killed where they stand.'

At the Battle of the Marne, French attacks persuaded the nervous German Commander, Moltke – over 150 miles away in Luxembourg – that his northernmost armies were overstretched and in danger. He ordered them to fall back. The Marne was the most decisive battle of 1914. France was saved and there would be no quick German victory. However, the Germans still occupied almost all of Belgium and the most productive industrial region of France.

Below left: This **pennon** was captured by British troops at the Battle of the Marne in September 1914.

Trophies of the German Army were much sought-after by British soldiers. One of them, James Dunn, recorded hunting for one in 1914:

'I dug myself a hole in a haystack where I kept quite dry. To me Williams remarked casually that he had seen a dead German grasping a lance on which was a pennon with a skull and cross-bones device. I dashed out to get this interesting souvenir, only to realise before I had gone ten yards that I had been sold, and Williams was sitting snuggly in my hole.'

The German leadership was well aware that the failure of the Schlieffen Plan was a disaster. Moltke himself suffered a mental breakdown. As his successor, Erich von Falkenhayn sardonically commented, 'Schlieffen's notes are at an end and therewith also Moltke's wits'. Meanwhile the German public were encouraged to look in a different direction – towards a great defensive victory which had been won against Russia. At the Battles of Tannenberg and the Masurian Lakes, the Germans had defeated an attempted Russian invasion of East Prussia. The victorious generals, Paul von Hindenburg and Erich Ludendorff, immediately became national heroes.

Above: General **Paul von Hindenburg** (front centre) poses for the camera. Behind his right shoulder is General **Erich Ludendorff**. Victories over the Russians made these men heroes in Germany. The stolid and reassuring Hindenburg soon began to rival the Kaiser as a patriotic figurehead. Ludendorff, ruthlessly ambitious but with a less-balanced personality, provided the brains of the partnership.

By the year's end the immense casualties had sapped the strength of the armies. The front lines began to stabilise. Soldiers had begun to seek shelter from artillery fire in trenches and dugouts. As winter set in, these took on an air of permanence. The war was undecided, and the terrible price paid in blood during 1914 meant that there could be no swift end to it. Few could now imagine peace without a victory to show for the sacrifices made. Yet the combatants had no strategies in place for fighting a prolonged war. They faced a costly learning process.

Above: Car flag flown at the Battle of Ypres by General Sir Douglas Haig. General Haig commanded 1 Corps, which bore the brunt of the German attacks at Ypres. Both the British and Germans were fighting at the limit of their endurance. At two crucial moments a German breakthrough was prevented at the last gasp by British counter-attacks. On each occasion Haig was aware that one more German push would have broken the British line. He carried this experience with him as he rose to high command; showing an unwillingness to break off offensives when he was convinced that the enemy was faltering.

The British Expeditionary Force

In August, a British Expeditionary Force (BEF) had been sent to fight alongside the French. Initially numbering just 100,000 men, it was only one twentieth of the size of the French Army. Small as it was, however, this force was the core of Britain's Army. As an island, Britain relied mainly upon its Navy. Unlike the Continental powers it did not raise mass armies by compulsory military service. Its army was a small, professional force. It was supported by the part-time volunteers of the Territorial Army and Yeomanry – intended for home service only.

The BEF was forced to follow the movements of the larger French Army, although its Commander, Sir John French, was under government orders not to put his army at risk of destruction. Deployed in Belgium, the BEF was soon forced into an anxious retreat; narrowly escaping disaster at the Battles of Mons and Le Cateau. By September it was exhausted and defeat had fostered ill-feeling between its commander and his French counterparts. But, after strong prompting from London, Sir John French got his men moving forward again at the Battle of the Marne.

In October the BEF was transported back to Belgium to meet a new German threat. Falkenhayn gambled on achieving a major victory in the West before winter arrived; driving newly-raised German forces at the Channel ports. British soldiers bore the brunt of desperate fighting around the town of Ypres. This was a battle fought in open fields and autumnal woods. The British regulars, now reinforced with reserves who had been recalled to the Army and by Territorial units which had volunteered for

Overleaf: Men of the 1st Battalion, Middlesex Regiment, come under shrapnel fire from German artillery on the Signy-Signets road during the Battle of the Marne on 8 September 1914.

overseas service, held off repeated German attempts to break through. Their enemies outnumbered them, but many of the Germans were elderly reservists or inexperienced young wartime volunteers, who mounted clumsy and costly attacks. Captain Harry Dillon of 2nd Oxfordshire and Buckinghamshire Light Infantry wrote home describing the defeat of one of these assaults:

> 'One saw the great mass of Germans quiver. In reality some fell, others fell over them, and others came on. I have never shot so much in such a short time [. . .] The firing died down and out of the darkness a great moan came. People with their arms and legs off trying to crawl away; others who could not move gasping out their last moments with the cold night wind biting into their broken bodies and the lurid red glare of a farm house showing up clumps of grey devils killed by the men on my left further down. A weird and awful scene.'

The British were just able to prevent a German breakthrough, but at a terrible cost. On 3 November Lieutenant Geoffrey Loyd of 2nd Scots Guards wrote: 'it is now only a very weak, a very sad and a very gallant little Army that holds the line'. Ten days later Loyd himself was killed in action.

1914 was a traumatic experience for British soldiers; even for regulars with experience of fighting in Britain's Empire. Surrenders accounted for a higher proportion of the Army's losses than at any other time during the war. Almost 90,000 men were killed, wounded or captured. Britain's pre-war Army was in tatters. The loss of experienced officers and non-commissioned officers – the Sergeant-Majors, Sergeants and Corporals – was particularly damaging. Only the arrival of an Indian Army expeditionary force – the first British Empire contingent to see action in Europe – enabled the BEF to hold the line as winter set in. If Britain was to keep fighting, it would need to raise and equip a new and bigger army.

Above: Jacket belonging to Company Sergeant-Major William Williams, 2nd Worcestershire Regiment. Williams suffered fatal wounds on 31 October 1914, when his unit made a counter-attack at Gheluvelt during the First Battle of Ypres. The counter-attack by the Worcesters was a crucial episode in the battle, preventing a German breakthrough. Williams is representative of the many irreplaceable experienced soldiers who were lost by the British Army during 1914.

Left: The German 42cm mortar. This huge weapon, the largest gun of its day, was nicknamed 'Big Bertha'. It was Germany's secret weapon in the invasion of Belgium. With it, they intended to smash the Belgian forts which blocked their advance. However, they had only four of these guns, and had to supplement them with 30.5cm mortars sent by Austria-Hungary. A Belgian witness described seeing 'Big Bertha' being fired at the Liège forts: 'The monster advanced in two parts, pulled by 36 horses. The pavement trembled [...] Then came the frightful explosion. The crowd was flung back, the earth shook like an earthquake and all the window panes in the vicinity were shattered.'

Original-Aufnahme vom Kriegsschauplatz.
Die durch ein einziges 42 cm Geschoss zerstörten Betondecken eines Panzerturmes des Forts Loncin

Kr. 86.
VERLAG VON
GUSTAV LIERSCH & C°
BERLIN, S.W.

Left: The wreckage of Fort Lonçin at Liège, caused by the explosion of a 42cm shell.

Left: Britain's **Indian Army** was the world's largest volunteer army. Throughout the war it provided a vital reservoir of manpower for Britain. At the outbreak of war the government of India despatched an Expeditionary Force to France. Arriving at Marseilles, it was transported to the front in Belgium in time for the First Battle of Ypres. This photograph shows Punjabi soldiers of 57th Wilde's Rifles in the line near the village of Messines. It was later realised that Indian troops were ill-suited to the harsh winters of France and Belgium, and most Indian units were withdrawn from the Western Front during 1915.

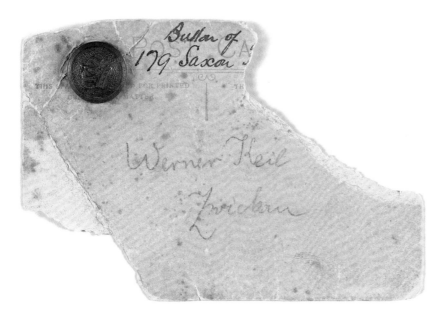

Left: This **German uniform button** was given to nineteen-year-old Corporal Eric Rowden of the Queen's Westminster Rifles on Christmas Day 1914 by a German soldier, Werner Keil. In his diary Rowden wrote: 'I went out and found a German who spoke English a little and we exchanged buttons and cigarettes and I had 2 or 3 cigars given me and we laughed and joked together, having forgotten war altogether.' This was just one episode in the Christmas Truce which occurred on sections of the Western Front in 1914. This extraordinary phenomenon was one of the last expressions of the old-fashioned, chivalrous warfare which many had expected.

Above: British and German troops during the famous Christmas Truce, Belgium, Christmas Day 1914

Civilians Begin to Suffer

Before the First World War, efforts had been made to agree internationally accepted laws on the conduct of war. One of the chief aims had been to protect civilians from unnecessary suffering. When war came however, civilians immediately became victims, just as they always had been in previous wars. This came as a terrible shock to people who had believed that Europe set an example of civilisation to the rest of the world.

In the East, terrified German and Austrian citizens fled the invading Russian armies. In Galicia the large Jewish population had good reason for doing so, as the Russian Army was notorious for its antisemitism. Those who failed to leave faced ill-treatment or deportation to the interior of Russia. When on Serbian territory, the Austro-Hungarian Army regarded all civilians as potential enemies. Horrible violence was meted out to many Serbian citizens. Reports of Russia's abuses of its Jewish population, or of massacres in the Balkans were nothing new to people in the rest of the world; but there was outrage when reports began to circulate of German atrocities in the West. During August and September 1914, German soldiers killed over 6,000 Belgian and French civilians. They also destroyed great cultural sites. The world-famous Louvain University library in Belgium, with its priceless collection of medieval manuscripts, was burnt to the ground, as the town was subjected to an orgy of destruction. In France, German shells left Rheims cathedral shattered.

German soldiers killed so many civilians because they had been primed by their leaders to be utterly ruthless with any civilian resistance, which their experiences in their 1870–1871 war with France had led them to expect.

There is no reliable evidence of any attack by Belgian civilians upon German forces, but many Belgians paid with their lives when nervous, and often drunken, German soldiers began to imagine such attacks in the confusion of their advance. But these were not random murders. They were intended to intimidate and German officers often directed them. One, who led an execution squad at Dinant where 674 people were massacred, recorded that:

'One woman clung to her husband and wanted to be shot together with him. I therefore decided to let her go free, together with her husband. One man had a child of about five in his arms, which was not his own [. . .] The child was taken from him and sent to the women. The man was shot with the rest.'

Above left: Civilian women pick their way over rubble and debris outside the ruined Hotel de Ville in Louvain, Belgium, September 1914

Above right: *After the Shelling, Louvain 1914*, by Grace Digby, 1914

As news of these atrocities spread, Belgians took to the road or to the sea. Almost 1.5 million Belgian refugees fled the country. Most crossed into France or the Netherlands, but 200,000 Belgian men, women and children sought sanctuary in Britain.

The world was appalled that Germany, a nation renowned for its culture, had ignored the international agreements intended to prevent such horrors – details of which became exaggerated in the telling. Britain and France could now reassure themselves that they were fighting to defend civilisation. This was how they began to portray their struggle to the rest of the world.

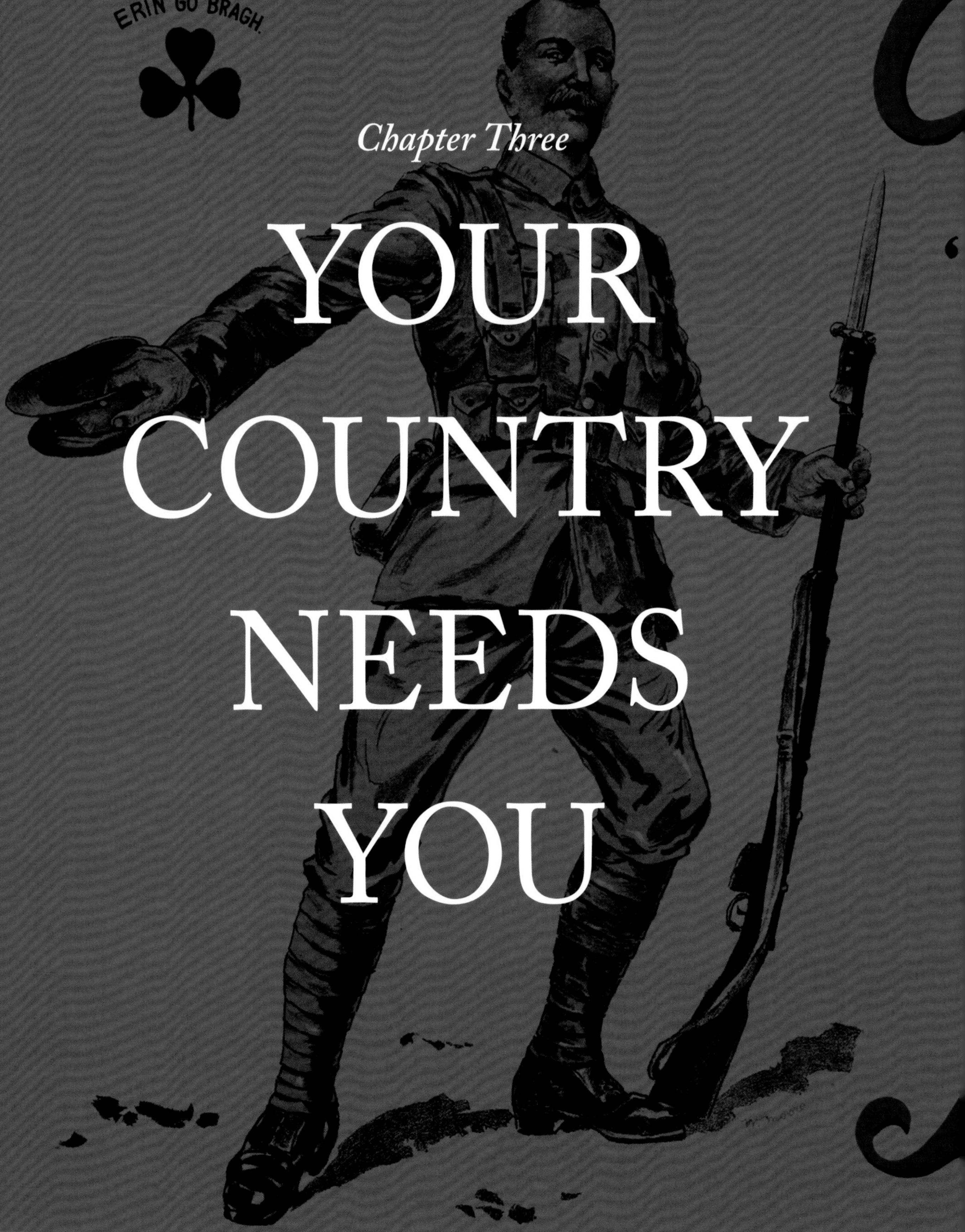

ERIN GO BRAGH.

Chapter Three

YOUR
COUNTRY
NEEDS
YOU

'Nothing would please me better than to die fighting for my country'

On Britain's first day at war, the Chancellor of the Exchequer David Lloyd George addressed businessmen, stating that the government would 'enable the traders of this country to carry on business as usual'. At this early stage many expected the war to follow the pattern of previous British participation in Continental wars. While small expeditionary forces might be sent to fight on land, Britain's strategy would be economic. A naval blockade of the enemy would be enforced while Britain loaned money and sold essential goods to its allies. Yet this turned out to be a very different type of war, in which the whole of society, and indeed the whole of the empire, would need to play a part.

At the outset the government took a radical step when it appointed as war minister one of Britain's foremost military heroes, Field Marshal the Earl Kitchener of Khartoum. Horatio Herbert Kitchener was in many ways a strange choice. He distrusted politicians and his vision of how the war must be fought could not have been more different from 'business as usual'. However the government grasped that a man of Kitchener's standing would provide a patriotic focus, simultaneously inspiring and reassuring, at a time of crisis.

Kitchener had made his reputation in Britain's wars in Sudan and South Africa around the turn of the century. By 1914 he was Britain's Consul-General in Egypt – effectively ruling Egypt and Sudan. He was paying a rare visit to Britain at the outbreak of war and on 5 August, at the request of Prime Minister Asquith, accepted the responsibility for directing Britain's war effort. On only his second day in office, he shocked his new cabinet colleagues by stating that 'we must be prepared to put armies of millions in the field, and to maintain them for several years'. Kitchener was not alone in fearing that the war would be a long one; although most people naturally hoped otherwise. However he was the first British leader to grasp that not only would victory take time, but that this war would require a far greater commitment of manpower and national wealth than any which had gone before.

Above: In First World War Britain, patriotic children might beg their parents to buy them this **doll in the image of Lord Kitchener**. Already a celebrity before the war, chiefly because of his victory in the Sudan in 1898, the popularity of 'Kitchener of Khartoum' reached new heights when he became war minister in 1914. He was worshipped as 'the great Englishman of the day' and 'the man the Kaiser fears'. The war office began to receive fan mail addressed to him, including marriage proposals. Kitchener's image adorned biscuit tins and teapots. His sculpted bust was even reproduced in soap.

Even before Britain's small Regular Army began to suffer its share of the terrible losses of 1914, Kitchener set about recruiting new soldiers. In fact he decided to create an entirely 'New Army'. He had reservations about the existing Territorial Army as a basis for this force – reportedly dismissing it as a 'town clerk's army' – regarding it more as an insurance against German invasion; something considered a real possibility at this stage of the war. Kitchener appealed for volunteers. By September this appeal was being reinforced by the image of 'K of K' himself on posters; his features invested with a steely gaze which he did not possess in real life, having a noticeable cast in one eye. Voluntary enlistment had got underway even before this initiative, and it continued at a healthy rate throughout the autumn, despite the evident dangers which British soldiers were facing at the front. By the year's end almost 2.5 million men had joined-up – the largest volunteer army ever raised by any nation.

Citizen Soldiers

Lord Kitchener's call was only one of many reasons for enlisting. For many men joining the Army was a solution to dire financial need. The uncertain economic situation at the outbreak of war had led to many workers being laid-off, and not only was a soldier paid, but his family received an allowance while he was on active service. Despite this, it is clear that most volunteers were moved by patriotic instincts and a sense of duty. They wanted to be seen to be 'doing their bit'. Twenty-two-year-old Bruce Seymour wrote to his father that 'nothing would please me better than to die fighting for my country [. . .] Do please say I can do this or I shall never respect myself again. It is worrying my conscience a very great deal.'

Outrage over Germany's actions in Belgium was an additional incentive. Private George Wakefield wrote that he had enlisted 'because, as an Englishman and a lover of freedom, I thought it was my duty at this time to give my services to the King and country for the reparation of Belgium and the defence of British policy'. German 'frightfulness' prompted churchmen to offer religious motives for enlistment. Sheffield Methodist minister the Reverend George McNeal preached of his hope that men would not merely 'fight for King and Country, but [. . .] for the principles of the religion of JESUS CHRIST, and to uphold the banner of His Cross.'

Below: There was a real fear that Germany might invade Britain in 1914. Many men who were ineligible to join the Army clamoured to be allowed to defend their homes. By November these men had been formed into Volunteer Training Corps (VTC). To their chagrin they were forbidden to wear khaki, and found that weapons were in short supply. Some had to carry **dummy rifles**. The VTC was regarded as a joke by some soldiers. The latter suggested that the royal 'G.R.' cipher on the red brassards worn by the VTC stood for 'Genuine Relics' or 'Government Rejects'.

Recruiting posters reinforced such sentiments with calls to 'Fall in' and 'Remember Belgium'. Others offered comradeship: 'Come along boys and join the Army – Our cheery lads need your help'. And posters were not the only influence. The resolve of some young men was surely stiffened by music hall artistes such as Minnie Elsie or Daphne de Marie, singing 'Be a soldier be a man', or 'Your King and Country need you more than I do'. However, none of these inducements would have created the rush to enlist had it not been for the adventurous instincts of their young, male audience. Many were desperate to get to the front with all possible haste, in case the war ended. For working class men the Army could offer a change from the daily grind of hard manual labour, and a chance to travel abroad – a thing entirely beyond their means in peacetime.

Similar rallying calls echoed across the empire. Men in the Dominions proved equally eager to join up. The prime minister of Australia pledged that his country would 'stand beside our own to help and defend Britain to the last man and the last shilling'. 332,000 Australians were to volunteer during the course of the war. Canada was to send 458,000. The high level of pre-war emigration meant that many of the soldiers from these two Dominions were British-born. New Zealand saw the most remarkable level of enlistment, with over half of the men eligible for service volunteering.

South Africa provided 136,000 white troops and 43,000 black South Africans. A reluctance to train black Africans to fight meant that the latter were used as a Labour Corps. But there was some dissent in South Africa, dating from Britain's crushing of the independent Boer Republics at the turn of the century. In October 1914 a rebellion by Boer hardliners had to be suppressed.

In India, a huge volunteer army existed even before the war, and the Indian government immediately began to send its best troops to fight for the empire. Further recruitment swelled the Indian Army to 1.5 million men as the war progressed.

STEP INTO YOUR PLACE

PUBLISHED BY THE PARLIAMENTARY RECRUITING COMMITTEE, LONDON — POSTER No 104   PRINTED BY DAVID ALLEN & SONS LD. HARROW, MIDDLESEX. W. 2844. 40 M. 9/15

AT THE FRONT!

Every fit Briton
should join our brave men
at the Front.

ENLIST NOW.

BRITAIN · NEEDS

YOU · AT · ONCE

THE VETERAN'S FAREWELL.

"Good Bye, my lad,
I only wish I were young enough
to go with you!"

ENLIST NOW!

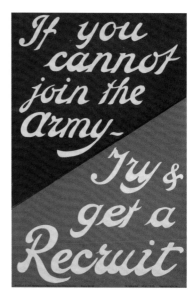

Above and left: A Parliamentary Recruiting Committee (PRC) was set up 'to give a powerful impetus to recruiting'. It sanctioned 160 different **poster** designs, of which 12.5 million copies were printed. Their messages make plain the main motivations which inspired those who enlisted – a sense of duty, a desire for comradeship and, for some, the prospect of adventure.

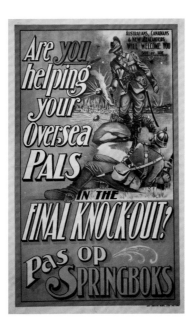

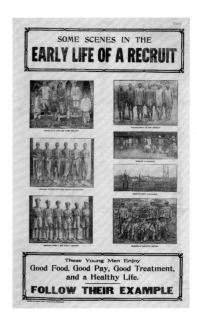

Above and left: The rush of volunteers for the Army was not limited to Britain. In the Dominions too, men answered the call. Even in South Africa, where many had been fighting against the British Empire only twelve years previously, men volunteered to fight for Britain's cause. The example set by their support for the mother country was used in Britain as yet another inducement to British men to enlist. India already possessed a huge volunteer army, but this began to expand when it was decided to send its best troops to fight overseas.

Kitchener's Army

After an initial stampede of recruits, enlistment continued through the autumn of 1914 at a steadier rate. Unfortunately Britain's military infrastructure was based on the needs of a much smaller army, and struggled to equip and train these new soldiers. Many of them found their enthusiasm dampened when they had to endure a cold winter crowded into tented camps or inadequate barracks. The resulting intermingling of different social classes provided an additional shock for many. Private Charles Jones, previously a solicitor's clerk, complained of nights in 'a small room covered with dirty lino on which we had to sleep packed like sardines and with one of the noisiest and [most] obscene collections of human beings it has ever been my misfortune to meet.'

As well as accommodation, suitable clothing and equipment were also lacking. Even rifles were in short supply. Many New Army volunteers had to begin their training with elderly or even dummy weapons. The excitement of joining up was followed by the drudgery of training, and few would see the front before the following summer. In the interim, Britain's small sector of the Western Front was held by the reinforced remains of the Regular Army and Territorials who had volunteered for overseas service.

To maintain the initial enthusiasm, special units were created to allow men to join up with their friends. Cities, towns, professions, businesses and sportsmen set up their own 'Pals' battalions. Men with particular skills such as engineering and driving could join specialist units. Units were even formed of 'Bantams' – men who did not meet the standard Army height requirement of five feet three inches (1.6m). In a country defined by class, only men from the upper and middle classes – in essence, those who had attended one of Britain's elite public schools – were appointed officers. In the rush to join the Army, a number of such men enlisted in the ranks, before subsequently applying for an officer's commission. Most of the new intake of men lacked any military experience. Re-enlisting former soldiers and the dwindling supply of regular officers and non-commissioned officers were heavily relied upon to train the New Army.

Above: A particular disappointment to many men who enlisted in 1914 was the lack of proper uniform to wear. They wanted to be 'in khaki' like the men at the front, but were forced to make do with old uniforms dredged out of store, or even their own clothes. Soon an emergency uniform of dark blue cloth was introduced; inevitably becoming known as 'Kitchener blues'. This pattern of jacket was worn with what one recruit described as 'a saucy little forage-cap, rather like a slice of melon in shape'.

Above: A group of **'Leeds Pals'** photographed at their training camp in the Yorkshire Dales shortly after enlisting on the outbreak of the First World War

Above: **Local unit badges.** Towns and cities all over Britain strove to outdo each other in raising men for the Army. The chance to fight alongside ones friends was a powerful inducement to enlist.

Local aristocrats, Members of Parliament, Industrialists and commercial and social associations also sponsored individual battalions. Many of these men got to wear badges which proclaimed their local identity. Some of the richer sponsors even paid for special badges for the first 1,000 men to enlist. Units raised in this way became known as 'Pals' battalions.

Top row from left: Collar badge issued to the first 1,000 recruits to the 16th Welsh Regiment, raised by the Lord Mayor and the Corporation of Cardiff;

Lapel badge worn on civilian clothing prior to the issue of uniform by volunteers of the 16th Prince of Wales's Own (West Yorkshire Regiment);

Badge of the 14th Royal Irish Rifles; largely formed from members of a Belfast Unionist militia, the Young Citizens' Volunteers of Ireland

Badge of the 13th East Surrey Regiment; raised by the Mayor and Borough of Wandsworth

Bottom row from left: Badge of the 28th London Regiment. Known as the "Artists' Rifles", this Territorial Army unit drew its soldiers from London's artistic community;

Badge of 17th The King's (Liverpool Regiment). Also known as the Liverpool Pals, this was the first 'Pals' Battalion to be formed;

Badge of the 15th Prince of Wales Own (West Yorkshire Regiment). Also known as the Leeds Pals.

Women & War.

How to Knit and Crochet Articles necessary to the Health and Comfort of our Soldiers and Sailors.

CONTENTS.

Knitted Balaclava
             Helmet.
Crochet Balaclava
             Helmet.
Abdominal or
           Cholera Belt.
Bedsock without Heel.
Knitted Sock.
Knitted Muffler.
Bed Sock.
Knee Cap.
Soldier's Mitten.

Price

1 D.

POSTAGE
ONE HALFPENNY.

"To women, work of pleasure,"
"Yet earning countless treasure"
"Of gratitude, forever,"
"From 'The Absent-Minded Beggar.'"

Published by
NEEDLECRAFT, LTD.
Manchester and London.

Left: This **penny leaflet** contains patterns for a variety of soldiers' comforts which could be knitted at home. Knitting for the troops became a mania. John Paterson from Cupar in Fife wrote that 'no woman dares to appear in the evening without a sock in her hand'. Even the Sabbath became a day for knitting. 'Every one knits on Sundays now, even the parson's wife', Essex vicar Andrew Clark observed wryly in December 1914.

Voluntary Efforts

The majority of citizens were denied the chance to join the armed forces by reason of their age, physical fitness or sex. Many of them still wanted to do what they could for the war effort. In Tunbridge Wells, Lady Annette Matthews was of the opinion that 'everyone has a purpose to help to the utmost of their powers.' She herself worked in a soldier's canteen and participated in a Red Cross scheme knitting clothing for wounded men.

Knitting was an extraordinarily popular mode of voluntary support for the war effort. It was something which women of all classes and incomes could do. Recommended patterns of socks, balaclavas and other woollen comforters were published in women's journals and by wool companies. In a throwback to the Crimean War, some knitted 'cholera belts', which had once been believed to ward off that disease by keeping the midriff warm. These appear to have been the least welcome knitted comfort among soldiers. Army Doctor Frederick Chandler wrote home 'Tell everybody you can not to make belly bands: there are far too many of them now, they are useless and they are a byword and joke! Helmets, scarves, mittens, socks and vests are invaluable.'

If home knitting represented one extreme of the comforts sent to troops, the other was exemplified by the Christmas 1914 Gift Box provided by a fund promoted by the seventeen-year-old daughter of the King and Queen, the Princess Mary. Intended as a gift for every person in the King's uniform at Christmas 1914, the magnitude of the task of production and distribution meant that these small brass boxes were still being handed out in 1916. The standard gift comprised a pipe, an ounce of tobacco, a packet of cigarettes, a tinder lighter and a Christmas card and photograph from Her Royal Highness. Different contents were assembled for the minority of men who were non-smokers, female nurses – who were presumed to be non-smokers – and for Indian troops; the latter varying according to their religion and customs.

Despite an increase in taxation to help pay for the war, people still put money into collecting boxes and bought pins and stamps for a host of war charities. These raised money for all kinds of causes: refugees, prisoners of war, wounded soldiers, wounded animals, or even the purchase of cigarettes for servicemen. The sums raised were phenomenal. Just one appeal, run by *The Times* newspaper, raised £1.65million in the first year of the war. There was no official registration of charities until 1916. Fraud

was therefore a danger, although duplication of effort was a more common failing. For example, 69 different charities all aimed at providing relief for Belgians were listed in 1916. In an effort to set an example of patriotic self-restraint, King George V himself pledged to give up alcohol for the duration of the war (although still taking a little for 'medicinal' reasons). Government ministers made the same promise, but proved even less able to keep it than their monarch.

The impulse to make sacrifices was not just felt in royal circles. Many civilians wanted to make working for the war effort their full time job. Joining a recognised voluntary organisation was the simplest way of achieving this. The British Red Cross and the St John Ambulance joined together to recruit volunteers to tend the wounded and to staff hospitals and convalescent centres. The Young Men's Christian Association (YMCA) provided food, drinks, and entertainments for resting soldiers behind the front lines. By this route, men too old or unfit for Army service could still get to the fighting fronts to 'do their bit'.

Above: This **tin of sweets** bears the message 'To Our Fighting Heroes with Best Wishes from British Grocer's Federation Xmas 1914'. Similar gifts were sent by commercial and patriotic associations all over the empire. Wealthy individuals also made gifts of cigarettes and other comforts.

Beyond the Call of Duty

For women, such direct involvement was more difficult to achieve. Expectations of how women could contribute were initially limited and unimaginative. This did not prevent some enterprising women from ignoring official disapproval and getting themselves to the war fronts. One of the most redoubtable was Dr Elsie Inglis, a supporter of women's suffrage who, most unusually for a woman of her generation, had studied medicine and qualified as a doctor. When war came she offered to organise female medical teams for the Army but was rebuffed by an official with the words 'My good lady, go home and sit still'. Undaunted, she secured funding from supporters of women's suffrage and set up the Scottish Women's Hospitals (SWH). Over the course of the war SWH units operated in France, Malta, Romania, Russia, Salonika and Serbia. In 1915 Inglis and some of her staff were captured by the enemy while working at the Serbian hospital. They were later repatriated and continued their work.

Another British woman was to make a dramatic sacrifice which galvanised public support for the war in late 1915. Edith Cavell was a leading figure in the nursing profession in Belgium. When the Germans occupied the country, she stayed behind to nurse the wounded of both sides, but became involved in efforts to smuggle stranded Allied soldiers out of Belgium. Betrayed to the Germans and arrested, she was executed by firing squad.

Cavell's execution was a worldwide sensation, and is still remembered today; but a less well known 'martyr' to Britain's cause was equally celebrated at the time. Charles Fryatt was captain of a ferry which travelled between Harwich and Holland. When ordered to halt by a German submarine, he attempted to ram it. The Germans responded by intercepting Fryatt's ship on a subsequent voyage and arresting him. On the basis that warlike acts were forbidden to civilians, they tried and executed Fryatt.

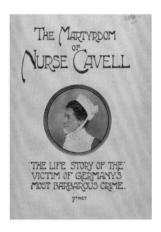

Above: This **book** is an example of a mass of popular literature which celebrated the life and death of British nurse Edith Cavell – shot by the Germans as a spy.

The accepted laws of war meant that Cavell's trial and execution were technically legal, but this did not prevent her death from causing outrage all over the world. It boosted recruitment in Britain and lowered Germany's reputation in neutral countries.

Overleaf: Maverick motorbike enthusiasts **Elsie Knocker and Mairi Chisholm** were taken to the front as dispatch riders for a nursing organisation called the Women's Emergency Corps. They soon left to set up their own first aid post in a cellar, a stone's throw from the Belgian front line near the village of Pervyse. There they stayed for over three years, earning a heroic reputation for treating the Belgian wounded at great risk to their own lives.

Hatred

The Germans protested that they were applying the accepted laws of war, but the fates of both Fryatt and Cavell caused outrage in Britain and inflamed anti-German feeling in neutral countries. They heightened the atmosphere of hatred towards Germany and all things German which had been building since news of the German Army's behaviour in Belgium had begun to spread. Belgian refugees arriving in Britain were interviewed to gather witness statements about war crimes. But their tales became exaggerated in the telling, and hearsay soon inflated them to an almost ridiculous level of horror. Belgian babies were said to have been bayoneted and nuns, nurses and young girls raped. Some monks, it was said, had been used as human clappers in cathedral bells. Real human tragedy was being grotesquely inflated into lurid propaganda material.

However British people were soon given their own reason to hate the Germans. In December 1914, German warships shelled the coastal towns of Scarborough, Whitby and Hartlepool. The shock, to a nation which had always regarded the sea as a protective barrier, was great. Once again the actions of the German 'baby-killers' – as they were dubbed by First Lord of the Admiralty Winston Churchill – became the basis of powerful propaganda.

Britain's popular press led a frenzy of anti-German feeling. Newspapers, books and leaflets overflowed with sensationalism and outrage. Manufacturers seized on the opportunity to produce anti-German knick-knacks and souvenirs. On a more elevated level, the government began to create an official propaganda machine; recruiting the services of popular authors such as Rudyard Kipling, HG Wells and Sir Arthur Conan Doyle. Germans were now almost universally referred to as 'Huns' on the home front. Kipling had used the term in a poem in September 1914, although the word had also been used by Kaiser Wilhelm himself in 1900, when he had compared his troops to the Huns of Attila. Rabble-rousing newspaper proprietor and former MP Horatio Bottomley went further, declaring that 'the Kaiser and his Hellish hordes are possessed by the soul of Satan'.

Above: This commercially-produced **parody of the famous German gallantry medal** the iron cross is embossed with a record of German destructive acts. One side refers to destruction in the cities of Louvain in Belgium and Rheims and Amiens in France. The other lists the British coastal towns of Scarborough, Whitby and Hartlepool, which were bombarded by German warships in December 1914. The Germans had hoped to draw part of the British fleet into an unequal naval battle, but 137 men, women and children were killed and buildings destroyed. The result was fury against the Germans and consternation that the Royal Navy had been unable to intervene.

Simultaneously Britain – or 'England' as it was invariably called – became the principal target of the German public's hatred. There was huge resentment in Germany at Britain's decision to enter the war on the side of countries to which it was not officially allied. This was mixed with fears about the effect Britain's financial and naval strength might have on German prospects of victory. Ernst Lissauer, a German poet and dramatist, penned a 'Hymn of Hate' against 'England', with the refrain:

> We love as one, we hate as one.
> We have one foe and one alone
> – England!

Copies of Lissauer's creation were sent to every serving German soldier. The Kaiser decorated him for his patriotic achievement. In Germany and Austria the slogan 'Gott strafe England' (God strike England) was seen everywhere. It even became a popular greeting – to be answered with the words 'Er strafe es' (so it will be).

Thus, in all the warring countries, the war immediately began to have deeper effects on society than anyone could have anticipated. In Britain, as amongst its friends and foes, humbug and hatred existed alongside heroism and self-sacrifice. Unheralded and unexpected, a home front had come into existence.

Right: Britain's children were also caught up in war fever. Nine-year-old Dublin boy Alfie Knight wrote this letter to Lord Kitchener, offering his services as a bicycle dispatch rider. He boasted that he could ride his bicycle 'jolley [sic] fast' and that he was 'a good shot with a revolver'. A reply from the War Office passed on Lord Kitchener's regrets that Alfie was 'not yet quite old enough to go to the front'.

Left: On 4 August 1914, Germany's Chancellor professed his exasperation that Britain had gone to war 'just for a scrap of paper' – namely the treaty guaranteeing Belgian neutrality. In Britain this outburst inspired a welter of posters, leaflets, and mock treaties referencing this 'scrap of paper'. Here we see the phrase accompanied by the Kaiser's (rather than his Chancellor's) face printed on a **novelty toilet roll**. This reflects attitudes to towards Kaiser Wilhelm in Britain, where people saw him as the evil-genius behind Germany's warlike actions.

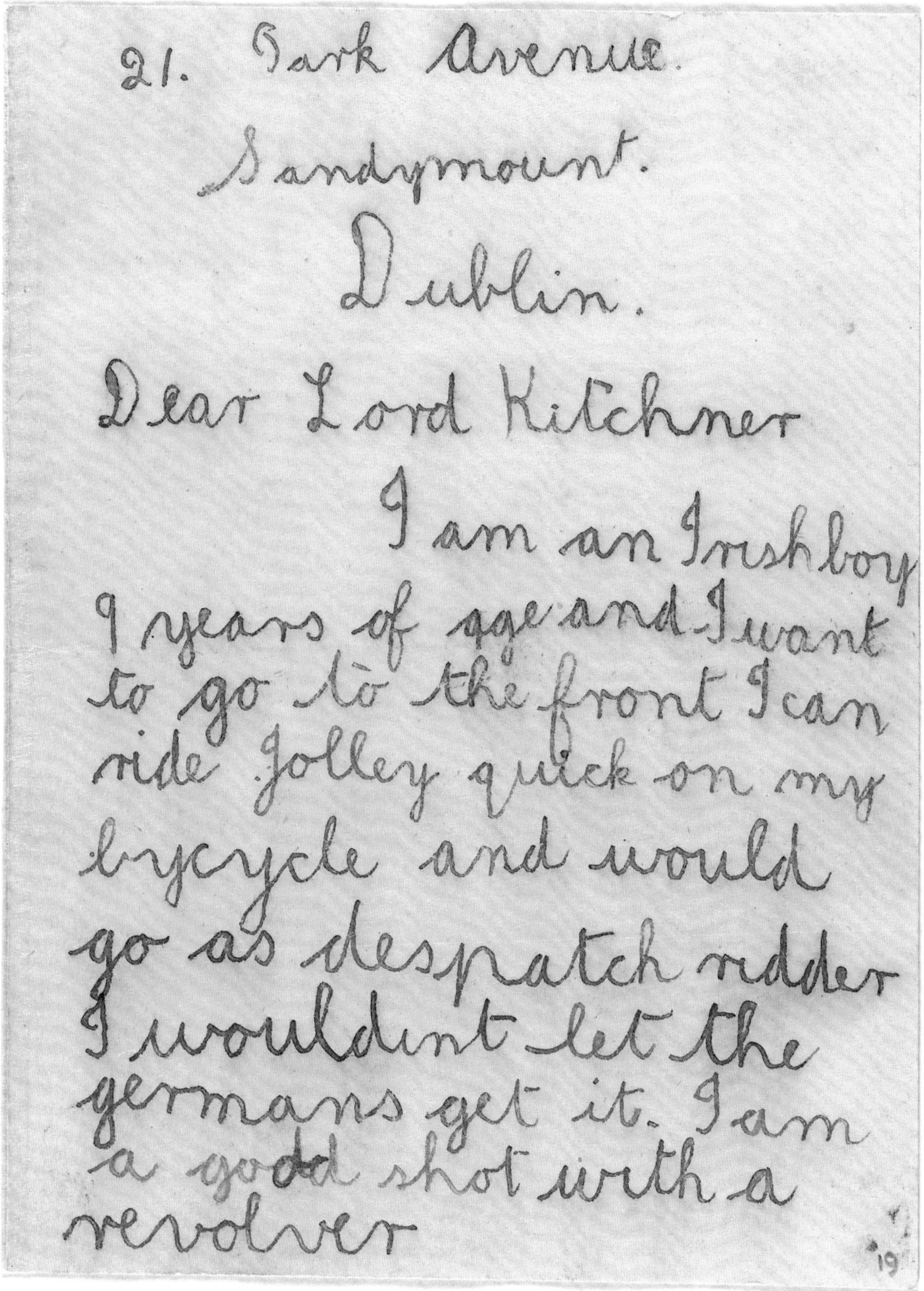

21. Park Avenue.

Sandymount.

Dublin.

Dear Lord Kitchner

I am an Irish boy
9 years of age and I want
to go to the front I can
ride Jolley quick on my
bycycle and would
go as despatch ridder
I wouldnt let the
germans get it. I am
a godd shot with a
revolver

19

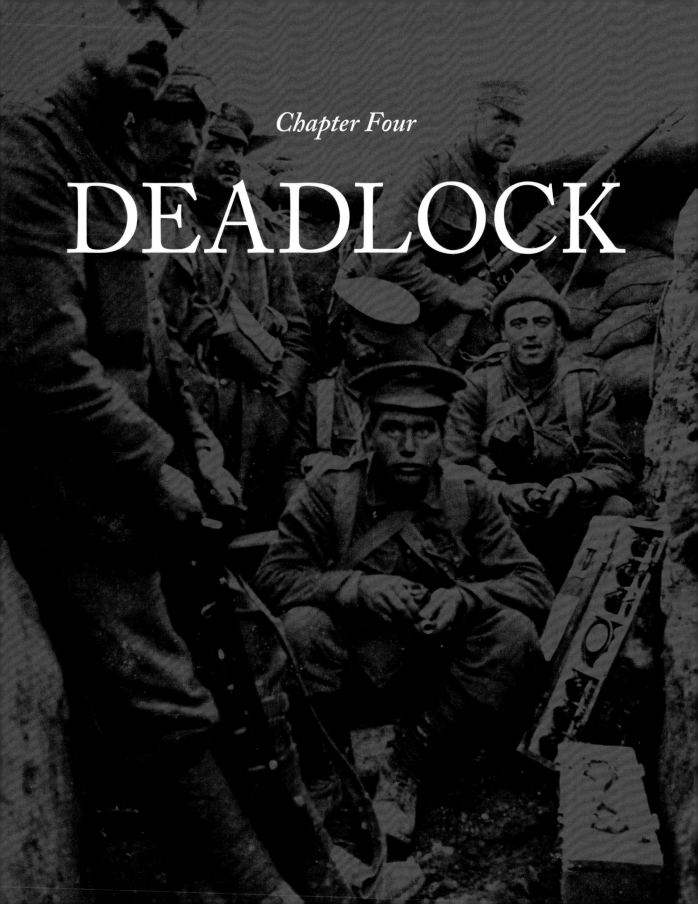

Chapter Four

DEADLOCK

'An endless and seemingly confused web. These are the trenches.'

By late 1914, the war in France and Belgium had become deadlocked. Neither side had achieved an outright victory on the Western Front. Their soldiers dug themselves into the earth to escape the murderous fire of modern weapons. Soon, vast trench networks snaked from the English Channel to Switzerland.

The German Army held rich, industrialised regions of France and Belgium. The French and British were determined to drive them out. But this was a new form of warfare and all armies sought desperately for new weapons and ideas which would allow them to win it.

'Digging, Digging, Digging'

'Digging, digging, digging, always bloody digging', sang the soldiers of the British Expeditionary Force. They had good reason, as by 1915 the chief occupation of front line troops of both sides had become the construction and maintenance of trenches.

Trenches neutralised the threat posed by the great killers of 1914: shrapnel and small arms fire. Trenches saved lives. While their squalor has given them an aura of horror in our modern memory, their immediate effect was to greatly reduce the number of casualties suffered. By early 1915 the trenches in Belgium and France had developed from simple ditches dug in the heat of action into integrated defensive systems. This swift evolution was possible because trenches were an accepted part of warfare and the science of 'field fortification' was well-known to all armies. Usually trenches had been dug by those besieging towns or fortresses, but temporary entrenchments had been a feature of many earlier battles. Never before, however, had they assumed such a permanent and extensive appearance as they now did on the Western Front.

In their most basic form, trench lines consisted of a 'fire trench', from which the enemy could be fired upon, and a support trench. Communications trenches, feeding into these, protected men as they moved up to the front line or brought up supplies. The 'parapet' – the top of the trench facing the enemy – was made bullet-proof with sandbags. Trenches were reinforced with wood or corrugated iron. Within them men were able to take cover in dugouts and shelters. These ranged from simple holes scraped in the side of a trench, to deep shelters reinforced with wood or concrete, capable of holding many men.

Trenches soon ran from the Channel coast of Belgium to the Swiss border. They were constructed in all terrains, from the mountain tops of the Vosges, through the forests of the Argonne and the accommodating chalk of the Somme, to the mining villages of northern France and the wet plains of Flanders. In the last region they often took the form of raised breastworks built from earth, wood and sandbags, as the high water table prevented deep excavations. In fact drainage was a problem everywhere, and soldiers suffered great hardships in waterlogged trenches before the introduction of wooden duckboards to walk on, and sumps cut into the trench floor to drain the water away. In some spots, bad weather always brought problems with water. Near Ypres in early 1916, Machine Gun Corps officer Vyvyan Board noted that 'in the fire trenches [. . .] you stand in thin mud about as thick as pea soup right up to the waist. I cannot imagine men in a more miserable state as the water is intensely cold. I saw men crying – and nearly all in great pain.'

Before the front line trench lay lines – eventually deep fields – of barbed wire. As the war progressed, armies identified a need for extra lines of trenches, to enable them to conduct defence in depth: if one line of trenches was captured, the fight could be continued from the second or even third lines. War correspondent Edmund Dane described the trench system in 1915:

> 'The observer who goes up in an aeroplane [. . .] sees the country below him marked by minute threadlike cracks, running here and there, into and out of one another; an endless and seemingly confused web. These are the trenches. Tangled though they appear to the unpractised eye, to the expert their confusion reveals a plan and a system [. . .] The maze of threadlike cracks looks deserted.'

The trenches created a formidable defensive barrier which attackers needed to overcome. On the Western Front the Allies could only win the war by driving the Germans out of France and Belgium. The Germans looked to defend the land they had taken until they could mass sufficient troops to win the war in the West. The fact that they were forced to fight on the Eastern Front at the same time meant that this had to be a long-term ambition. Their trenches in the West were therefore intended for long-term occupancy, and tended to offer more comfort and shelter than many French and British trenches. Moreover, as the Germans stood on enemy territory, they could choose what to hold and what to give up. They selected the position of their trench lines to maximise their ability to observe and fire upon the Allies. They made sure to occupy high ground wherever possible, to assist their artillery observers. The French and British felt unable to give up so much as an inch of Allied territory. French General Émile Fayolle lamented the lack of flexibility shown by his superiors: 'Never have they consented to a rectification of the line. One dug-in where one was, however precarious or difficult the situation. Sometimes it would have sufficed to fall back 40 meters to be solidly and safely emplaced.'

Above: Barbed wire was a feature of all entrenched positions. First used to control cattle in the American West in the 1870s, it was now used to hinder attacking troops or to channel them into areas swept by machine gun fire. British manuals specified entanglements at least ten metres deep in front of trenches. This wire was set up and repaired during the hours of darkness. Soldiers working in wiring parties wore special **wiring gloves** to protect their hands.

Trench Artillery

Faced with a trench-bound battlefield, the combatants struggled to find ways of continuing to kill their enemies and, perhaps, to break out of the deadlock altogether. Artillery remained the dominant weapon and it now fired at targets which it could not directly view, relying upon observers in the front line or, increasingly, in the air. Trench warfare forced gunners to change their ammunition. High explosive shells now replaced shrapnel as the chief killer. These could blow up trenches and sometimes penetrate shelters. A soldier's training or experience offered little protection against the unpredictable threat of shellfire. All armies looked to maximise the amount of heavy guns available to them, as these guns could deliver the most effective high explosive firepower.

Commanders soon saw a need for an artillery piece that was portable and concealable enough to be used from the front line; firing directly upon the enemy trenches. The answer was the 'Trench Mortar'. Mortars had been used in siege warfare for centuries; they fired their bombs at a high trajectory to clear enemy city walls. The Germans had such a weapon in service in 1914, called the *Minenwerfer* (mine thrower). It became much feared by Allied soldiers. Its range was tiny compared with conventional artillery pieces, but its bombs were extremely effective. Lieutenant Colonel James Jack, commanding an infantry battalion in France, made the following diary entry on 13 September 1916: 'Some of the trenches have again been badly mauled by minenwerfer fire, three men being blown to bits by one bomb. These heavy trench mortar shells, with their terrific explosion[s], are intensely disagreeable.' The Allies began to develop mortars of their own, but it would be 1916 before they got truly effective types into widespread service.

Below left: The **3-inch Stokes mortar** was invented by an engineer from Ipswich, Wilfred Stokes. First appearing in 1916 it finally gave British troops a weapon superior to the German mine throwers which had plagued them since 1914. Simpler, more portable and cheaper to make than its German counterparts, it also boasted a higher rate of fire. An experienced crew could put as many as nine bombs in the air simultaneously. Mortar fire usually drew swift retaliation from the enemy. British artillery officer Edward Beddington Behrens wrote home describing trench mortar crews as 'the Suicide Club [. . .] Those who have been in it sometime[s] seem like desperate men, brave as anything – rather nervy though'.

Below: German 17cm Minenwerfer

Close Combat

The desire to provide portable explosive firepower to front line infantrymen saw the revival of another weapon previously associated with seventeenth century siege warfare – the hand grenade. Grenades could be thrown into enemy trenches or down into dugouts. They could reach where rifle-fire could not. Many armies had some sort of grenade in service in 1914, but struggled to meet ever increasing demands for them from the front. Prior to 1916 many hastily-designed, or even home-made grenades were pressed into service. They were frequently almost as dangerous to the users as to their enemies. To be selected as a 'bomber', as grenade throwers were called in the British Army, was not an enviable fate. However, when reliable grenades, with safety mechanisms, became widely available, they became the dominant infantry weapon. Commanders became alarmed that bomb-throwing had supplanted rifle skills among their men.

A man using hand grenades could not easily carry a rifle; he needed something to defend himself with if the enemy got close. All armies faced shortages of pistols, so the answer came in the form of two of mankind's most primitive killing tools – the club and the knife. These weapons were well-suited to the nature of war in the trenches, which often brought men face to face with the enemy in a manner rare in open warfare. This was especially true as the armies developed a policy of launching raids across the 'no man's land' which separated the opposing trenches. These raids could gather intelligence about the enemy, perhaps even bring back prisoners, but frequently they were seen as a means of gaining a moral superiority over the opposition. The aim was to dominate no man's land. The soldiers involved in raids had varying reactions to such activities. For many they were an unwanted, terrifying, intensification of the risks they faced daily. For some they provided a thrill that the humdrum routine of trench warfare denied them.

Clubs were such a basic weapon that they could be improvised in the front line, although most were made in army workshops. Some of their users seem to have taken delight in making clubs of frightful appearance, studded with nails or wire spikes, but all trench clubs were ultimately intended to crush skulls. They might be supplemented in action with tools such as spades or axes, which could make effective weapons. Warfare took on a grimly personal tone.

Below: Of all the weapons of trench warfare, the most basic and primitive was the **trench club**. Clubs provided an easily-made means of self-defence for men such as 'bombers', who could not carry rifles as they needed both hands to throw grenades. They were also used on trench raids and patrols. In night raids on the enemy lines they allowed killing to be carried out silently. This German club is a relatively sophisticated design, using a coil-spring to increase the power of the blow delivered by the club's iron head.

Killing with a knife was perhaps the most intimate and potentially disturbing aspect of trench warfare. Swiss-born poet Blaise Cendrars, who fought in the French Army, gave a visceral account of the experience:

'I have defied torpedoes, guns, mines, fire, gas, machine guns, all the anonymous, demonic, systematic, blind machinery. I am going to defy man. My own kind. A monkey. Eye for eye, tooth for tooth. Just him and me now. Just fists, just knives. No mercy. I pounce on my antagonist. I deliver a terrible blow. His head almost comes off. I have killed a Boche. I was fiercer and faster than he. More direct. I struck first. I live in the real world, me, the poet. I acted. I killed. Like someone who wants to live.'

The French and Germans were the first to see a need to equip their men with fighting knives. Their armies purchased them in huge quantities. The French even resorted to buying cheap lock-knives or butcher's knives to maintain supplies. Both eventually developed standard patterns of 'trench knife'. The British Army was not enthusiastic about knives, but this did not stop officers purchasing them privately. Some went so far as to buy enough to hand them out to their men. British nurse Vera Brittain was shocked to be shown such a knife by her fiancé Roland Leighton. She confided to her diary that 'the sight of the dagger (for trench raids) in the hand of one of the most civilised people of these ironically-named civilised times depressed me to morbidness'.

Below left: The British Army lacked an efficient hand grenade in 1914, and struggled to issue such weapons when trench warfare made them vital. The so-called **hairbrush grenade** was a 1915 attempt to provide a 'bomb' which could not only be manufactured at home, but also produced by the Royal Engineers at the front. It consisted of a metal box of explosive fixed to a wooden handle which aided throwing. Many early grenades proved dangerous to their users. Most used flame or friction to ignite a length of time-fuze. These ignition systems sometimes caused premature explosions and didn't work well in wet weather. The hairbrush grenade benefited from a fuze that was activated by a spring-loaded striker.

Left: The French led the field in the large scale issue of knives to their troops. This is a **butcher's knife** – one of over 200,000 purchased before purpose-designed trench knives became available. The French Army's early experiences of launching attacks on trench systems taught them the need for special teams of 'moppers-up' known as '*nettoyeurs des tranchées*' (trench cleaners). Their task was to ensure that no Germans remained alive in a captured trench. One of them, Private Louis Corti recorded that 'we were armed with a dagger, a revolver or rifle and a bag of grenades [. . .] the watchword was "No Mercy".'

The Return of Armour

Just as trench warfare saw a revival of ancient weapons; it also witnessed a return to the wearing of armour. As army medical departments analysed the types of injury suffered by soldiers, they identified a high proportion of head wounds caused by shell fragments. This prompted the development of steel helmets. The French led the way, introducing a helmet in July 1915. By 1916 all armies were issuing steel helmets to their troops. These helmets did what they were intended to do; reducing the number of head wounds caused by small shrapnel balls, shell fragments, stones and other debris. Yet they were not bullet proof. Any headgear capable of withstanding rifle and machine gun bullets would have been too heavy to wear.

Some armies issued cumbersome body armour to soldiers engaged in especially hazardous duties. The British Army did not do so, but this did not stop some soldiers from purchasing their own armour. A number of patent body armours were marketed as the war progressed. However, practical considerations stopped the wearing of armour from becoming universal, despite public figures such as Sir Arthur Conan Doyle campaigning for its introduction. One officer, signing his letter 'In Action' explained the problems in *The Times*: 'Nothing else but a quarter-inch

Left: Of all the steel helmets issued during the First World War the British '**Brodie helmet**' was the most effective. It was made of higher quality steel than its German counterpart and, unlike the French helmet, gained strength from being stamped from a single piece of metal. The helmet was based on a design patented by John Brodie. It was later refined to include a less sharp, folded rim and a more comfortable liner. The shallow, rounded contours of the helmet were designed to deflect missiles and the steel was capable of stopping a shrapnel ball descending from above.

steel plate would be of any use, and plates to cover the heart and abdomen alone would weigh some 15lb, and considerably hamper the movements. With rifle, ammunition, equipment, empty sandbags, bombs and other paraphernalia the soldier is already overloaded.'

With regard to privately-acquired armour, this correspondent fired his own revolver at a 'body shield' which he had been sent and 'the ordinary lead service bullets went clean through it, carrying jagged splinters with them'.

The Empty Battlefield

Many soldiers were struck by the 'emptiness' of the battlefield in this new form of warfare. Once the armies had dug trenches, men seldom saw, let alone got the chance to shoot at, their enemy. If they fired upon him, it was likely to be with 'indirect fire', using weapons capable of firing at targets not visible to their crews – artillery, trench mortars or even machine guns. One notable exception to this was the sniper, a rifle-armed marksman whose job was to kill unwary enemy soldiers who exposed themselves above the level of the trench parapet. Snipers frequently used optical rifle sights to shoot from long range. But they could also operate closer to the enemy; from hides built into the parapets of trenches, or lying in open ground, concealed in camouflage clothing. The Allies were forced to work hard to catch up with the early lead which the German Army established in the field of sniping. The latter exploited their highly developed optical industry to provide telescopic sights. Many men within its ranks were also experienced users of hunting rifles. The Allies not only had to train snipers, but to begin the manufacture of optics on a scale capable of supplying this and other military needs.

The static nature of the warfare on the Western Front also saw the birth of a new military art: camouflage. The chief need was to disguise guns and munitions dumps from enemy observation. This was usually achieved with a mixture of screens, netting and foliage. As the war progressed pieces of military equipment ranging from huge guns down to individual steel helmets were painted in 'disruptive' camouflage patterns – some of them unexpectedly colourful at close range. In the front line itself, efforts were made to disguise the layout of trenches and emplacements and to spy out those of the enemy. Because they frequently lacked control of high ground overlooking the battlefield, the British and French became particularly

Right: **Periscopes** were a response to the dangers of exposing one's head over the trench parapet. As well as box periscopes of the type shown here, there were mirrors designed to clip onto a soldier's bayonet. Private Kenneth Garry of the Honourable Artillery Company recorded his own experience of the Ploegsteert area of Belgium not long after this photograph was taken there:

'It is of course unhealthy to look over the parapet during the day, but by employing a periscope, the German trenches can be seen. The best of all is the penny glass in a metal clip to fix on a bayonet or stick. The Hun takes a fiendish delight in spotting periscopes, it gives him great delight to see bits of glass fly into the air as a result of a well-directed shot.'

inventive in developing camouflaged hides for observers. These could take the form of trees – set up at night in no man's land to replace an existing one which would be removed – dead horses, or even the corpses of men.

Completely concealed from observation, another war was fought beneath the ground. Both sides attempted to tunnel towards the enemy and blow up his trenches. This was done with 'mines' in the form of excavated chambers packed with high explosive. Tunnelling and mining was dependent upon suitable soil and topography, so was more common in some parts of the front than in others. In these areas it created an added level of anxiety for soldiers manning the trenches. Being buried alive by an explosion was a major fear of many men. But the tunnellers themselves also faced the threat of their tunnels being blown-in by the enemy, or even of hand-to-hand fighting in the claustrophobic confines of their underground labyrinths. The British Expeditionary Force exploited the expertise of the many miners in its ranks and of mining engineers from all over the empire. By 1917, it had established a mastery of the art of underground warfare.

Left: In areas where tunnelling and mining could be attempted, both sides were often active simultaneously, and attempted to hamper each other's efforts by planting explosives to blow-in enemy tunnels. Fighting even took place in these cramped underground galleries. Allied military miners used geophones to listen for German activity. The **geophone** was a French invention, intended to magnify sound waves in the ground. It consisted of a stethoscope connected to two discs containing mercury. By pressing the discs to the earth and using a compass, an experienced listener could work out the location of any underground sound. He might hear talking or digging. A period of silence could mean that a mine was about to be detonated.

Gas

On both sides inventive minds sought ways out of the trench deadlock. In early 1915 Germany took the dramatic step of releasing poisonous chlorine gas to commence an attack against Allied positions around Ypres. This initially caused panic when it drifted into the Allied lines, but its impact was reduced by the Germans' failure to take full advantage of the confusion caused. In fact this battle, which became known as the Second Battle of Ypres, was actually a diversion to cover the transfer of German troops to the Russian Front. However, the use of chemical weapons caused international revulsion. Germany had an advanced chemical industry, and its scientists had promoted gas as a more humane method of waging war. In one sense they were correct as, in the war as a whole, gas was not a great killer. But soldiers and civilians alike did not see it in that way, regarding the use of gas as plumbing new depths of inhumanity. Even among the many other horrors of modern warfare, killing with gas seemed uniquely abominable. British soldier Elmer Cotton described chlorine gas victims he saw in 1915 as 'black, green and blue, tongues hanging out and eyes staring – one or two were dead and others beyond human aid, some were coughing up green froth from their lungs'.

Almost inevitably the Allies swiftly set about developing their own poison gasses. The British released chlorine on a large scale at the Battle of Loos in September 1915. This was an attack launched in support of major French offensives elsewhere on the front. It would be the largest British attack so far, but the BEF lacked sufficient heavy artillery to provide a suitable preparatory bombardment. It was hoped that the gas would have sufficient impact to make up for this failing, but wind conditions diluted its effect. While some advances were made, the attack failed when British commanders mishandled the way in which their reserves were fed into the battle, which resulted in 50,000 British and Empire casualties.

Overleaf: This remarkable photograph was taken on 25 September 1915, the opening day of the Battle of Loos. It was taken by a soldier of the London Rifle Brigade, and shows British troops of the 46th Division advancing towards the cloud of chlorine gas which has been released in the direction of the German lines. On this part of the front, the gas worked quite well, but in others the wind failed to carry it into the German positions, or even blew it back onto the British attackers. The battle proved that gas was no substitute for adequate artillery support.

The use of gas created a technological race, in which the scientists of both sides rushed to develop new gasses and countermeasures to combat them, such as gas masks and respirators. Soon gas shells were introduced, superseding the release of gas from cylinders. Britain developed the Livens Projector – a tube dug into the ground from which gas bombs could be fired. This weapon was much feared by German soldiers as, fired as part of a group, it could completely saturate an area with gas with no warning. Newer and more deadly types of gas were introduced. The final development was another German initiative copied by the Allies. Mustard gas, introduced in the autumn of 1917, was intended to hinder and incapacitate the enemy, rather than kill him. It attacked the eyes or sweaty areas of the skin, causing burns, sometimes through to the bone, and temporary blindness. It left behind a sticky residue, which would also burn, and which could coat clothing and equipment, or persist for days in shell holes or trenches.

These new weapons, combined with ever greater quantities of heavy artillery, meant that trenches were to become progressively less effective as a defensive barrier, or even as a place of safety for their defenders. In late 1915 however, many of these developments were in the future. There appeared to be no way around the deadlock on the Western Front.

Right: This photograph was taken in the aftermath of the **Battle of Loos** in a captured German position, known as Big Willie Trench. The Guards Division held it against German counter-attacks. These men are fortunate in being provided with boxes of the new Number 5 grenade – otherwise known as the Mills Bomb. This grenade was far safer and more efficient than previous British designs. Some units had been put in dangerous situations during the Loos battle when it was found that the wet weather had ruined the igniters of their grenades. The Mills Bomb was superior because it was set-off by a spring-loaded striker, which did not activate until the grenade had left the thrower's hand.

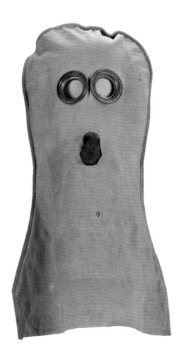

Left: From 1915 the British Army issued 'helmets' to protect against poison gas. British scientists willingly risked exposure to deadly gasses while testing these helmets, and some were poisoned. The helmets had to be upgraded as the Germans replaced chlorine gas with phosgene, which was ten times more deadly and almost undetectable except for a faint whiff of mouldy hay. The **'PH' or 'Tube' helmet** was impregnated with chemicals to counter phosgene gas. The wearer breathed in through his nose and exhaled through a metal tube held in his mouth. Captain Geoffrey Donaldson of the Royal Warwickshire Regiment wrote home that wearing these helmets 'was like an appalling nightmare as you look like some horrible kind of demon or goblin'. The PH helmet was difficult to see out of and, during 1916, was superseded by the 'Small Box Respirator', which had a separate face-piece and gas filter, linked by a tube.

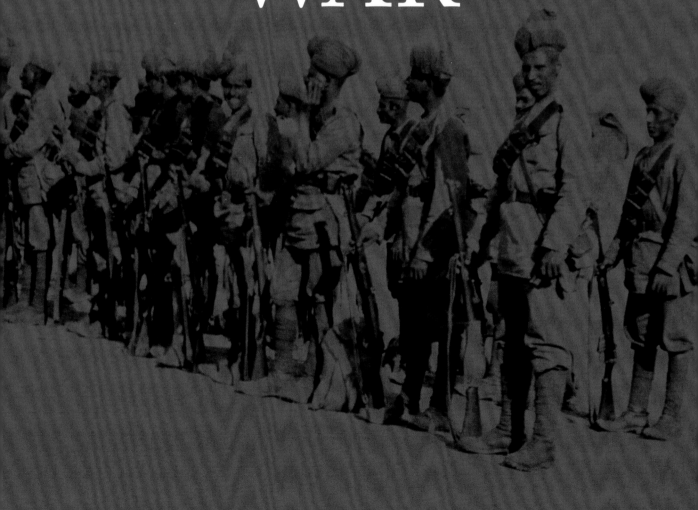

Chapter Five

WORLD WAR

'Lips crack and heads go dizzy in the stifling heat'

The war which had started in Europe in August 1914 swiftly spread across the globe. Britain, France and Germany all possessed overseas empires which were vulnerable to attack. Britain's declaration of war inspired German efforts to strike at the British Empire. For some in Britain, this widening of the war seemed to offer a chance of winning a victory away from the deadlocked Western Front.

The focus was further shifted from the Western Front by a German attempt to knock Russia out of the war, and by new fronts being opened up as Italy and Bulgaria joined the fray. And from the first days of the war Britain and Germany began a struggle for mastery of the sea.

Above: This flag was captured from Turkish troops who attacked the Suez Canal in January 1915, threatening the key link between Britain and its most prized possession, India. The attack was beaten off, but Turkish forces remained a threat until they were defeated at the Battle of Romani in August 1916. The British followed the retreating Turks across the Sinai desert. It was an arduous campaign. Private Stanley Cooke wrote home:

'One of the fellows [...] had written home stating the troubles we had to get water [...] his people replied asking why he did not fall out & get a glass of milk at one of the farmhouses on the way. If his people could only see this desert they would understand the howl that went up when he mentioned it.'

Germany's Global Strategy

Germany had been both enraged and alarmed by Britain's decision to go to war. Its leaders decided to strike at the British Empire to divert its attention and resources from the Western Front. When British involvement had first become a possibility Kaiser Wilhelm himself had written 'Our consuls in Turkey and India, our agents etc., must rouse the whole Muslim world into wild rebellion against this hateful, mendacious, unprincipled nation of shopkeepers; if we are going to shed our blood, England must at least lose India.' The key to this strategy was Turkey. The Ottoman Empire, to give it its proper title, had long been in decline, and had recently lost its remaining lands in Europe as a result of the Balkan Wars of 1912–1913. It was ruled by a Sultan, but real power lay in the hands of a nationalist group, the Committee of Union and Progress (CUP). These men were desperate for a strong European ally in their mission to restore Turkey's greatness. The Germans did not see the Turkish Army as useful in itself, regarding Turkey as 'a military nonentity'; but they could see that the Ottoman Empire's geographical position could be used to strike at Britain. Sprawling across the Middle-East, its borders with British-controlled Egypt and with Persia (Iran) offered the opportunity to threaten Britain's links with India, or to send agents to inspire trouble in India itself. The Ottoman Empire also shared

a border in the Caucasus with Russia, meaning that the latter would have to fight on a new war front. Turkey could also stop supplies being shipped through its waters to Russia's Black Sea ports.

A secret treaty of alliance was swiftly signed between the two countries, but Turkey only entered the war when two German warships, the *Goeben* and the *Breslau* took refuge in Turkish waters. They were transferred to the Turkish Navy and, on 29 October 1914, with the covert agreement of the CUP, bombarded the Russian port of Sevastopol. Turkey had now entered the war as one of the Central Powers. Its army was slow to move into action but, by the beginning of 1915, was poised to threaten Britain's most vulnerable link with India – the Suez Canal.

Military operations were only one strand of German strategy against the British Empire. The Turkish Sultan claimed leadership of all Muslims, and was persuaded to declare a Holy War – *Jihad* – calling upon the millions of Muslims in the Allied empires to rebel. In reality most Muslims outside Turkey were unimpressed by this call to arms.

Above: The Central Powers hoped that Turkey's call for Jihad would create chaos in India, but most Indian Muslims did not recognise the authority of the Ottoman Caliph. One serious outbreak of disorder did occur in Singapore however, when an Indian regiment mutinied and briefly took over the city. The mutiny was put down and 200 mutineers were court-martialled. Forty-seven of them were executed by firing squad. Others were imprisoned or sent to penal colonies.

One Muslim officer in the Indian Army wrote to his brother, 'what better occasion can I find than this to prove the loyalty of my family to the British Government? Turkey, it is true, is a Muslim power, but what has it to do with us?' The only serious threat was posed by the already radical Senussi sect, which had been fighting the Italian occupation of Libya with Turkish aid, and now invaded Egypt. British Empire forces were diverted to the Western Desert to drive them out and, in 1916, a further force had to be sent to crush a Senussi rising in Sudan.

Turkey's leaders did not share Germany's strategic aims. They wanted to establish a stronger empire and bring the Turkic peoples currently ruled by Russia into it. Their major military effort of late 1914 was an attack in the Caucasus. But their armies were too poorly equipped and supplied to sustain a winter campaign in such mountainous territory. The Russians inflicted a terrible defeat on them and, as Turkish soldiers froze to death in their thousands, began to invade Ottoman territory. Turkey's defeat in the Caucasus brought catastrophe to the local Armenian population. Up to two million Christian Armenians lived in the eastern part of Turkey. They were generally treated as second class citizens and had been the victims of violence during the previous century. When war came, some Armenians fought alongside the Russians, and all fell under

Left: One ship from Germany's East Asia Squadron, the light-cruiser *Emden*, set off on a lone commerce-raiding campaign in the Indian Ocean. Her captain, Karl von Müller, became a hero in Germany and even earned the respect of the British public. The *Emden* caused havoc and delayed the departure of Australian troopships. She was eventually caught and destroyed by the Australian cruiser HMAS *Sydney*. One of the *Sydney*'s sailors, Richard Broome, painted the scene on the inside of a **chocolate tin**. His diary recorded that 'she was a total wreck, on fire from the bridge to the stern [...] her sides perforated by gaping holes and her upper deck a mass of twisted steel'.

THE ILLUSTRATION OF THE GREAT EUROPEAN WAR. NO 38. THE JAPANESE GENERAL JAMAD'S ARMY OCCUPIED CHIUO FORTS AT TSINGTAU.

Left: Tsingtao (Qingdao) in China was the chief German naval base in the Pacific Ocean. Germany leased the surrounding region from the Chinese government. To deprive German cruisers of this haven, Britain called upon the aid of Japan, with which it had been allied since 1902. Japan agreed to attack Tsingtao as it was eager to establish its own power in China. A small British contingent also took part in the siege. This **Japanese print** depicts the storming of a section of the German fortifications. The German garrison surrendered a week after becoming surrounded by the Allied troops, despite Kaiser Wilhelm declaring that 'it would shame me more to surrender Tsingtao to the Japanese than Berlin to the Russians'.

suspicion of sympathising with Turkey's enemy. Armenian soldiers in the Turkish Army were now disarmed and either shot or worked to death. From spring 1915 Armenians were forcibly deported from their homes. This process was accompanied by massacre and rape. Those who survived faced starvation and disease. The number of Armenians killed during the course of the war is much disputed, but historians estimate the figure at around one million.

Germany's other global strategy was to attack British shipping on the high seas. It had warships poised to do this. Most of these cruisers were concentrated in the East Asia Squadron, based in the German controlled port of Tsingtao in China. Under the command of Admiral Maximilian von Spee, this force sailed south until it encountered and destroyed a British naval force off Coronel, on the coast of Chile. This defeat caused shock and dismay in Britain, and two modern battlecruisers were sent to hunt down Spee. These ships had the firepower of a Dreadnought battleship, but sacrificed some of its armour for a greatly increased speed and range. They caught the Germans as they were about to attack Port Stanley in the Falkland Islands. Spee's squadron was completely outgunned and was destroyed. By the end of 1914 Britain had re-asserted its naval dominance and Germany's cruisers had been driven from the seas.

Control of Germany's strategy lay in the hands of Erich von Falkenhayn. He was a realist who understood that Germany did not have the strength to defeat all the Allies simultaneously. He therefore planned to force one of them into a separate peace during 1915. His choice fell on Russia – largely because the Russian Army was putting Germany's ally Austria-Hungary under extreme pressure. When the Germans began their offensive in May, their use of massed artillery came as shock to the Russians, who had exhausted their own supplies of shells during 1914. Russian industry was unable to make good this lack, or to provide adequate supplies of weapons during 1915. A Russian general complained that 'the Germans plough up the battlefields with a hail of metal and level our trenches and fortifications, the fire often burying the defenders of the trenches in them. The Germans expend metal, we expend life.' In successive blows the Germans drove the Russians back in what the latter came to call 'the Great Retreat'. The French, assisted by Britain's growing army, launched attacks on the Western Front in an attempt to draw German troops away from Russia. They were desperate to keep their ally in the war. Although these efforts did little to change the situation in the East, the Tsar remained unshaken in his loyalty to his allies and Russia ignored German peace feelers. However, the gravity of the situation persuaded him that he should take the fateful step of taking supreme command of his army. His reputation began to suffer from his personal association with military failure.

Overleaf: A succession of defeats suffered by the Russian Army in the summer of 1915 combined to create what the Russians called '**the Great Retreat**'. By September they had retreated 300 miles and suffered 1.4 million casualties. This photograph of retreating Russian infantry was taken by Englishwoman Florence Farmborough, who enlisted as a Red Cross nurse in Russia. She had been working as an English tutor to a family in Moscow when war broke out. She recorded the following conversation between two Russian officers: 'We have learnt the art of retreating!'. . . 'Exactly, and, God knows, the lesson has been of long enough duration!'

Left: The Russian Army which marched to war in 1914 was well-equipped, but Russian industry was ill-prepared to make up the losses which would be sustained in combat. By 1915 the Russians were desperately short of ammunition, guns, machine guns and even rifles. As one officer explained, 'A third of my men were in the first trench, and they had rifles. All the rest had no rifles – their duty was to go forward, one by one, and pick up the rifles of those who were killed.' This crucial weakness was exploited by the better-supplied forces of the Central Powers. Still more equipment was lost as the Russian Army retreated.

This **Russian Maxim machine gun** was captured by the Germans. They re-chambered it to accept their own military ammunition and used it on the Western Front, where it was eventually captured again by British troops.

VIVAT
MACKENSEN.

2.MAI.
SIEG bei GORLICE
WEST-GALIZIEN

ZUM BESTEN DES
ROTEN KREUZES
VERLAG
AMSLER u. RUTHARDT.
BERLIN. W 8.

·VIVAT·
DAS BEFREITE
GALIZIEN

1915·

VIVAT
IWANGOROD
IST GEFALLEN !

OFFIZIELLES
BAND

VIVAT!

PRZEMYSL
3. Juni.

19   15

VIVANT
DIE BEZWINGER
·WARSCHAU·
·IWANGOROD·

·1915·

VIVAT
das 14·Korps

VIVAT
KOWNO

VIVAT
IWANGOROD

Above and left: In wartime Germany and Austria-Hungary, members of the public purchased **silk ribbons** – *Vivat bänder* – to celebrate military victories. They were produced on behalf of war charities such as the Red Cross, to whom the profits went. These ribbons commemorate German and Austro-Hungarian victories against the Russians during 1915. Triumphs came thick and fast during that summer and autumn for the Central Powers, but the Russian Army was too big to destroy in a single campaign.

British Counter-Strategy

Britain looked to counter Germany's global strategy. The first priority was to protect its sea communications from attack by German cruisers. This did not merely mean sending naval forces to hunt the enemy down. A second element of the strategy was to seize German colonies which provided harbours and coaling stations for the cruisers and in which transmitters had been built to maintain wireless communications with them. In China and the Pacific, German-held territory was swiftly seized. However, attempts to take Germany's African colonies developed into longer campaigns.

South African forces had conquered German South-West Africa by mid-1915 and an Anglo-French Army had seized Togoland and Cameroon by early 1916. The attempt to capture German East Africa developed into a mobile war which was to outlast all other military campaigns of the First World War. It ravaged much of south-eastern Africa and brought death to hundreds of thousands – civilians as well as soldiers – largely due to disease rather than wounds. Both sides employed Africans as soldiers, but the highest death rate was among over a million Africans pressed into service as porters. These men were the key to maintaining the armies in areas in which horses could not survive. It took three porters to carry the food and supplies to keep one soldier fighting.

Left: Britain employed over a million **African porters** and labourers to support its armies in Africa. Many had little choice but to join up, as the British authorities simply demanded that local African leaders fill recruiting quotas. Porters were necessary because little motor-transport was available, and horses could not survive in areas infested with tsetse fly. Terrible conditions were suffered by these men, as little proper thought was given to their health and nutrition. An Indian Army volunteer, Gerald Cooke, wrote of 'the toil and sufferings of the wretched porters who are the only form of transport up here, and these human beasts of burden do get some thick times, poor beggars'.

Back-breaking toil, inadequate nutrition and disease contributed to the deaths of over 100,000 of these non-combatants. One in four of those recruited by Britain in Kenya failed to return. In Africa it was more dangerous to carry supplies for the British Empire than to bear arms for it.

Britain's other priority was to protect India. The Indian government was alive to the possibility of a threats coming from Turkey via Persia and Afghanistan and it sent an Indian Army Expeditionary Force to the Persian Gulf even before Turkey's declaration of war. Their fears were well founded, as the Germans and Austro-Hungarians sent agents across neutral Persia (Iran) to stir-up trouble in Afghanistan. In November 1914 this force landed in Turkish controlled Mesopotamia (present day Iraq) and occupied Basra. By the summer of 1915 weak Turkish opposition had encouraged the War Office to order an advance up the River Tigris, in the direction of Baghdad. But, by this time, all eyes in Britain were fixed on another part of the Ottoman Empire.

Gallipoli

For some of Britain's leaders, the entry of Turkey into the war seemed to provide an opportunity to follow a traditional British strategy based on sea power. Foremost among them was Winston Churchill who, as First Lord of the Admiralty, controlled the Royal Navy. He promoted a plan to send a naval force through the Dardanelles straits and force Turkey to surrender by bombarding its capital, Constantinople. This plan had seemed to offer a way around the deadlock of the Western Front. As Churchill himself wrote, 'Are there not other alternatives to sending our armies to chew barbed wire in Flanders?' The French, fearful of their ally gaining too much influence in the eastern Mediterranean, sent a contingent of their own.

The Dardanelles campaign got underway in February 1915, but met with problems from the first. The straits were defended by a combination of mines and guns. Allied battleships risked being sunk by the mines if they closed in to bombard the guns – and the guns prevented smaller vessels from sweeping the mines. Ships were lost. In April the fateful decision was taken to land troops on the Gallipoli peninsula to clear the way. The landings were notable as the baptism of fire of the volunteers from Australia and New Zealand. Once the men were ashore fierce Turkish resistance locked them into a trench-bound war every bit as static as the

Western Front. A secondary landing in August did nothing to break the deadlock. Soldiers on both sides not only faced the dangers of battle, but had to endure extremes of heat during the summer. Bombardier George Dale wrote in his diary that 'a great brass sun beats down from a clear sky, and we soon learn what the term "thirst" really means. Lips crack and heads go dizzy in the stifling heat.' The heat later gave way to autumnal storms and cold capable of causing frostbite. Shortages of food and clean water and debilitating sicknesses like dysentery also had to be faced.

By the year's end it had been decided to evacuate the British and empire troops at Gallipoli. This was achieved with little loss, but the evacuation was an admission of failure and the defeat was a huge blow to British prestige. The campaign had cost the two sides half a million casualties between them, roughly equally shared. And this was not the only humiliation which British power had to suffer in early 1916. The advance in Mesopotamia had also run into trouble and the leading Indian Army forces had become besieged in the town of Kut. On 29 April, after spending almost four months cut off from aid, the Kut garrison surrendered, with 13,000 starving soldiers entering Turkish captivity. Many of them would not survive it. According to the verdict of British General Sir William Robertson, 'a more mismanaged expedition never was – except Gallipoli'.

Left: This **cloth map** was produced by a British newspaper, the *Manchester Guardian*. It shows the strategic situation of the **Gallipoli peninsula** at the mouth of the Dardanelles, and the sites of the Allied landings. In the distance lies the ultimate goal of the campaign – the Turkish capital Constantinople. Prominence is given to Australia and New Zealand, for whose troops this was the first time in action.

Above: This photograph shows Australian soldiers of 4th Australian Infantry Brigade behind Quinn's post, one of the most dangerous and exposed positions on the **Gallipoli** battlefield. It was the scene of repeated fighting and, on the day this photograph was taken, the officer for whom it was named, twenty-seven-year-old Major Hugh Quinn – in peacetime a Queensland accountant and amateur boxing champion – was killed there. Gallipoli cost the lives of 56,707 Allied soldiers. 11,430 of them came from Australia and New Zealand.

New Blood

Since the outbreak of war, both sides had been making diplomatic efforts to influence neutral countries in their favour. Four of these nations, Italy, Romania, Bulgaria and Greece, were looked upon as potential allies. They received approaches from both the Allies and the Central Powers, which essentially attempted to bribe them either to join in or to stay neutral. And they were not immune to such inducements, as Prime Minister Asquith acidly remarked, 'All these little Powers hate one another cordially, but when the carcase is ready to be cut up each wants as big and juicy a slice as it can get'.

Italy had been a member of the Triple Alliance with Germany and Austria-Hungary, but had refused to go to war in 1914, asserting that neither of the other signatories had been attacked. Italy had fought Austria for its independence during the previous century. It still coveted the Italian-speaking Trentino and the port of Trieste, which lay within Austria. Italy also had ambitions for a northern border demarcated by the Alps, control of the Adriatic Sea and influence in the Balkans. Britain and France were happy to offer all these things in the event of an Allied victory in which Italy participated. They duly did so in the secret terms of the Treaty of London, signed with Italy in April 1915. On 23 May Italy declared war on Austria-Hungary, and attempted to invade Austrian territory. The Italian Commander, Luigi Cadorna, dreamt of marching his men into 'the heart of the Hapsburg Monarchy'. But his army, although large, lacked equipment and training. Furthermore the terrain favoured the defenders. Along Italy's northern border little could be gained among the high mountain peaks and glaciers. Snow, ice and avalanches threatened soldiers' lives here as much as guns. The main fighting took place to the east, along the valley of the River Isonzo, where the Italians mounted a series of costly offensives. The terrain here ranged from mountains in the north, via a barren plateau, to the tempting target of the border city of Gorizia. At the southern end of this front the road to Trieste was blocked by the forbidding rockbound Carso plateau, where dynamite was required to excavate a trench and where flying rock fragments magnified the effect of every shell. The Italians swiftly found themselves facing the same deadlock as their allies on the Western Front.

In September the Central Powers won a diplomatic victory of their own, by bringing Bulgaria into the war on their side. Bulgaria was offered Serbian territory – land which it believed was rightly its own. Bulgaria had been impressed by German success against Russia and requested that a renewed attack on Serbia should be conducted under German leadership. In October Serbia was invaded from two sides by Bulgarian and Austro-Hungarian and German armies. The Serbian Army, already weakened by disease, could not withstand such an attack. The Serbian government decided that the Army at least must be saved even if the country was overrun. What followed was an agonising retreat across the wintry mountains of Albania in which half of the Army was lost. Meanwhile the whole of Serbia came under a harsh occupation. The Central Powers now formed a continuous bloc stretching from the North Sea to Persia.

The French and British made a belated attempt to aid the Serbs by sending troops into the southern part of Serbia. This involved landing troops at Salonika in Greece in breach of Greek neutrality. Political strife now paralysed Greece, as its king – who was Kaiser Wilhelm's brother-in-law – struggled to keep his country neutral in the face of opposition from a pro-Allied faction. The Allied landing was too late to save Serbia, but the troops remained on what became known as the Macedonian Front. They were later joined by the remnants of the Serbian Army, which had been evacuated by Allied ships from the Albanian coast. The Allies could not afford to give up on the Balkans, as the most powerful nation in the region, Romania, was still uncommitted. Romania possessed a large army and valuable resources of oil and food. The growing power of Germany obliged Romania to begin selling its produce to the Central Powers, but it stayed out of the war for the time being.

Right: This **poster** reflects the nationalistic motivation behind Italy's decision to enter the war. Italy's leaders wanted to incorporate Italian speaking parts of Austria into Italy and to push Italy's northern border to the Alps. They also hoped to control the Adriatic Sea and exert influence in the Balkans. The prospect of war also excited visionaries like Gabriele d'Annunzio, who proclaimed 'Blessed are the young who hunger and thirst for glory [. . .] Blessed are the merciful, for they shall be called upon to staunch a splendid flow of blood and dress a wonderful wound.' Not all of his fellow Italians shared his enthusiasm. For the rural poor in particular, forced to give up their sons to the Army, the war promised only hardship.

Overleaf: This photograph sums up the horrors of the **retreat of the Serbian Army** through the mountains of Albania in late 1915. Infantry escorting a baggage train trudge grimly through the snow, oblivious to the sick or exhausted man stumbling at the roadside. The Serbian Army was 420,000 men strong when the Central Powers launched their invasion in September 1915. Only 155,000 survived to be evacuated by Allied ships from the Albanian coast.

SEMPRE AVANTI !!

The War at Sea

After the scare briefly caused in 1914 by the German cruisers had passed, the war at sea settled down into a war of blockade. Britain used its naval dominance to seal off the English Channel to surface vessels and patrolled the approaches to the North Sea to prevent supplies from reaching Germany. The aim was to starve Germany, initially of resources which might feed its war industry, ultimately of food for its people. Anglo-French naval forces imposed a similar blockade upon the Central Powers in the Mediterranean. The Germans responded by launching underwater attacks on Allied ships, using submarines and mines.

The German High Seas Fleet could not break the Royal Navy blockade. It was outnumbered by the British Grand Fleet which, for fear of torpedoes and mines, had established its main base at Scapa Flow in the Orkney Islands. In reality submarines offered only a limited threat to fast moving modern warships, although Germany scored some early successes in picking-off vulnerable older vessels. The German Navy soon realised, however, that the most effective use of submarines was to mount a counter-blockade by attacking merchant ships carrying food, raw materials and munitions to Britain.

'Blockade work is unspectacular, uninspiring, but exceedingly dangerous.' So said Rear Admiral Sir Dudley de Chair, commander of Britain's main blockading force, the 10th Cruiser Squadron. The danger came from the sea itself. To seal off the North Sea, British ships patrolled the area between Scotland, Iceland and Norway, where heavy seas and foul weather were a constant menace. The danger was increased by the procedure employed when a suspect vessel was intercepted. A boarding party was sent to inspect it and, if 'contraband' was found, take it into a British harbour where the cargo would be seized. The boarding party would be sent out in an open rowing boat led by an officer wearing a sword and pistol. Surgeon Probationer James Shaw witnessed an accident involving a boarding party boat:

'In lowering some mistake [was] made [. . .] she capsized and all crew were thrown into [the] water. Lieutenant Clarke was under the boat but managed to get hold of her rudder which had come loose. But he had an awful struggle to get at it. He had heavy clothes and was wearing a sword and revolver. He managed to relieve himself of revolver. Sub-Lieutenant Inglis with one or two of the crew got aft and were in danger from the propellers.'

De Chair deployed his ships in patrol lines, with ships positioned at twenty mile intervals. No vessel could pass between them without being seen. Over 6,000 vessels, ranging from modern cargo ships to tiny trawlers, were intercepted during 1915 and 1916. The task, however, proved wearisome for those enforcing the blockade. Alexander Scrimgeour in de Chair's flagship, HMS *Alsatian*, wrote that 'we have had a few exciting incidents, but on the whole the North Sea and the adjacent waters are not very thrilling spots, and sometimes it is very monotonous, especially as we have no mails, and only occasional fragments of news by wireless'.

The blockade was a long term strategy, and its effects were slow in manifesting themselves. In the meantime it created diplomatic problems for Britain. Neutral countries viewed the blockade as an illegal restraint upon trade. To a certain extent Britain could bully the European neutrals into acceptance or even co-operation. But America was a different matter. President Wilson of the United States was a strong believer in the 'freedom of the seas' and repeatedly protested against the British blockade. Luckily for the Allies however, the Germans ensured that most of Wilson's anger was directed against them.

German submarines – U-boats – also threatened the freedom of the seas, but they did not stop at just hindering merchant ships, they sank them. From February 1915, they adopted a policy of 'unrestricted' submarine warfare. No longer did the U-boats give a warning to vessels which they attacked. Now they shelled or torpedoed them without warning. The reason given was that the British were using Q-ships – merchant vessels with concealed guns which flew neutral flags to lure U-boats into approaching, before revealing their guns and opening fire. The German sinking of ships without warning appalled America. International outrage was heightened when a U-boat sank the civilian liner the *Lusitania*.

All but 764 of the huge vessel's 1,959 passengers perished. The dead included 128 Americans. Wilson now began to exert pressure on the Germans to halt unrestricted submarine attacks. In August, the sinking of another liner, the *Arabic*, with further American casualties brought the matter to a head and, for fear of enraging the USA further, the German government ordered the Navy to halt the campaign.

Many people had expected the naval war to result in a decisive battle between the British and German battle-fleets in the North Sea. This did not happen, as both sides had too much to lose from such a battle. Britain had no reason to risk its domination of the oceans and the German fleet would risk destruction if it fought the whole of the greatly superior British Grand Fleet. This did not stop the Germans from attempting to lure parts of the British fleet into an ambush, or into minefields or the paths of waiting submarines. Coastal bombardments and attacks upon Britain's fishing fleet were mounted in the hope of achieving this.

Above: At first the Royal Navy used elderly cruisers to enforce the blockade of Germany, but they could not hold the sea for long periods in heavy weather. They sustained damage and their crews were wracked with cold and sea-sickness. Soon these cruisers were replaced with what were known as Auxiliary Armed Cruisers – passenger or cargo vessels with guns mounted on them. Some of the new ships, such as this vessel, HMS *Changuinola*, were former banana boats, and 10th Cruiser Squadron became known in the Navy as the 'Banana Fleet'. But this motley collection of ships, protected by the battleships of the Grand Fleet within easy sailing distance, proved a highly effective force.

The Battle of Jutland

In late May 1916 the Germans made a foray into the North Sea in the hope of luring the British Battlecruiser Squadron, commanded by the aggressive Admiral David Beatty, into action against the entire High Seas Fleet. Unbeknown to them, British Naval Intelligence had long been in possession of German naval code books and was able to predict their movements by intercepting their wireless signals. Thus, instead of ambushing the battlecruisers, the Germans found themselves facing the entire Grand Fleet. A running battle ensued.

The Battle of Jutland, named for the nearest coastline, in Denmark, came as a shock to the Royal Navy and the British public. Fourteen British ships were lost, including three of the powerful battlecruisers. Over 6,000 sailors went to the bottom with them. Fighting at sea could be every bit as terrible as being in the trenches. Thomas Bradley was a Roman Catholic chaplain who was in the battlecruiser HMS *Tiger* during the battle:

Left: This **camisole** was worn on 7 May 1915 by Margaret Gwyer, one of the passengers of the doomed liner RMS *Lusitania*. Gwyer had recently married the Reverend Herbert Gwyer in Canada, and the couple were returning to England. During the sinking Gwyer was sucked into one of the ship's funnels, but blown out again by an explosion in the boiler room. Both she and her husband were rescued. The camisole still bears stains from oil and soot.

'The cries of the wounded and burnt men were very terrible to listen to. They were brought in sometimes with feet or hands hanging off. Very soon the deck of the distributing station was packed with wounded and dying men and when fresh cases were brought in one had some difficulty in avoiding stepping on the others [. . .] little pieces of limbs under your feet as you walked ankle deep in the water.'

German losses were less severe but, still outnumbered, their principal aim was to make good their escape to their home ports.

The balance of losses allowed the Kaiser to boast that 'the spell of Trafalgar is broken!' The British Commander, Admiral John Jellicoe, was criticised in some quarters for his caution, but strategically he had done

Left: The Royal Navy battleships *Warspite* and *Malaya*, shortly before going into action at Jutland. These were two of the most modern and powerful battleships in the world. With their sister-ships *Barham* and *Valiant*, they formed the 5th Battle Squadron, which, because of the high speed of its ships, fought alongside the Battlecruiser Squadrons under the command of Admiral Beatty. The battlecruisers suffered shocking losses at Jutland, but *Warspite* and *Malaya* both survived despite suffering damage. Commander Humphrey Walwyn was inspecting damage sustained by *Warspite* when a '12 inch [shell] came in through the starboard side and burst with a terrific sheet of flame, impenetrable dust, smoke, stink and everything seemed to fall from everywhere at once'.

the right thing in not putting his fleet at too great a risk. The day after Jutland the Royal Navy controlled the North Sea even more firmly than it had before the battle; for Jellicoe remained in a position to put as many as twenty-four Dreadnoughts to sea, while the Germans had only ten fit to fight. An American journalist wrote trenchantly, 'the German fleet has assaulted its jailor, but it is still in jail'. The blockade of Germany remained unbroken. It also meant that the Allies continued to enjoy a monopoly of commercial contacts with the USA. The Allies, using Britain as an intermediary, purchased not only cotton, grain and raw materials from America, but also firearms, ammunition and explosives. Even more significantly they were able to fund their war efforts with the aid of credit raised on Wall Street. British naval power gave the Allies a tremendous advantage.

Chapter Six

FEEDING
THE
FRONT

'Our old traditions are all being uprooted'

Britain was now committed to fighting a global war, but it also remained committed to fighting alongside its allies France and Russia at the heart of the conflict – in Europe. Fulfilling this commitment required a rapid expansion of the Army. This created a seemingly insatiable demand for men, weapons, supplies and food. Yet in 1915 recruitment dropped, and the Army's guns ran short of shells. To sustain the struggle the whole country would need to be put on a war footing. Britain was about to undergo a transformation which would have been unthinkable before 1914.

The Defence of the Realm

Before the war, British people had been accustomed to little governmental interference in their lives. From August 1914 this situation came to an end, as the state began to intervene in almost every aspect of society and industry. The first inkling of this change was to be found in the Defence of the Realm Act (which soon became known by the acronym DORA); first passed on 8 August 1914. This insignificant-looking paragraph of legislation would enable the introduction, over time, of a host of new restraints on daily life in Britain.

Initially many of these restrictions were a straightforward response to the widespread fear of German invasion and German spies. Many beaches were closed; it was forbidden to sketch near ports and harbours. To prevent spies sending signals and messages, the use of fireworks and the burning of bonfires were restricted and pigeon-keeping was regulated. Instructions were even issued for the evacuation of people and livestock in the event of an invasion. But DORA soon spread its tentacles wider. Railways and docks were taken under government control to prioritise the movement of weapons and troops. Factories capable of producing material for the war were liable to be commandeered in the same way. Above all, the government gave itself the right to put on trial anyone whose actions were interpreted as likely to harm the armed forces or assist the enemy, or even anyone spreading information 'likely to cause disaffection or alarm'.

This was an extraordinary departure from the personal freedoms for which Britain had become renowned; as was the introduction of censorship of letters and newspapers. Perhaps even more extraordinary was the general public acceptance of these interventions, although they were not endured entirely without complaint. Ethel Bilbrough, a well-to-do woman from Kent, made the following diary entry in October 1915, 'If there is one thing more than another that a man feels a private personal right to, it is his own letters!! [. . .] our old traditions are all being uprooted. To have strange prying curious eyes reading ones' own letters (that concern no one else) is exasperating!!!.'

In March 1915, the Chancellor of the Exchequer David Lloyd George declared, 'we are fighting Germans, Austrians and Drink, and so far as I can see the greatest of these deadly foes is Drink'. He was exaggerating for effect, but the government really feared that Britain's drinking culture would hamper war production. To curb drunkenness, brewers were ordered to reduce the strength of their beer and pub opening hours were limited. There was even a ban on 'treating' – the buying of rounds of drinks for friends. A few protested. One critic blamed the restrictions on 'a noisy clique of teetotallers' acting with the 'oppressive tyranny of the killjoy'. A more popular measure was the introduction of daylight saving time. On 21 May 1916 the clocks were put forward one hour for the first time in Britain. Lighter evenings saved gas and electricity, which was as welcome to the householder as it was to industry.

People could be fined or imprisoned for breaking any of the hundreds of new regulations. A Stratford-upon-Avon man, Albert Brooks, was fined £5 with the alternative of a month in prison for 'spreading false reports as to an alleged disaster to the Warwickshire Yeomanry at the Dardanelles'. Ethel Bilbrough was given further cause to question the workings of DORA when a soldier found her drawing a view of the Dorset coast and seized her sketchbook.

State intervention also hit Britain's citizens directly in the pocket. The rate of income tax rocketed. The standard rate, which had stood at 6 per cent of income in 1914, had risen to 30 per cent by 1918. The number of people liable to pay it also rose. Further money was raised by introducing an amusement tax on cinema and theatre tickets.

Right: As soon as Britain went to war, Parliament gave the government powers to impose controls on 'enemy aliens'. Britain in 1914 had a large population of German immigrants, many of whom had become naturalised British subjects. There were smaller numbers of Austrian, Hungarian and Turkish civilians. Men of military age were confined in internment camps, while the others, as this **proclamation** shows, had their movements restricted. Many of the latter were also interned periodically, when the press and the public demanded harsher treatment. An extreme exponent of anti-German agitation was Horatio Bottomley, proprietor of the newspaper *John Bull* who, in the wake of the sinking of the *Lusitania*, called for 'a vendetta against every German in Britain – whether naturalised or not [. . .] you cannot naturalise an unnatural beast, a human abortion, a hellish fiend. But you can exterminate him.'

City of London Police.

NOTICE TO ALIEN ENEMIES.

BETWEEN THE HOURS OF 9 P.M. & 5 A.M.

male alien enemies are required, with effect from 18th May, to remain at their registered places of residence unless furnished with a permit from the Registration Officer of the Registration District in which that place of residence is situate.

The Police are directed to enforce this restriction.

CITY POLICE OFFICE,
26, OLD JEWRY,
LONDON, E.C.

17th May, 1915.

J. W. NOTT-BOWER,

Commissioner of Police for the City of London.

Charles Skipper & East, Printers, 49, Great Tower Street, E.C.

8319.

Men

By 1915, the supply of volunteers for the armed forces was dwindling. Roughly 19,000 men were joining up per week, when 35,000 were required just to keep the Army up to strength. In July 1915, Kitchener called for recruits in a highly publicised speech to a cheering City of London audience. He appealed to men to ask themselves, 'have I a real reason for not joining the Army, or is that which I put before myself as a reason, after all only an excuse?' An increasingly forceful recruitment campaign and intense public pressure sought to cajole, bully or humiliate those who hadn't yet joined up. Posters echoed Kitchener's words, asking 'Have you a reason, or only an excuse for not enlisting?' One imagined a troubled future for men who refused to enlist, when their children asked 'Daddy, what did you do in the Great War?'

Nevertheless, at the time of Kitchener's speech there were still over two million single men of military age not in uniform. For many in Britain, following the lead of a hostile press, these men were nothing but 'shirkers' and 'slackers'. But many men had powerful reasons for not enlisting. Apart from the obvious dangers of fighting, many were reluctant to give up a good wage or business, or feared for the welfare of their families. More significantly for the war effort, thousands of men were working in vital industries and therefore expressly forbidden to enlist in the armed forces. Nevertheless, by early 1916, Army recruiting officers had stripped Britain of nearly thirty per cent of its workforce. Throughout the war there was fierce competition between the Army and industry for manpower. No matter how much the government sought to control the situation, there were only so many men to go round. This problem was to endure for the remainder of the war, occasionally threatening to escalate into a full-blown crisis.

A partial solution could have been found by employing women in war industries, but initially there was no official apparatus to allow this. Since the outbreak of war, many women had been demanding the right to play a full part in the war effort. Among the most vociferous were two champions of women's suffrage, Emmeline Pankhurst and her daughter Christabel. Within days of Kitchener's call for more male volunteers, they were leading a march in London demanding war work for women. By this time 80,000 women had already filled out registration forms declaring their willingness to take on war work, but only 2,000 of them had been

Right: Many thousands of men were prevented from joining the armed services because they worked in jobs which were vital to the war effort. As well as those who actually manufactured weapons and munitions, they included miners, railwaymen and even bootmakers. The government arsenals and commercial companies who employed these men had **lapel badges** made for them to indicate that their work was of national importance, and to protect them from public scorn for appearing not to be 'doing their bit'.

taken on. Lloyd George, at least, was aware of women's potential, and addressed the marchers with the words, 'without women victory will tarry, and the victory which tarries means a victory whose footprints are footprints of blood'. This was important, as Lloyd George would soon be in a position to convert his words into action.

But, during 1915, public debate was most regularly focused on the means by which sufficient men could be provided for the Army. Military men, many politicians and most of the press called for compulsory military service to be introduced. In this they were supported by a majority of the public, including the ever-opinionated Ethel Bilbrough, who wrote 'I don't see why we should [. . .] let a lot of lazy loafers hang about at home while others braver and better are doing their work. But I doubt if the present government would dare demand a big thing like conscription!' Many in government were indeed reluctant to take such a step; especially Liberal ministers, who saw it as alien to the traditions of their party.

In October 1915 one last great effort was made to recruit volunteers. The Director of Recruiting, Lord Derby, called upon men aged 18 to 41 to sign 'attestation' forms declaring that they would serve, on the understanding that they would be called up only when necessary and that unmarried men would go first. In the event, married men who attested, many with young families, were furious to discover that thousands of single men were still not attesting. In November an appeal from the prime minister hinted that, if more single men did not enlist, conscription would be introduced. By the year's end, less than half of those eligible had registered.

Conscription began to look like the only solution, but it would not be introduced without opposition. The pacifist Independent Labour Party and others who believed that the war itself was wrong were obvious opponents, but there were plenty of people who viewed conscription as a grave threat to Britain's traditions of personal choice and freedom. An organisation called the No Conscription Fellowship distributed leaflets and held meetings to voice their intention to 'deny the right of any government to make the slaughter of our fellows a bounden duty'. But the loudest voices were raised in favour of the measure – often in intemperate language. The *Daily Express* railed that, 'no honest man who has ever attended one of these pretended anti-conscription meetings can be under any illusion as to its real object. The so-called anti-conscriptionists are fighting against this country as much as if at this moment they were trying to poison gas the British Army in the trenches'.

Right: The white feather had been popularised as a symbol of cowardice in a 1902 novel *The Four Feathers*. During the period of voluntary recruitment, many women took to handing white feathers to young men not in uniform, in an attempt to shame them into enlisting. This letter, containing a white feather, was sent to pacifist Bernard Taylor. Hate mail was also sent. Mr E Brooks, a Bath railway porter, received a postcard from the 'Scout Mistress of the Bath Girl Scouts' – or more likely someone purporting to be her – which reads, 'seeing that you cannot be a man not to join the Army, we offer you an invitation to join our Girl Scouts as washer up'.

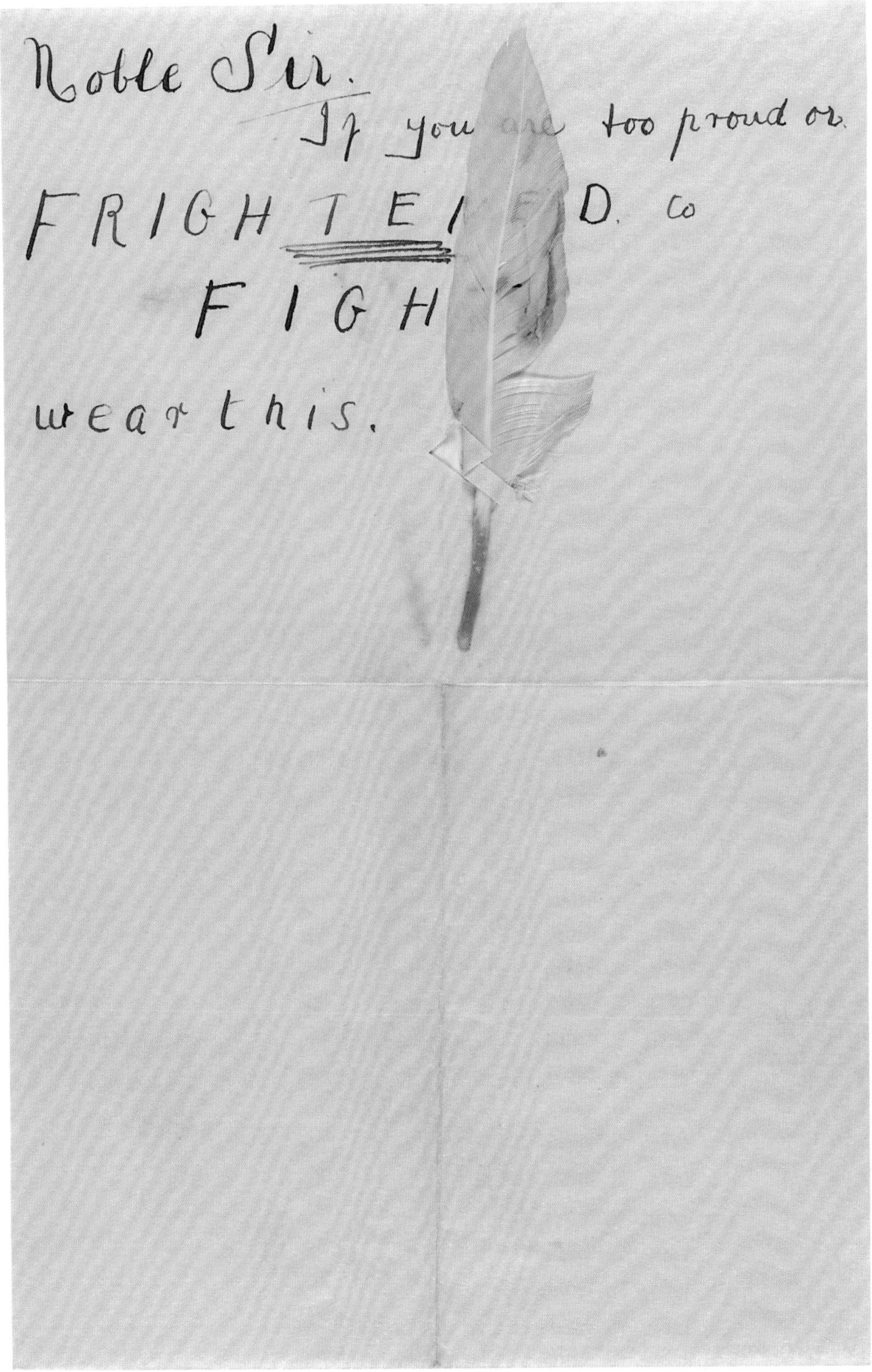

Noble Sir.

If you are too proud or

FRIGHTENED to

FIGHT

wear this.

On 27 January 1916, the Military Service Act was passed, making all single men aged 18 to 41 liable for military service. Four months later, it was extended to married men in the same age range. The legislation made these men members of the armed forces by default, although exemptions could be granted by local tribunals. In fact, in the year from March 1916, nearly 80,000 men were exempted. Most were engaged in work of 'national importance' or deemed to be medically unfit. Also excused were many men who were sole providers for dependents. Exemptions could be absolute, conditional or temporary. Those with religious or political objections to conscription were also considered; 16,500 of them appeared before tribunals. Most were given some sort of exemption, or were directed to take up vital work such as agriculture, or to carry out non-combatant duties at the front. But 6,000, who became known as 'absolutists' refused to accept conscription or even to recognise these tribunals. Most of these men acted out of political, rather than religious principle. They were jailed, often repeatedly, receiving harsh treatment. Their willingness to endure it testified to the depth of their convictions.

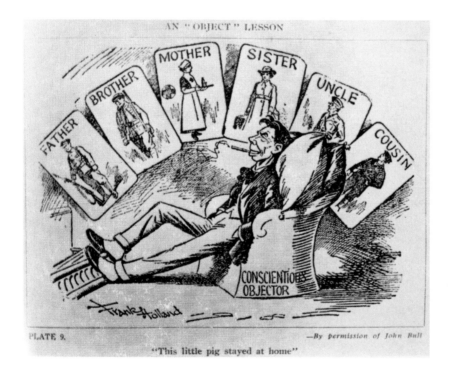

AN "OBJECT" LESSON

FATHER BROTHER MOTHER SISTER UNCLE COUSIN

CONSCIENTIOUS OBJECTOR

Frank Holland

PLATE 9.   —By permission of John Bull

"This little pig stayed at home"

Left: This **cartoon** appeared in the rabidly patriotic paper *John Bull*. It shows a conscientious objector indolently smoking at his fireside while his entire family is engaged in fighting the war. The depiction of the conscientious objector mirrors earlier satirical characterisations of 'shirkers'. His dandyish clothes and cigarette holder identify him as a social type known as a 'Knut'. These supposedly idle and foppish young men had been the object of amused scorn in pre-war years. The stereotype is used here to arouse revulsion against the concept of conscientious objection.

Conscientious objectors featured heavily in press reports at the time, but they represented only a tiny fraction of the six million men who served in the forces during the war. Conscription was therefore looked upon as a success and was emulated in Canada and New Zealand. The Australian government attempted to introduce it, but the public rejected the measure in two referendums. Ireland was a special case. For fear of inflaming Irish nationalism, conscription was never implemented there.

Shells

The nature of the fighting on the Western Front meant that the Army's guns had a limitless appetite for shells. In May 1915, BEF Commander Sir John French blamed the failure of an attack at Aubers Ridge on a shortage of high explosive shells. His cause was taken up by the influential military correspondent of *The Times*, Charles Repington, who wrote 'the want of an unlimited supply of high explosive was a fatal bar to our success'. His newspaper and the *Daily Mail* both attacked the War Office and its chief Lord Kitchener for the shortage. Kitchener had made efforts to expand Britain's war production; munitions production had increased almost twentyfold since the outbreak of the conflict – but it was not enough. The Army was 92 per cent short of its requirement for high

Left: This **poster** sums up the manpower challenge faced by Britain. The Army was desperate for men, but without fully staffed factories and transport networks, it would not get the weapons it needed to fight the war. Both workers and soldiers were 'needed to serve the guns'. This poster, as well as calling for men, is careful to give equivalent status to the munitions worker and the soldiers at the front.

explosive shells. The War Office was not helped by Kitchener's resentment of interference, and his failure to follow normal ministerial procedures led to him being nicknamed 'K of Chaos'.

The 'Shell Scandal' failed to destroy Kitchener's reputation with the public, but it prompted a change of government. Asquith dissolved his government and formed an all-party coalition to oversee Britain's 'full mobilisation and organisation' for war. The most significant change in the short term was that Kitchener lost responsibility for war production to a new Minister of Munitions – the former Chancellor of the Exchequer, David Lloyd George. This highly ambitious man staked his career on finding a solution to the most pressing problem of the day. His immense energy and powerful position within the new government enabled him to centralise every aspect of munitions production – from raw material purchases and inventions, to employment practices and workers' welfare – in the hands of his ministry. It began to build huge government munitions factories. At the same time, thousands of businesses, from railway carriage and bicycle manufacturers to family jewellers were converted to 'controlled establishments' churning out guns, limbers, fuzes and shells. All across Britain, vast quantities of shells and guns poured out of factories. Railways, canals and ships pumped this essential equipment to the front line.

Lloyd George was still forced to negotiate with Kitchener over the allocation of manpower, but he did not forget the potential addition to his workforce that was offered by women. The employment of women was nothing new. Before the war, almost 6 million British women had been in work. The textile industry employed many thousands but, as the war began to effect trade, began to lay them off. Many other women were in domestic service; working long hours as maids or cooks in wealthy households. The expanding munitions industries, offering guaranteed work and regulated conditions at higher wages than women generally earned, proved an attractive proposition. The novelty of the Munitionette caught the public's imagination. The very fact that working class women might be able to earn a good living in such a way came as a surprise. Madeline Ida Bedford's poem 'Munitions Wages' purported to speak with the voice of a Munitionette:

Previous page: The production of shells involved a number of distinct processes. Shells were made at one location and their fuzes at another. They were filled with explosive at specialised filling factories. The largest of these, the **National Shell Filling Factory at Chilwell in Nottinghamshire**, is shown in this photograph. Chilwell was a wholly new factory built in late 1915. It employed 10,000 people, many of whom were women who had formerly worked in the local lace industry. Chilwell's task was to fill heavy artillery shells, and by the war's end it had filled almost 64 per cent of all those produced.

Earning high wages?
Yus, Five quid a week.
A woman, too, mind you,
I calls it dim sweet.

Ye're asking some questions –
But bless yer, here goes:
I spends the whole racket
On good times and clothes.

However, not all of those recruited for munitions work were working class women with experience in the labour market. Some middle class women also volunteered. They were frequently appointed as factory supervisors. One of them, Monica Cosens, wrote with wonder that, 'the ranks of Lloyd George's army of shell-workers are made up of parlour maids, clergymen's daughters, laundry hands, step-washers, artists, publicans' daughters, nursemaids, charwomen, authors, barmaids, board-school teachers, dukes' daughters, flowergirls, South Africans, Canadians, in fact of women from every walk in life'.

There was resistance to this influx of female labour. According to a 1915 report, male workers saw women as 'interlopers' and 'unfair competitors'. They expressed their views through their unions; especially with regard to 'dilution' – the training of unskilled workers, many of them women, for skilled work that had previously been exclusively theirs. At the outbreak of war the Trades Union Congress had promised not to call any strikes. However workers still downed tools over pay and conditions. The July 1915 Munitions of War Act made strikes illegal in 20,000 'controlled establishments', but in general Lloyd George was careful to keep the powerful unions happy. He was forced to give in to the pay demands of powerful groups like the South Wales Miners and even rushed to Glasgow on Christmas Day 1915 in the hope of calming industrial unrest among shipyard workers in Clydeside. Guarantees were given that women would not permanently replace the men whose jobs they had filled. As it was, men still provided two thirds of the workforce and usually took home better wages than the women. Lloyd George thought pay equality 'a social revolution which [. . .] it is undesirable to attempt during war time'.

Above: This **fretwork figurine** depicts David Lloyd George as Minister of Munitions; a shell under each arm. Lloyd George had stood on the radical Left of the Liberal Party before the war, but now began to alienate many of his former admirers as he strove to suppress labour unrest which threatened production. He wrote expressing his exasperation:

'The whole of this very serious and menacing trouble is but part of the price we are paying for running a great war on what is known as the 'voluntary' system. An undisciplined nation is fighting the best-disciplined country in the world, and some of our politicians think this terrible handicap is a real advantage. I wish they could have a few weeks experience of the Munitions Department.'

Government control of production and the need to accommodate female workers prompted state intervention in working conditions and workers' welfare. The Ministry of Munitions appointed a health committee. An official publication was frank about the thinking behind this, stating that 'without health there is no energy, without energy there is no output'. Larger factories had to provide separate canteens and washrooms for men and women and even crèches for working mothers. 'Townships' were built around some of the new government factories. These were busy and social places, with housing, schools, shops, cinemas and banks. Even around older munitions-producing centres like the Woolwich Arsenal, model housing estates were constructed to house the ever-growing workforce. Munitions factories produced rule books and enforced strict discipline. A Women's Police Service, another wartime novelty, routinely searched women arriving for work for forbidden items – particularly matches which might cause disaster in a shell filling factory.

Even with such safeguards, munitions production was dangerous. In January 1917, 73 men and women were killed in an explosion at the Silvertown high explosive factory in East London. In July 1918 an even bigger blast tore through the massive shell-filling plant at Chilwell in Nottinghamshire, killing 134 workers. Only 32 identifiable bodies were found. The chemicals used to make explosives were a more insidious threat. As a task which did not require much physical strength, the filling of shell casings with explosive paste became largely a female job. This mixture could cause blood disorders and liver damage, turning the skin yellow. Sufferers were known as 'canaries'. Over 100 munition workers died of TNT poisoning before its dangers were identified.

Lloyd George successfully applied his energies to building upon and rationalising the work begun by Kitchener. By mid-1916 the Army was no longer short of shells. Yet even as his efforts began to come to fruition, Lloyd George was catapulted into a new role – when he succeeded Kitchener as Minister for War. On 5 June 1916 Kitchener had boarded the cruiser HMS *Hampshire*, which was to take him on a visit to Russia. Within hours the ship sank, after striking a mine which had been laid by a German submarine. To the great distress of the nation Lord Kitchener perished, along with most of HMS *Hampshire's* crew.

Below: Special protective clothing had to be supplied for female munition workers. Those engaged in heavy or particularly active work were equipped with overalls like these. The sight of so many women in trousers was a great novelty at the time, but was accepted as a wartime necessity. *The Times* reported that the phenomenon was greatly approved of by a visiting delegation of French women who had not imagined the British to be 'quite so daring and unconventional'.

Above: An official guide to munition workers' welfare suggested that 'if opportunities of wholesome amusements, refreshments and recreation are not provided, the public-houses and less desirable places of entertainment may benefit, but everyone else suffers'. This photograph shows a **football team formed by female workers** at the AEC munitions factory at Beckton, London. Its captain Grace Werner (with the ball), had formerly acted on the London stage under the stage-name Gracie Sinclaire.

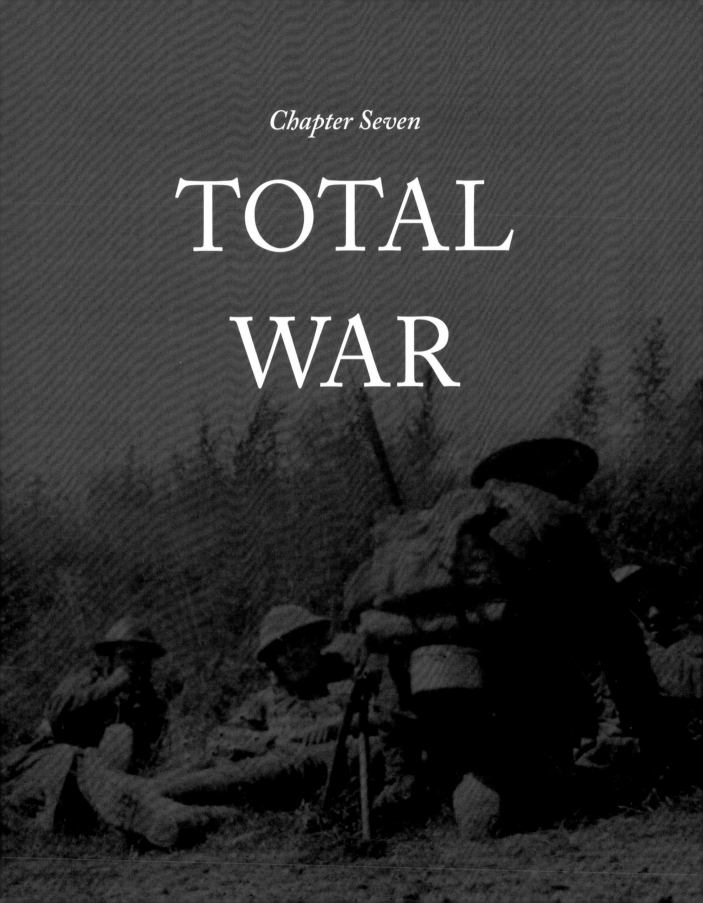

Chapter Seven

TOTAL
WAR

'The whole horizon seemed to be on fire, the bursting shells blending with the smoke from the burning villages'

1915 had been a year of setbacks for the Allies. Russia had been repeatedly defeated; Serbia had been overrun by its enemies; Britain had become involved in distracting and indecisive campaigns in the Middle-East; Italy had failed in its attacks upon Austria. Nevertheless, the Allied leaders held high hopes for the coming year. For the first time they agreed to co-ordinate their strategy. With their war industries now producing plenty of guns and shells, they would try to win the war by attacking the Central Powers on all fronts. But their enemies would strike first.

War Winning Plans

In December 1915 the Allied generals met at Chantilly in France. There they agreed a joint strategy proposed by General Joffre. All of them would launch major attacks against Germany and Austria-Hungary during the following spring and summer. They were confident that their combined efforts would overwhelm their enemies. The British role would be to mount an offensive alongside the French in northern France. It would take place where the River Somme met the German front line. The Somme was a rural region, largely untouched by war, and it was where the British and French armies stood alongside each other. The British had not yet taken part in an attack on this scale, and there was a fear in the French high command that their allies would not commit themselves fully unless the two armies fought together.

The Germans, however, had a plan of their own for 1916. Despite his failure to force Russia into peace negotiations, Germany's military chief Erich von Falkenhayn still sought to knock one of the Allies out of the war. He regarded Britain as Germany's most deadly foe, but decided that if he could first destroy the French Army, he would be knocking 'England's best sword' from its hand. He ordered an attack on the French fortress city of Verdun. German forces there were well placed to receive supplies by rail, while the French defenders would be hampered by poor

LES GRANDES BATAILLES DE VERDUN

AVOCOURT - MORT-HOMME - BETHINCOURT - BOIS DES CORBEAUX - FORGES - BRABANT sur MEUSE - CÔTE DU POIVRE - DOUAUMONT - FORT DE DOUAUMONT - VERDUN - VAUX

WOÊVRE

MEUSE

AVOCOURT	MALANCOURT	BETHINCOURT	FORGES et BOIS DES CORBEAUX	BRABANT sur MEUSE	VACHERAUVILLE VAUX-DAMLOUP	CÔTE du POIVRE	FORT DE DOUAUMONT	VERDUN	DÉFENSE DE
MORT-HOMME		FRONT DU 4 et 5 MARS		ASSAUTS 22 FÉVRIER 1916		25 FÉVRIER	28 FÉVRIER au 5 MARS	BOMBARDEMENT LE 20 et 21 FÉVRIER	VAUX 27 FÉVRIER
COMBATS et ASSAUTS MARS AVRIL 1916	CUMIÈRES — BETHINCOURT		6 et 8 MARS	PERTE DU BOIS des CAURES	FRONT du 25 FÉVRIER		DOUAUMONT VILLAGE		
	6 au 13 AVRIL 1916			23 FÉVRIER 1916	ASSAUT DE SAMOGNEUX 24 FÉVRIER 1916		3 AU 5 MARS		
				ÉVACUATION DE BRABANT 24 FÉVRIER 1916					

transport links. Falkenhayn looked to draw the French into counter-attacks which would expose their men to an overwhelming concentration of artillery. In short, he hoped to make the murderous nature of the war on the Western Front work in favour of the German Army.

In February 1916, the battle opened with a devastating artillery bombardment. French General Philippe Pétain was ordered to save Verdun at all costs. The French government feared that defeat would destroy the country's morale. The battle became a struggle to save France itself. The Army clung on to deny the city to the Germans, but its sufferings as the battle dragged on were terrible. Lieutenant Henri Desagneaux wrote in his diary for 25 June, 'the blood flows, the heat is atrocious, the corpses stink, the flies buzz – it's enough to drive one mad. Two men of the 24th Company commit suicide.' Coming out of the line five days later he wrote, 'our time at Verdun has been awful. Our faces have nothing human about them [. . .] Despite our joy at being alive, our eyes reveal the crazy horror of it all.'

Above: This French **poster** uses an aerial perspective to aid public understanding of the Battle of Verdun. The Germans hoped to place their artillery on the commanding heights to the east of Verdun, but had to capture some of the underground fortresses which ringed the town to do so. The fall of Forts Douaumont and Vaux were terrible blows to the morale of the French people, but their army held on, and was able to recapture the two forts in the autumn. The fighting at Verdun set new standards for horror, due to the massive amount of artillery concentrated on a relatively small battlefield.

But the French did not suffer alone. The Germans were never able to seize the commanding positions from which their artillery could dominate the battlefield, and Pétain concentrated his own artillery upon the attackers to deadly effect. German casualties ran at a level not far short of those of the French. The battle was to last for ten months at a cost of 700,000 French and German lives.

Falkenhayn's plans suffered a further blow in June when the Russian Front sprang dramatically into life. Russia had achieved wonders over the winter and spring in re-equipping and reinforcing its defeated armies. Its shell production had increased tenfold between 1915 and 1916. Now it was ready to play its part in the Allied plan for 1916. On 4 June General Alexei Brusilov launched a massive offensive against the Austro-Hungarians in Galicia. Over half a million Russians attacked on a 300 mile front. The Austro-Hungarian Army was ill-prepared. To Falkenhayn's fury, his Austrian counterpart Conrad had transferred many of his best troops west, for an unsuccessful attack on the Italians.

The forces facing Brusilov were overwhelmed; losing 1.35 million men – mostly as prisoners. Germany was forced to rush troops to the area and, from this point onwards, Austria-Hungary was unable to take any military initiative without German approval and support. As an Austrian officer, Karl Schneller bluntly put it, 'we are now totally and completely under the thumb of the Germans'. Brusilov's success had the additional effect of encouraging Romania to enter the war on the Allied side.

Now it was the turn of France and Britain to launch their attack. But plans for the Somme battle had been altered due to the heavy commitment of the French Army at Verdun. It had become clear that the British Army would have to take the leading role in the offensive. Britain's New Army, composed of the volunteers recruited since 1914, would undergo its first great test. It would be equipped with new guns and ammunition supplied by the Ministry of Munitions. The British Army on the Western Front would also be led by a new commander. Following the Battle of Loos the government had lost faith in Sir John French. On 19 December 1915 he was replaced by Sir Douglas Haig, who had played a central part in the battles at Ypres in 1914 and at Loos. Haig was immediately thrown into planning the largest operation which the British Army had ever mounted.

There was uncertainty as to the aims of the offensive. Haig hoped that his 'Big Push' would break the German Army in France. The French realised that their reduced contribution to the joint attack made such a result highly unlikely. They looked only to wear down Germany's strength. In this they were echoed by the man chosen by Haig to take day-to-day control of the battle, General Sir Henry Rawlinson. Rawlinson expressed the view in his diary that 'the attack is to go for the big thing. I still think we would do better to proceed by shorter steps.' The British objectives for the battle were therefore a compromise. In May, Haig informed his generals that 'however confident of success, it would not be sound to base our plans on the expectation of definitely destroying the enemy's power in one campaign'. If this could not be achieved, the goal should be to 'wear out the enemy' while training Britain's inexperienced army and, because of Verdun, to 'support the French'. This was sensible; but the failure to go wholeheartedly for one outcome or the other bedevilled the planning of the huge bombardment with which the battle would commence.

The Somme – A Costly Apprenticeship

The British would use 1,500 guns in the biggest bombardment that they had yet mounted. It was intended to last for five days but was extended to seven, due to bad weather. The bombardment was expected to destroy the German defences, giving the infantry an easy task when they attacked. Tragically this was to prove wishful thinking. The British Army still lacked enough heavy guns for the task in hand. The effects of this shortage were worsened by the fact that Haig insisted that both the German first and second lines should be hit simultaneously; hoping that both could be breached in the initial attack. The already limited firepower was dispersed over a too great an area of the battlefield.

The soldiers waiting to attack were nonetheless enthusiastic; particularly the volunteers of the New Army, who were about to fight en-masse for the first time. Lance Corporal Norman Tattersall of the 20th Manchester Regiment wrote home:

> 'Our boys are jubilant, you would think they were going to a football match [. . .] We are confident of giving them a good hiding. We will sacrifice many of our lives, but it will be for the sake of those at home [. . .] Our Battalion is over the top first and you will read of a grand success.'

Below left: Heavy guns like the British **9.2-inch Howitzer** made the difference between victory and defeat on the Western Front. Howitzers fired large shells at a high trajectory, bringing them plunging down on the enemy. Effective against trenches and all but the deepest dugouts, they were also used for the essential task of destroying enemy artillery. The bombardment which started the Battle of the Somme was far bigger than any yet fired by the British. Lieutenant Adrian Consett-Stephen marvelled at it in a letter home:

'My Lord the gun! He lives in a lair that takes a month to build [. . .] an army toil to feed him with long rows of glistening shells. Men and gun are one and indivisible. My Lord the Gun has come into his own, and his kingdom today is large – it is the world.' However there were still not enough heavy guns to make the bombardment effective.

In the early morning mist of 1 July 1916 the infantry attack was launched. By the afternoon of a sweltering day, the British Army had suffered the greatest disaster in its history. Almost 20,000 soldiers were killed, among them Norman Tattersall's brother, Albert. A further 37,646 were reported wounded or missing. Few obtained their objectives. In most instances the Germans had remained unscathed in deep shelters excavated in the chalk which characterised the region. In many places the artillery had also failed to cut the barbed wire. Almost a third of British heavy artillery shells turned out to be 'duds', failing to explode due to their hasty manufacture. These circumstances, combined with the inexperience of many of the troops and their officers, were the cause of the disaster. This point is proved by the relative success of the French on their sector of the Somme front. They enjoyed a great victory at light cost, due to their excellent artillery support and their greater experience of mounting such operations.

Above: This **helmet** was worn by the French soldier who advanced immediately to the right of the British forces on the first day of the Battle of the Somme. He was a private named Berenger. It is not known how he sustained the damage to his helmet. Berenger's commander, Commandant Le Petit was reported to have walked towards the German front line with his arm linked with that of the commander of the neighbouring 17th Liverpool Regiment, Lieutenant Colonel Bryan Fairfax. The French benefitted from experience of fighting large battles and, despite deploying fewer troops than Britain on the Somme, they performed with greater efficiency; capturing more men and guns than their allies did.

Left: These rare images were taken on an officer's personal camera. They show soldiers of the British 18th Division in action on 1 July 1916. This division enjoyed success on that day. The second photograph shows men of 55th Brigade after capturing their objective, a trench known as 'Montauban Alley'. General Sir Walter Congreve, who commanded the Corps which included 18th Division, called it 'A perfect day', declaring 'I am proud of my splendid fighting troops'.

Left: An officially sponsored film, *The Battle of the Somme*, was shown in cinemas from August 1916. One scene, from which this **still** is taken, made a particularly lasting impact on audiences, showing a wounded man being brought in by a comrade. *The Battle of the Somme* was the first feature-length documentary ever made, and was phenomenally successful. An estimated 20 million people saw the film within a few weeks of its release. It was not shown without controversy however. Herbert Hensley Henson, the Dean of Durham, wrote to *The Times*, protesting 'against an entertainment which wounds the heart and violates the very sanctities of bereavement'. He was answered by Sir Arthur Conan Doyle who observed that 'the theatre is filled constantly with the relatives of the men portrayed, and I do not think they feel that there is any desecration in the performance'.

Watching the barrage falling on the French sector of the front, Captain Rowland Feilding observed that 'the whole horizon seemed to be on fire, the bursting shells blending with the smoke from the burning villages'. The British units who attacked closest to the French – some of whom benefited from French artillery fire – also captured parts of the German line, but here Rawlinson's lack of belief in a breakthrough meant that no action was taken to exploit their success. The reaction of those who fought that day was mixed. Lieutenant Edward Beddington-Behrens wrote home the next day: 'I am sure you must be bucked with our success! We are – it was fine seeing the Boches prisoners come in. But the casualties were terrible.'

The tragedy of 1 July 1916 still dominates Britain's memory of the First World War, but it was just the first day of five months of fighting. As summer turned to autumn the Anglo-French armies subjected the Germans on the Somme to a merciless pressure, including major attacks in mid-July, September and November. Artillery Officer Adrian Consett-Stephen wrote home explaining that 'one can compare [. . .] our whole offensive to a little boy who sets out to climb a big tree. On failing to reach further than the first bough he takes out a pocket knife and proceeds to cut it down. That is what we are doing.' The British and French had little choice but to continue, as their Allies Italy and Russia were playing their part in the joint plan by attacking on their respective fronts, and Romania had joined the Allies and invaded Hungary. The Somme battle also meant that the Germans were unable to mount further attacks on Verdun.

Britain's soldiers were joined on the Somme by Imperial troops from Australia, Canada, New Zealand and South Africa. Tiny Newfoundland had already paid a heavy price when its regiment had sustained 91 per cent casualties on 1 July. In common with their British comrades, none had previously experienced a battle on this scale. An Australian, Corporal Oswald Blows, recorded his reaction in his diary:

> 'The terrors of war are awful and Britain is paying a terrible price in blood for the deserved peace. We can win, and we will. If it were man to man, we would absolutely walk over them, but it's their artillery which infantrymen cannot hit back at, and the cruel and apparently inexhaustible supply of shells [. . .] which breaks up and demoralises a man, and cruelly maims thousands.'

Left: This **jacket** was worn by **British officer Second Lieutenant Harold Cope of the 7th Border Regiment**. In early August 1916 Cope's unit was involved in heavy fighting for the shattered remains of Delville Wood, which occupied a commanding position on the Somme battlefield. On 7 August Cope was seriously wounded. The sleeve of his jacket was cut away to allow his wound to be dressed. Had he received his wound in 1914, Cope might well have died. But British Army medical services had learned to get the seriously wounded quickly from the battlefield to Casualty Clearing Stations near the front line for life-saving operations.

Above: **Canadian soldiers** played an important part in the British attacks on the Somme. This photograph shows Canadians after their first action there, near the village of Courcelette. They are riding on an American-built Autocar truck. The sergeant in the front passenger seat is wearing a German helmet and also has a captured bayonet. A Canadian soldier, Private John Brice – formerly a bank clerk in St John, New Brunswick – wrote home saying 'I can't help but feel impressed by the tremendous force which seems to be behind this drive of the British [. . .] the guns, horses, men and supplies of all sorts seem to be inexhaustible'.

In fact the whole Army was forced to learn how to conduct a major offensive through bitter experience. One of the commanders on the spot, General William Furse, lamented that 'we are squandering our men [. . .] partly because of indifferent Art[illery], partly because of indifferent ammun[ition], partly because of indifferently trained infantry'. A French officer noted that 'our neighbours, the British, are slower than us because less experienced. Their superb infantry, superbly equipped, is very brave but undergoing a costly apprenticeship.'

British planning and infantry tactics improved as the battle progressed, as did their use of artillery. Major successes were won on 14 July and 15 September, although neither brought a breakthrough. Worsening weather saw the battle sink into a muddy stalemate before it was called off in November.

Previous page: By 1916 the **Indian Army** units sent to the Western Front in 1914 had been transferred to Mesopotamia, apart from the cavalry, which remained. This photograph shows the **20th Deccan Horse** on 14 July 1916, shortly before taking part in the only cavalry action of the Battle of the Somme. Alongside the 7th Dragoon Guards, they advanced into a gap which had opened up between German units. A cavalryman, Shah Mirzah, wrote home of his experience:

'What I saw in the course of the advance I shall never forget. We had to pass amongst the dead bodies of men who had fallen during the morning's attack, and the trenches were full of German dead [. . .] the Dragoon Guards and Deccan Horse [. . .] had an engagement with a party of Germans. One troop of each regiment charged, killing sixteen Germans and taking forty prisoners [. . .] Our losses among the cavalry were not heavy.'

Left: For many men the war was an adventure from which they wanted to bring home souvenirs to show off to their families. The most sought-after personal trophy was the **spiked German Pickelhaube helmet**. This one – the helmet of an infantryman from Württemberg – was captured on the Somme by Lieutenant Jack Best of the Machine Gun Corps. Many trophies were scavenged from the battlefield, but a major offensive like the Somme provided an opportunity to take them directly from German soldiers. Military units also laid claim to captured equipment. Guns seized from the enemy were a sign of success on the battlefield.

The Decision Brought Nearer

On the last day of 1916 British General Sir Henry Wilson made the following diary entry, 'The last day of a year of indecisive fighting [. . .] both sides claiming victory; on the whole victory inclining to us, and the decision brought nearer.' While few would dispute that the battle of the Somme had been indecisive, had it brought an Allied victory nearer? As far as the British Army was concerned, this was certainly the dominant opinion. Wearied though they were by the long and bloody struggle on the Somme, most soldiers believed that they now had the skills and the equipment to beat the Germans. A visiting observer from neutral America reported that 'the general feeling seems to be one of disappointment that more was not accomplished, but also of satisfaction that marked superiority had been shown to the Germans in much of the fighting'. Edwin Montagu, who had succeeded Lloyd George as Minister of Munitions, wrote that 'there is not a soldier I meet who does not believe that this German force is a beaten one'.

For the Germans the lessons of the Somme were very different. The battle had caused around 600,000 Allied casualties, but the Germans had suffered over 500,000 themselves. This was more than a third of their entire losses for 1916. Their front on the Somme had held, but the German Army's policy of giving no ground willingly and of counter-attacking to regain any they lost had kept its casualties high. The Germans had not expected the French to be in any fit state to attack while the Verdun battle still raged, and they had not considered the inexperienced British capable of mounting such a massive operation at all. The sheer scale of the Allied attack had come as a blow to them. During the first ten days of the Battle of Verdun, the Germans had sustained 25,989 casualties. In the first ten days of the Somme they suffered 40,187. What shocked them most of all was the new intensity of the Allied artillery fire. A German military analysis in August 1916 concluded that 'the most difficult factor in the battle is the enemy's superiority in munitions. This allows their artillery, which is excellently supported by aircraft, to level our trenches and to wear down our infantry systematically'. German soldiers began to look upon the Somme front with fear, and outbreaks of indiscipline were reported. Lieutenant Colonel Albrecht von Thaer confided to his diary:

'We have had sad experiences with two Rhineland regiments. Driven to extremes by the horrendous enemy artillery fire, whole companies have refused to advance again, have 'disappeared' in the dark; for the first time, there have also been incidents within our area of command of men firing at their own officers. – Such things are best kept to ourselves.'

The Somme played a major part in the collapse of Falkenhayn's strategy. It confirmed the failure of his Verdun scheme, and was the most dangerous of the Allied offensives which beset the Central Powers on all sides. The imminent entry of Romania into the war, which would put another 650,000 men into the line against the Central Powers and cut off vital supplies of food and oil, was the final straw. The Kaiser replaced Falkenhayn with Germany's greatest military heroes, Paul von Hindenburg and Erich Ludendorff. Ironically Falkenhayn went on to play a major role in the surprisingly swift defeat of Romania by the combined armies of the Central Powers during the autumn of 1916. At the same time the failure of his strategy was emphasised by French attacks at Verdun which recaptured much of the ground taken by Germany early in the year.

Hindenburg and Ludendorff visited the Western Front in August and were horrified by what was happening on the Somme. The impressions they gained were to guide their decision-making as they got to grips with the challenge of winning the war for Germany. Immediately they gave orders for the construction of a new and improved defensive position in northern France. This was to become known to the Allies as the 'Hindenburg line'. Withdrawing to this shorter line, which they did in early 1917, would allow them to save troops for use elsewhere. But it meant abandoning a battlefield which Germany had expended thousands of lives to hold only months before. This was just the first sign of the fateful influence which the experience of the Somme was to exert on German strategy.

The Battle of the Somme had been the bloody centrepiece of a year in which the Allies had seized the strategic initiative from Germany. From now on, the German High Command no longer controlled the pattern of the war as it had done in 1914 and 1915. Instead Germany's leaders were to struggle to find an answer to the Allied ability to wage industrial warfare on a huge scale. While indecisive on the battlefield, the Somme marked a turning point in the war as a whole.

Right: Tanks,
Muirhead Bone, 1916
Muirhead Bone was Britain's first official war artist. He was sent to record British efforts on the Somme. His drawings proved hugely popular, as they had greater authenticity than the efforts of artists whose pictures appeared in the illustrated press, but who had never been to the front. This picture of a British tank made a particular impact. This new weapon was first used on 15 September, when forty-nine of them took part in a major attack around the villages of Flers and Courcelette. Early tanks lacked the range and reliability to be truly war-winning weapons, but they caused a sensation both at the front and among civilians at home.

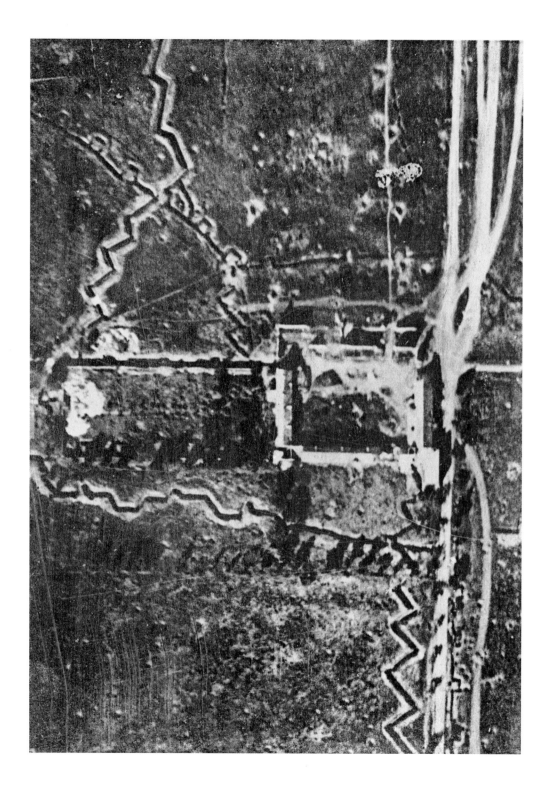

Left: Artillery relied heavily upon aerial observation to identify and map their targets. Most air combat revolved around the need to attack or protect aircraft which were carrying out photographic reconnaissance missions. By 1916 it had also become possible for observers in the air to maintain direct wireless contact with artillery units – guiding their fire onto target. These **two photos** show **Mouquet Farm on the Somme, before and after** it was fought over. For most of the Battle of the Somme the Allies enjoyed air superiority, due the effectiveness of their fighter aeroplanes. A German infantryman's diary for 16 August reads 'everybody is wishing for rain or at least bad weather so that one may have some degree of safety from the English aviators. One daren't leave one's hole all day or else one immediately gets artillery fire on the trench for half an hour.'

Left: *A Grave and a Mine Crater at La Boisselle, August 1917*
William Orpen, 1917
William Orpen was an artist who enjoyed privileged access to the Western Front due to his friendship with British Commander-in-Chief Sir Douglas Haig. He painted this picture of the Somme battlefield in 1917, following its abandonment by the Germans:

'Never shall I forget my first sight of the Somme in summer-time [...] The dreary, dismal mud was baked white and pure—dazzling white. White daisies, red poppies and a blue flower, great masses of them, stretched for miles and miles. The sky a pure dark blue, and the whole air, up to a height of about forty feet, thick with white butterflies: your clothes were covered with butterflies. It was like an enchanted land; but in the place of fairies there were thousands of little white crosses.'

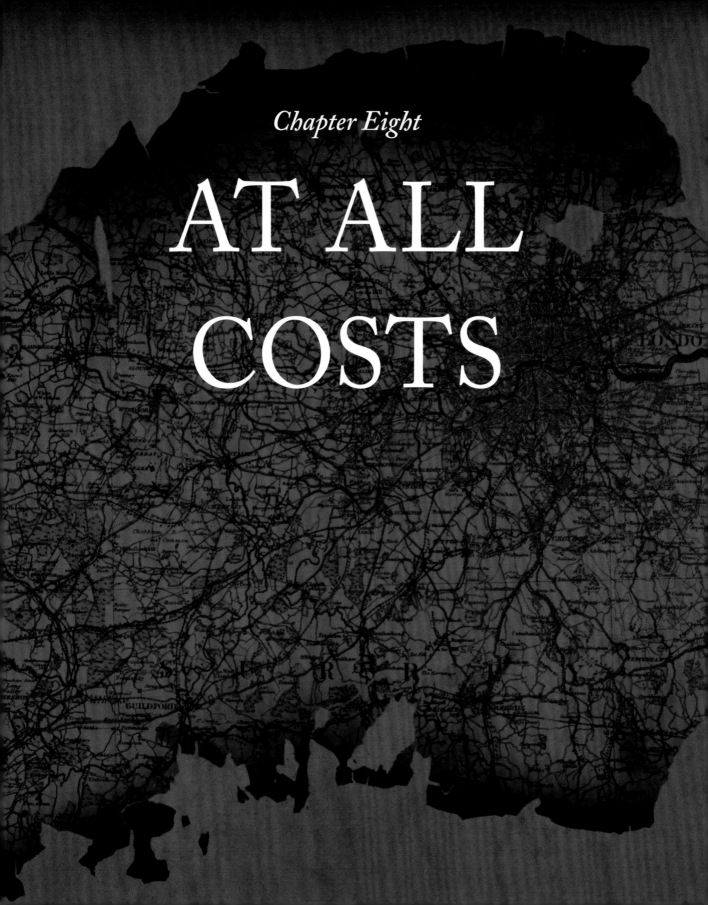

Chapter Eight

AT ALL
COSTS

'Not a soldier's or civilian's war, but the whole nation's war'

The immense battles of 1916 did not bring an end to the war; in fact they only succeeded in intensifying it. In both Britain and Germany new leaders were given control of the war effort. They were even more focused on winning outright victory than the men who had preceded them.

In Britain nobody could escape the impact of war anymore. Women kept the country going, taking on work usually done by their fathers, brothers and sons. Even children played their part in the war effort. Civilians increasingly found themselves in the front line: people were bombed in their homes; fighting broke out on the streets of a British city – Dublin; and German submarines brought the threat of starvation.

New Leaders

By the end of 1916 the industrial, economic and manpower resources of all sides were fully committed to the war effort, but victory did not come, and the toll of casualties continued to rise. This did not deter most people from supporting the war, but the apparent stalemate led to the fall of both Germany's and Britain's war leaders. Their strategies and policies were seen to have failed and both countries turned to men whom they felt would pursue victory at all costs.

In Germany the change took place as early as August 1916, when General Erich von Falkenhayn paid the price for the failure of his strategy. Kaiser Wilhelm was forced to replace him with the popular heroes of the Eastern Front, Paul von Hindenburg and Erich Ludendorff. He did so with reluctance, fearing the former as a rival figurehead and object of public adoration, and hating the latter for his naked ambition and non-aristocratic origins. Steady and reassuring, Hindenburg was already worshipped by the public and, once in charge of the war effort, usurped the Kaiser in their affections, just as the latter had feared. Ludendorff was the 'brains' of the partnership, but was more volatile. What both shared was a belief that complete victory must be won. They were convinced that anything less would result in their greatest fear: a political crisis which would result in the fall of the monarchy and a socialist Germany.

The first job for Hindenburg and Ludendorff was to deal with the immediate dangers facing Germany. The threat from Romania was swiftly neutralised, while in the West preparations were made to withdraw to a new defensive line – the Siegfried Position – the construction of which they immediately ordered. This system of fortifications, which the Allies called the 'Hindenburg Line', was intended to secure the Western Front against Allied attacks in 1917. Meanwhile Hindenburg and Ludendorff took radical steps to completely mobilise Germany for war. Based on the principal that all Germans had an equal responsibility to work for victory, they proceeded to militarise the German war effort. No sacrifice was too much to demand to keep the Army fighting. Army officers replaced civilians in control of war production and the incredibly ambitious 'Hindenburg Programme' was initiated, in the vain hope of doubling production of munitions and trench mortars and tripling that of artillery and machine guns. A 'Patriotic Auxiliary Service Law' made all men aged between 17 and 60 liable to work in war industry if necessary, although, to Hindenburg and Ludendorff's disgust, the demands of the trade unions had to be taken into account to get the law passed.

In Britain the change in leadership came in December 1916. The country had become bewildered by the apparent lack of progress towards victory, and public opinion, both led by and represented in the newspapers, demanded greater efforts. In introducing conscription and increasing government control over society through DORA, the coalition government had been following rather than leading public opinion. Prime Minister Herbert Asquith was seen as lacking the dynamism to be an effective war leader.

The ambitious David Lloyd George, having boosted his reputation as Minister of Munitions, was frustrated by the limited powers accorded to him at the War Ministry. Supported by the newspapers he began to campaign for the war to be run by a small committee, which he hoped to chair. Asquith agreed in principle, but was determined to chair the committee himself. At this point Lloyd George resigned – undermining support for Asquith within the coalition. On 5 December Asquith himself stepped down. He was replaced not by one of his Conservative rivals, but by David Lloyd George who, in the words of the *Daily Mirror*, was 'the man the nation wants [. . .] a man who can organise the country for

Right: Field Marshal Paul von Hindenburg became a patriotic icon for the German people – largely replacing the Kaiser in the affections of the public. He seemed to embody German military values of loyalty, strength, decency and chivalry, but also an iron will to achieve victory. His features could be found on souvenir china, and his image adorned film and **war loan posters** like this one. Hindenburg held the view that 'the entire German people should live only in the service of the Fatherland'. But his attempts to control manpower and war industries on military lines largely failed.

victory'. A less fulsome endorsement came from social historian Barbara Hammond, who wrote in a letter that, 'I've come to think that the Asquith regime means certain and moderate disaster, the Ll. G. [regime] either absolute disaster or success'.

Lloyd George immediately created a small, all-party war cabinet to make major decisions. He set up new ministries to control shipping, labour, war pensions, food and other aspects of the war effort. He also took the revolutionary step of bringing in successful men from outside the world of politics – 'men of push and go' – to run them. Lloyd George was a skilled political operator. As chancellor before the war he had been a hate figure for the Conservatives: he now relied upon their support. Lloyd George was not convinced by the insistence of Britain's generals that the war could be won only by costly efforts on the Western Front. But his Conservative colleagues and the press supported the generals, meaning that he never felt able to make a decisive intervention in military strategy.

A Nation at War

By 1917 no one on the British home front was untouched by the war. Its signs were everywhere. Edwin Montagu, who had replaced Lloyd George as Minister of Munitions, wrote that this 'was not a soldier's or civilian's war, but the whole nation's war'. One very obvious sign of this was the number of visibly wounded soldiers recuperating in war hospitals across the country. Many of these men were missing limbs or were disfigured. Disability, once confined largely to the poor and undernourished, now struck thousands of otherwise healthy young men. Wounded soldiers were treated as heroes, but the sheer numbers of them put a huge strain on medical services. From the Western Front alone, over one million British and Empire troops were evacuated to Britain for medical treatment. Most of the British hospitals nursed men who had already received emergency treatment behind the front and who had been shipped home to recover. The more active of these convalescents could be seen on the street, in cinemas and music halls or in parks. They wore a distinctive uniform known as 'hospital blues'. This served the dual purpose of identifying them as men who had made a sacrifice for their country and making it difficult for them to go on drinking binges or absent without leave.

Below: Medical experts were faced with the problem of the rehabilitation of wounded men. One answer was occupational therapy, in which men were encouraged to create pieces of craftwork. The intention was to exercise both limbs and minds. Frequently this began at an early stage in their recovery. Even men confined to bed and in pain might be given needlework to do. This **figurine of a VAD nurse** was made at a charity set up to rehabilitate disabled servicemen, the Lord Roberts Memorial Workshops. It was made on a fret-saw driven by a foot pedal. These saws were found useful for building up muscles in damaged legs. The committee in charge of the workshops claimed that it 'decided to start Toy-making as the staple industry, thus serving two purposes, namely, training the men, and capturing this pre-eminently German trade'.

The existing military medical services could not hope to staff so many hospitals; so much reliance was placed on the 70,000 volunteers of the Voluntary Aid Detachments (VADs). Many VADs were young middle and upper class women. They encountered a scale and intensity of pain and suffering for which their comfortable upbringings could not have prepared them, and a life that was far removed from popular perceptions of nursing. VAD Vera Brittain explained to her fiancé that, on a surgical ward, there was 'much work to be done in a great hurry [. . .] the mixture of gramophones and people shouting or groaning after operations drowns everything else [. . .] One does not often have to play the bedside Angel of Mercy of sentimental story illustrations'.

The munitions industry had been taking on female workers since 1915, but women soon began to find active roles in other areas of employment. The sight of women in offices was nothing new, but their numbers more than trebled during the war, whilst an even greater novelty was female employment in more visibly 'masculine' jobs such as on public transport. A further revolution was the recruitment of women to make good the shortage of agricultural labour which had been caused by men joining the Army, whilst the final stage in the integration of women into the war effort came in 1917, when the Army and Royal Navy both began to recruit female volunteers into new auxiliary branches.

Left: Glasgow tramways conductress's hat. The war saw the first employment of women in public transport. Although the numbers involved were not huge, they made a huge impact on the public. The sight of women drivers or ticket collectors was a much greater novelty than that of female factory workers – and this was not the only men's work they were taking over. Londoner Joe Hollister wrote:

'There was a flutter of excitement at Gracechurch street the other day at two girls with trouser overalls cleaning the windows of shops, the railway companys have employed them of course for a long while, tramcars, omnibuses, mail-vans, motor cars [. . .] all the caterers, newsvendors, bootblacks, lamplighters, latherers in barber shops, in fact in almost every sphere of activity, when 'Tommy' comes home he will be keeping house and minding the kids while the missus earns the pieces.'

Left: This photograph shows members of the **Women's Royal Naval Service (WRNS)** preparing floats for mine-nets. 1917 witnessed the creation of female branches of the armed services in Britain. The Women's Army Auxiliary Corps (WAAC) was established in March. WAAC volunteers took on roles such as bakers, cooks, clerks and drivers; releasing men for front line service. The WRNS was formed in November. In total, over 100,000 women joined Britain's armed services.

Children were also playing an increasing part in the war. They were encouraged to donate their pocket money to war charities, or use it to buy war savings stamps. Boy scouts watched the coast for signs of espionage or invasion, or guarded the transport network against sabotage. Many children went out to work. Laws governing the employment of children varied from region to region. Technically, the school leaving age was fourteen, but children younger than that worked on factories and farms. With so many fathers and brothers away fighting on low Army pay, a child's earnings could provide much needed income. In August 1917, Education Minister Herbert Fisher expressed concern that 600,000 children had been put 'prematurely' to work.

Left: In May 1915 a **Women's Land Service Corps** was established, and in February 1917 this was renamed the **Women's Land Army** (WLA). The 113,000 women who joined the WLA became farm labourers. The work was exhausting, dirty and badly paid. Many farming communities suspected women workers of loose morals. WLA organisers advised 'Land Girls' that 'you are dressed like a man, but remember that just because you wear a smock and breeches, you should take care to behave like an English girl'. Most Land Army recruits were middle class women who did not need to seek munitions work, where the wages were higher.

Left: British people were encouraged to lend their money to the government to finance the war. War Bonds offered wealthier citizens tempting rates of interest if they were willing to commit their money to a long term investment. Poorer people could also contribute by buying sixpenny war savings coupons which could be converted into war savings certificates. Even children were not left out. One of these colourful and collectable **stamps** was given out with each sixpenny war savings coupon purchased by a child. Various series were produced, covering subjects such as VC winners, women's work and the Royal Navy. These attractive items were intended to 'appeal to every child', but realistically would have been affordable only to children of well-off parents.

By 1917, Britain's war spending had quadrupled in just two years to nearly 70 per cent of its economic output. Taxes had been rising since 1914 and the government was increasingly forced to borrow heavily from abroad, mainly from the United States. A major contribution to funding the war was actually made by the very industries that were being paid to manufacture war materials. An Excess Profits Duty was imposed on them, permitting the government to apply a high rate of tax (80 per cent by 1917) to any profits made by these industries over and above an agreed amount.

The public were also called upon to lend money to the government by buying war bonds. If Britain defeated Germany, lenders would get their money back, with generous interest. Yet in 1917, it was by no means certain that Britain would be victorious or that, with national debt mounting, the government would be able to repay its people for their support. This did not prevent vast sums from being raised. A war bond floated in January 1917 raised £1,000million. Real tanks were displayed around the country in a fund-raising campaign. A 'Tank Week' held in Glasgow in January 1918 raised the astonishing sum of £14million.

Those with less disposable income were not left out, and a National War Savings Committee was established in 1916. This committee made lending to the government more affordable by offering war savings certificates for small sums of money. But inflation was eating into the incomes of working people. Food prices were rising fast and the influx of workers into industrial towns was pushing up rents. These concerns, combined with long hours and tough working conditions, prompted strikes in mines, shipyards and some war industries. Rather than crush the strikes, Lloyd George addressed their demands; raising wages and controlling rents. Front line soldiers frequently expressed bitterness at the attitude of the strikers, feeling that they were failing to 'do their bit'. But, in reality, patriotism ensured that fewer working days were lost to strikes during the war than in the years which had preceded it.

Death on British Streets

British civilians also faced the dangers of war in their own homes. East coast towns had suffered naval bombardments in 1914, but a greater threat came from the air.

In January 1915 German airships, known as Zeppelins, began to make raids on British towns and cities. Their aim was to terrorise the population by bombing them, and their long range enabled them to strike almost anywhere. Zeppelins built a sinister reputation by attacking at night, from altitudes which made them almost invulnerable to attack. Not until 3 September 1916 was a German airship shot down, when William Leefe-Robinson, a twenty-one-year-old Royal Flying Corps officer, earned the Victoria Cross by destroying the airship SL11. Leefe-Robinson wrote to his father that, as the airship plunged to the earth in flames, he became aware of

> 'thousands, one might say millions of throats giving vent to thousands of feelings [. . .] All the sirens, hooters and whistles of steam engines, boats on the river, and munition and other works all joined in and literally filled the air – and the cause of it all – little me sitting in my little aeroplane above 13,000 feet of darkness!!'

In 1917 a new terror struck, in the form of raids by bomber aeroplanes. These bombers could only reach London and South-East England, but they were far more efficient at their task than the airships had been. People became angry at the lack of any proper warning system. There were no shelters, so people crowded into public buildings, including the London Underground. There were not enough searchlights or guns to bring down the German aircraft, and the government had to order the reluctant Army to send fighter aircraft home from the Western Front. These aircraft forced the Germans to switch from day to night bombing, but the raids continued into 1918. By the end of the war, air raids of all types had claimed the lives of 1,413 men, women and children, opening a new chapter in the history of warfare. Yet although they caused fear and, occasionally, panic, German air raids failed to inflict significant damage on Britain's war effort, or to deter British people from pursuing victory over the 'Hun babykillers'.

A further, shocking, intrusion of the war into the home front saw fighting on the streets of a British city in 1916, when an Irish Republican rebellion took place in Dublin. Mainstream Nationalist politicians – having been promised an Irish Parliament – had thrown their support behind the war in 1914. However some Republican activists saw the war as an opportunity to achieve not just Home Rule, but total independence for

Above: The Germans used two types of airship to attack Britain, the aluminium framed Zeppelin and the wooden framed Schütte-Lanz. The former were operated by the Navy and the latter by the Army. This **charred map of London** was recovered from the wreckage of Zeppelin L31, shot down over Potters Bar, Hertfordshire, on 1 October 1916 by Second Lieutenant Wulfstan Tempest. As the airship fell, 'roaring like a furnace', the crew were seen 'leaping vainly for their lives, and in the glare presented a hideous sight as they fell and were broken horribly upon the meadows while the watching crowds, exultant, roared out the National Anthem'. Among the dead was the leading German airship commander Kapitän-Leutnant Heinrich Mathy. In a premonition of his own end Mathy had earlier written 'if anyone should say that he was not haunted by visions of burning airships, then he would be a braggart'.

Ireland. Germany, hoping to cause a crisis in Britain and to draw British troops away from the Western Front, secretly undertook to send them guns, and an armed rising was planned for Easter 1916. One of its leaders, James Connolly, declared that, 'the time for Ireland's battle is now, the place for Ireland's battle is here'. But the German ship bringing the arms was intercepted. With plans going awry, some of the Republican leaders attempted to call off their action, but others went ahead regardless. On Easter Monday they seized public buildings and declared the establishment of an Irish Republic.

The rebels were never strong enough to achieve their aims, and divisions among Nationalists prevented the rising from spreading. Within a week the Republicans had been forced to surrender. The rising resulted in the deaths of 160 soldiers, 60 rebels and 300 innocent civilians. Most shockingly of all, artillery had been fired on the streets of a major British city – with serious damage caused to central Dublin. The rebel leaders were tried by Court Martial and shot by firing squad. Like the execution by the Germans of Cavell and Fryatt, this application of military law, while technically correct, had negative political consequences for those who ordered it. The unnecessary brutality of the executions, even more than the rising itself, fanned the flames of Irish Nationalism. Thousands of Irishmen continued to fight for the empire as part of the British Army, but many in Ireland now began to look beyond the policies of the moderate Nationalists, and dreamt of a future for Ireland outside the United Kingdom.

Below left: In 1917–1918 South-East England came under attack from a German bomber unit known as the **England Geschwader** (England Squadron), based near Ghent in Belgium. Their main weapon was the Gotha bomber. The first Gotha raid on London in June 1917 left 162 dead and 432 injured. The Gotha's speed and altitude made it very difficult for British fighters to attack. The England Squadron also had small numbers of the gigantic Zeppelin-Staaken bomber-plane, which was effectively invulnerable to attack and could carry a 1,000kg bomb. The Gothas created such fear that 300,000 people sheltered in the London Underground nightly. This **memorial napkin** records the deaths of 18 primary school children, killed when a Gotha bomb hit Upper North Street School in Poplar on 13 June 1917.

Below: A view of a Zeppelin, probably L 50, coming out of a hangar

In order to prevent the further slaughter of Dublin citizens, and in the hope of saving the lives of our followers now surrounded and hopelessly outnumbered, the members of the Provisional Government present at Head-Quarters have agreed to an unconditional surrender, and the Commandants of the various districts in the City and Country will order their commands to lay down arms.

Left: This **note** confirms the surrender of the Irish Republican leaders in Dublin at the end of the **Easter Rising**. Styling themselves as members of the 'Provisional Government' they offer unconditional surrender in the hope of 'saving the lives of our followers, now surrounded and hopelessly outnumbered'. The leadership themselves were aware that their own fates were likely to be trial and execution. The first signature is that of Patrick (Padraig) Pearse, followed by those of James Connolly and Thomas MacDonagh.

The Submarine Threat

In the spring of 1917 British people faced the gravest threat yet to their ability to continue the war. The battles of 1916 had proved that Germany could not win the war on land while all of its enemies remained united. Its new military leaders, Hindenburg and Ludendorff, were determined to 'save the men from another Somme battle'. They therefore gave their backing to a Navy plan to strangle Britain into submission with submarines. Britain was heavily reliant upon imported food – especially North American grain. Germany's admirals were confident that a complete U-boat blockade would bring about starvation and civil collapse in Britain within months and force the British government to the negotiating table. This would mean recommencing unrestricted submarine warfare, to which American protests had brought an end in 1915. Politicians pointed out the risk that a renewed campaign of this nature might bring the USA into the war. Hindenburg and Ludendorff countered that the tiny US Army would take years to prepare for a European war, and the Navy promised that its submarines would stop it ever reaching France. The Kaiser was persuaded by these arguments and took what turned out to be the fateful decision to approve the policy.

On 1 February 1917 the Germans announced an exclusion zone around Britain in which all shipping was liable to be sunk without warning. In Germany the U-boat men became national heroes. At last a way seemed to have been found to strike effectively at the hated 'English'. Some, however, understood the gamble which had been taken. Evelyn, the English wife of German aristocrat Prince Blücher, recorded the reaction in Germany in her diary, 'everyone is excited about the submarine question [. . .] Germany is playing her last card'. At first, it looked like it might be a winning card.

Germany had many more submarines than in 1915, and they carried more torpedoes. Ship after ship, both Allied and neutral, was sunk. By April the level of shipping losses was becoming critical. Between February and April 1917, U-boats sank two million tons of merchant shipping carrying valuable cargo. Britain really did begin to see the spectre of starvation looming, and some of its leaders began seriously to doubt the country's ability to continue fighting. Admiral Jellicoe, now First Sea Lord, stated bluntly that 'they will win unless we can stop these losses – and stop them soon'.

Opposite and left: To counter the U-boat threat, British marine artist Norman Wilkinson invented dazzle-painting. He expressed its intention in a letter to the Admiralty: 'The proposal is to paint a ship with large patches of strong colour in a carefully thought out pattern and colour scheme, which will so distort the form of the vessel that the chances of successful aim by attacking submarines will be greatly decreased.' Wilkinson's idea was taken up and most vessels were carrying these extraordinary paint schemes by 1918. Wilkinson supervised the painting of these **small models** to provide approved paint-schemes for all types of ship. The effectiveness of the schemes was tested by looking at the models through a miniature periscope.

Relief came when the desperate Admiralty changed its strategy, introducing a policy it had previously resisted – the convoy system. Ships would no longer sail alone, but in groups under naval command. This greatly reduced the likelihood of U-boats finding their targets, as they found it just as difficult to locate a convoy as a single ship. If they did find a convoy, their task was now more difficult and dangerous, as, when the convoys approached Britain, they were met by naval escort vessels and aircraft which guarded them from attack. The rate of sinkings plummeted and, although the U-boat threat remained until the end of the war, Britain's survival was no longer at stake. This victory came at a cost. Over 14,000 merchant seamen lost their lives in the U-boat war. Of these, 4,000 were lost in the dreadful period between February and April 1917.

Opposite: The German public seized upon the 1917–1918 campaign of unrestricted submarine warfare with huge enthusiasm, as this **poster** for the film *U-Boats Out!* shows. The U-boats seemed to offer a technological means of winning the war which did not involve the massive loss of life which land battles entailed. However the German Navy's conviction that such a campaign could bring Britain to its knees had been based on over-optimistic calculations.

America Goes to War

The most momentous effect of the new U-boat campaign was to push the United States to the brink of war. Even at the beginning of 1917 this had looked an unlikely scenario. President Wilson had been re-elected in 1916 with the campaign slogan 'He kept us out of the war'. American investors were warned not to place too much faith in an Allied victory. This was likely to have serious consequences for Britain, through whom the Allies had been raising huge loans on the US money market. The return of unrestricted submarine warfare changed everything. Wilson was infuriated by this renewal of German attacks upon neutral shipping and broke off diplomatic relations with Germany. He still hesitated to go to war, however, knowing that many of the American people – particularly the eight million who had German ancestry – were not convinced of the need to do so.

Soon though he was given the opportunity to act by another example of German recklessness. On 19 January 1917, German foreign minister Arthur Zimmermann had sent a coded telegram to Germany's ambassador in Mexico. It made a bizarre proposal. The Mexican government was to be informed that, should war break out between Germany and America, Germany would welcome Mexico as an ally and would reward it with the states of Texas, Arizona and New Mexico. British naval intelligence was intercepting all German communications, and the British government was only too happy to bring the Zimmermann note to Wilson's attention. The latter's fury was increased when he discovered that the Germans had sent one version of it via a telegraph machine in the US Embassy in Berlin, which he had made available to them to conduct peace discussions during the previous year.

On 2 April Wilson addressed Congress:

> 'The right is more precious than peace, and we shall fight for the things which we have always carried nearest our hearts – for democracy, for the right of those who submit to authority to have a voice in their own governments, for the rights and liberties of small nations, for a universal dominion of right by such a concert of free peoples as shall bring peace and safety to all nations and make the world itself at last free.'

Four days later, the USA declared war on Germany. The news was received with joy by the Allies and with enthusiasm by most Americans. It also had an instant effect on the war. The Allies were offered unlimited credit at affordable rates of interest by the US Treasury. Merchant ships of the Central Powers which had been impounded in US ports were turned over to Britain – easing the shipping shortage. And America committed its own powerful navy to the fight. Small warships were immediately thrown into the battle against the U-boats, joining the Royal Navy in escorting convoys. By the year's end a Squadron of US battleships had joined the British Grand Fleet at Scapa Flow – confirming once and for all the Allied domination of the vital North Sea.

The Germans had been right in considering that the US Army was unprepared for a European war, and it would be many months before it was ready to fight on any significant scale. With Allied help, however, it was made ready more speedily than anyone had expected, and the success of the convoy system meant that it could be safely transported across the Atlantic. The decision by Germany's leaders to attempt to win the war using U-boats had brought fearful consequences for their country.

Right: This **poster** calls upon men to volunteer for the US Army – using the powerful image of a mother and baby drowning as a result of Germany's submarine warfare campaign. However, the majority of American soldiers were drafted. This form of conscription of men chosen by ballot was selected by President Wilson as the fairest means of raising a large army.

In early 1917 the US Army was small, lacking in essential weapons such as heavy artillery and aircraft, and had limited experience of combat. When the need came however, the USA achieved the astonishing feat of creating and equipping an army of four million men – half of whom had been shipped to the Western Front by the war's end. Help came from the Allies. France supplied artillery and aircraft, Britain transported most of the American Expeditionary Force across the Atlantic.

Chapter Nine

LIFE AT THE FRONT

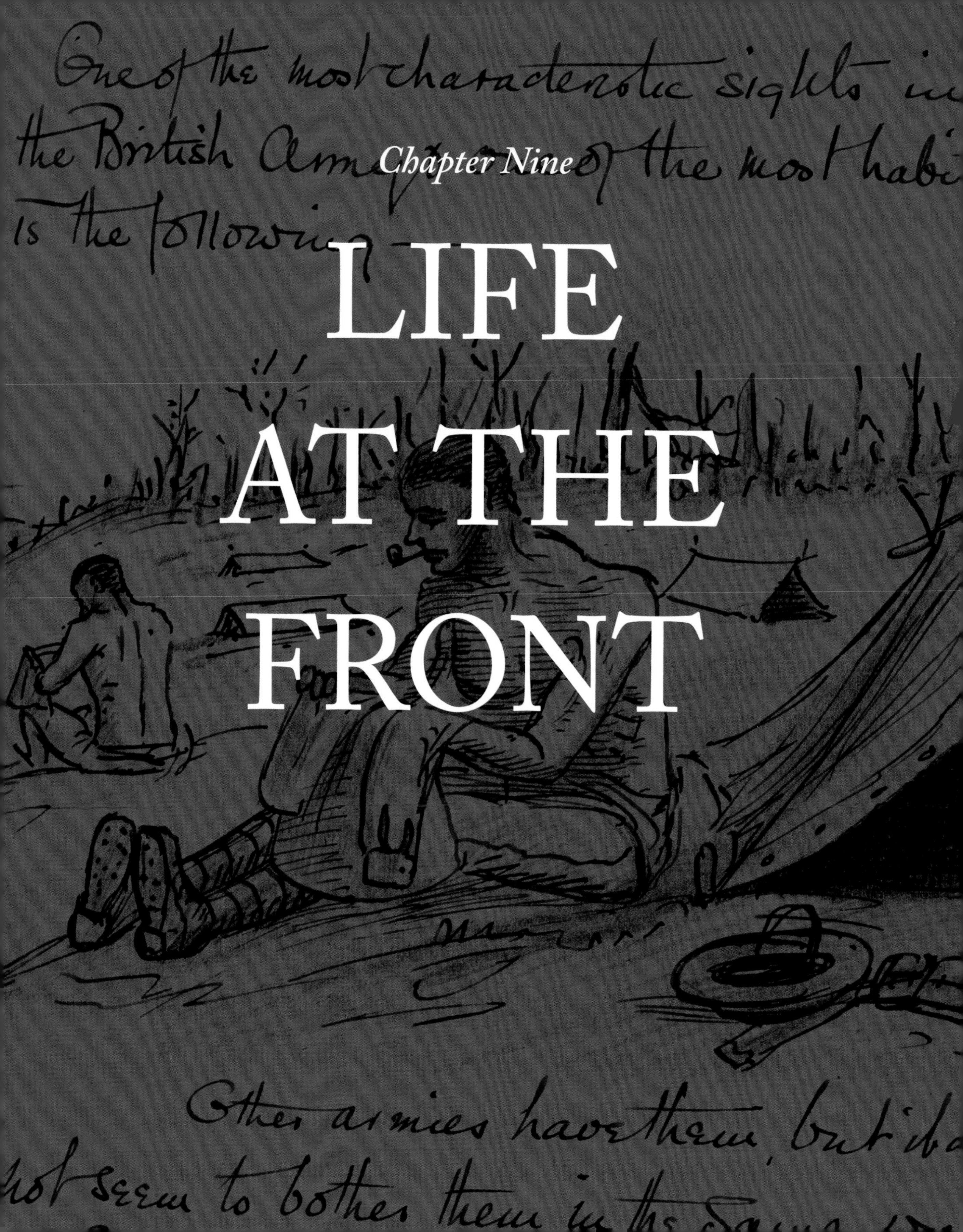

'If you are fit to lead them they will follow you'

During the fifty months of the First World War the British Army developed into a unique social organism, with new men – both volunteers and conscripts – being grafted onto the remains of the Regular Army. In some respects it was a massive social experiment. The traditions of the Army had to accommodate the expectations of civilian soldiers, and the social classes were mixed together in an unprecedented manner. While some women and a significant number of older men were to be found at the front, life as a fighting man was primarily an experience undergone by young men. Their youth helped them to endure hardship and exhaustion; it also accounts for their enthusiastic participation in any activity which offered relief from the drudgery and dangers of Army life.

Officers and Men

The Army was broadly divided into officers and men, the distinction between the two founded on social class, meaning that officers were often younger than the men they were commanding. During the initial phase of enthusiastic volunteering, many middle and upper class men had willingly taken up arms as ordinary soldiers. But while anyone might choose to serve in the ranks, officers were drawn from men educated in Britain's public schools and universities, and represented a tiny percentage of the country's population. As casualty rates rose, this requirement was relaxed and men educated in state-funded schools were given officer's commissions.

Officers were responsible for the lives of their men and, to a great extent, needed to earn their respect to lead them effectively. Junior officers – Lieutenants and Captains – were the ones who had daily contact with their men. A soldier would rarely come into contact with the Lieutenant-Colonel who commanded his unit, and he might never see a General. So the relationship between the junior officers and their men was crucial. If they proved incompetent, cowardly, or imposed discipline unfairly, they would be despised. But brave, fair leaders earned real devotion. Despite their youth, officers eager to discharge their duty of care towards their men generally aimed at establishing a paternalistic relationship with them. One Lieutenant, Francis Snell, wrote that 'one may stand in relation to these men as a father or an elder brother [. . .] if you are fit to lead them they will follow you'. Junior officers more than shared the dangers faced by their men. Expected to lead from the front, they were twice as likely to be killed.

Nonetheless, personal bravery was a means by which many leaders inspired their men. In the British Army even senior officers, who should have known better, sometimes took this to the point of recklessness. Seventy-eight British generals were killed in action – more than in the larger French and German armies. Even without this heightened threat of death, the responsibilities facing a young officer were daunting. The newly-commissioned officer was advised to regard himself as a mere 'blot on the earth' until he proved himself, and that he should 'assume the attitude of the new boy at school' in the company of more senior officers. Inexperienced officers relied on their battle-hardened non-commissioned officers, the Corporals and Sergeants, to coach them in the ways of trench fighting and Army life.

Below left: Officers had traditionally been expected to direct the fire of their men, rather than to fight themselves. The pistols they carried were a symbol of their rank, but were usually weapons of last resort. Officers could purchase their own pistols. These were usually revolvers in the service .455-inch calibre, like this **Webley Mark VI**. However some officers purchased different types of pistol and provided their own ammunition.

Trench raiding and other opportunities for close combat made pistols more important, and by the end of the war many officers were taking a serious approach to pistol shooting techniques. The war witnessed the issue of pistols to increasing numbers of enlisted men, such as 'bombers' or the crews of machine guns and mortars, who could not carry a rifle in addition to their other weapons. British manufacturers could not keep pace with the demand, so American and Spanish pistols were imported.

Officers were responsible for purchasing their own uniform and equipment, although they received an allowance to assist with this. As the dangers of modern warfare became clear, officers in the front line began to dress increasingly like their men, so that they could no longer be singled out by snipers. Writing home in 1917 Captain Graham Greenwell complained about 'all officers providing themselves with Tommies' uniforms as a sort of disguise [. . .] it is a sad departure'. When not in the front line, many young officers eagerly spent their money on the very latest in military fashion and gadgetry. Rules covering the cut and colour of officer's uniforms were bent or broken. Military outfitters offered countless desirable accoutrements such as complicated pocket knives, flashlights, cigarette cases and other smoker's requisites. Canes or walking sticks were also carried by virtually all officers – in and out of the line. These items were as much fashion accessories as practical devices. More senior officers sought to clamp down on the fashionable fads of their juniors. Lieutenant Colonel James Jack wrote, on taking command of a new Battalion, 'my officers [. . .] must be an example to their men in every respect [. . .] Proper officers' canes, a present from me, have replaced on parade a miscellaneous collection of walking sticks'.

The lowly 'Tommy', serving in the 'other ranks', had no such choice in his clothing and equipment. He was issued with everything he wore or carried and, although the British Army's kit compared well with that of other armies, the technology of the day meant that it was heavy and uncomfortable. The British soldier effectively carried his life with him; much of it in a haversack. Full kit included rifle, bayonet, ammunition, greatcoat, blanket, entrenching tool and food rations, which meant that a man typically carried half his own weight when on the march. Lance Corporal Roland Mountfort, of 10th Battalion Royal Fusiliers, described it as 'a cruel, unnatural weight that no man should be forced to carry'. Nevertheless, British soldiers were at least able to spread the load with the aid of a well-designed system of belt, braces and pouches.

Wet weather increased the soldier's burden, soaking into the heavy greatcoat and rough serge uniform. Officers preferred light waterproofed coats for winter wear, and they were not burdened down on the march like their men. An officer was allowed to take up to 35 kilograms of baggage to the front. This was transported for him. He also benefited from the assistance of a 'soldier servant' – a member of the other ranks deputed to cook and clean for him. The Tommy, by contrast, had a constant struggle to keep himself clean. Baths were a luxury, usually taken communally in improvised bath-houses behind the front line. Meanwhile men's clothing became infested with lice and fleas. Certain standards were maintained even in the front line however; with daily shaving compulsory in all but the most dangerous situations. Special attention was given to the care of the men's feet, which were vulnerable to debilitating attacks of 'trench foot' if soaked in water for long periods of time.

Life at the front was above all a shared life. A unit's officers would maintain the brotherly traditions of the officer's mess – where they ate, drank and relaxed together – even at the front. Sergeants kept their own mess too. The other ranks fought, worked, played, slept, ate and drank side by side. Privacy was non-existent. Men from different walks of life mingled in a way unknown in civilian life. A listing of men in just one Battalion, the 2nd Durham Light Infantry, recorded the peacetime lives its soldiers had left behind. Within its ranks butchers, artists, tea-tasters, jewellers, hairdressers, clerks and journalists lived and fought alongside each other. This shared existence gave rise to strong loyalties, both between soldiers and between men and the units in which they served. Many became fiercely loyal to their battalion, regiment or whatever 'mob' they found themselves serving in. Deep friendships were forged in the stress of battle and in the hardships of trench life. A hatred of common enemies – the Germans, unpopular officers, or men in safe jobs behind the front lines – was also a unifying factor.

Below left: The **1908 Pattern Web Infantry Equipment** worn by British infantrymen had set new standards when it was introduced. It was made from woven canvas, instead of the leather used in other armies. It placed no restrictions upon the soldier's chest, and when in 'fighting order' – in which the pack was removed and left with the unit's baggage – it allowed great freedom of movement. The whole equipment could be taken off in one piece like a waistcoat when at rest. The rapid expansion of the Army led to shortages of this equipment and many New Army soldiers were initially issued with a leather substitute pattern.

Left: The British soldier was usually plentifully fed; but he had plenty of complaints about the type of food he got. The basic ration was based on beef – normally boiled, but frequently tinned corned beef, known as 'bully'– bacon, tea, bread or hard army biscuits and jam. Soldiers constantly sought to vary this monotony. **Tinned foods** such as this **meat stew** were highly prized. Parcels from home could contain other delicacies. Units foraged for fruit and vegetables locally. Some even managed to keep their own cows to milk. When off duty on the Western Front soldiers flocked to canteens run by organisations like the YMCA, or to the local estaminets. At the latter, run by local people who exploited the business opportunity offered by the presence of thousands of hungry and thirsty men, soldiers could enjoy egg and chips, washed down with something not provided in official canteens: wine and beer.

Above right: Working party of British troops on muddy ground near Bernafay Wood, November 1916

Left: The outdoor life at the front, accompanied by a monotonous diet and occasional shortages of water, meant that minor ailments were common among soldiers. Colds and flu caused misery, digestive disorders abounded and constipation was the almost universal curse of the front line. Medical officers at the front could offer only the most rudimentary treatments, so those who could afford it used medicines purchased at home. These **gelatine 'lamels'** were carried at the front by a British officer. They provided various **medicines** in a stable and portable format, which were dissolved in water when used. They included such substances as cocaine – 'for tickling cough or sore throat' – and nux-vomica (better known as the poison strychnine) as a 'general tonic'.

Hard Labour

British soldiers at the war fronts did not spend every day in action. In trench warfare it was normal for a unit to spend three to seven days in a front line trench; followed by similar periods of time in a support trench and even further back in a reserve trench. This would be followed by a week spent 'out of the line' in a safe rear area. The latter period was known as 'rest' but, both in and out of the line, the soldier's daily life involved a lot of hard work. In the front line, repairing trenches and barbed wire, and moving vital trench stores – tools, wire, ammunition, signalling equipment – were constant chores. Such work was usually carried out under cover of darkness; although seldom without the risk of attracting enemy fire. Behind the lines, 'rest' could mean the very opposite of the word, with an exhausting, dreary schedule of 'working parties' and 'fatigues', such as unloading ammunition or maintaining and cleaning accommodation. For artillery men the movement of guns and shells and the digging of emplacements for them entailed constant toil. Ever growing numbers of Army Service Corps (ASC) men worked to feed the insatiable appetite of the fighting front for supplies. There was always a shortage of labour at the front, despite many older men being formed into pioneer battalions, for whom such work took the place of fighting. As the war progressed additional labour was provided by 'Native Labour Battalions', raised in the empire. These men were Indians, Egyptians and black South Africans. Even the vast population of China was tapped for manpower – by agreement with the Chinese government, Britain recruited 100,000 men to serve in the Chinese Labour Corps on the Western Front.

Left: With large armies of citizen-soldiers in the field, the burial and identification of the dead became an important consideration. Failure to inform loved ones of the fate of dead fathers, sons and brothers would have meant that the state was not fulfilling its duty towards those who were making such sacrifices to defend it. A crucial element in the procedure was the issue of **identity tags** to every man. Early in the war, these consisted of a single aluminium or fibre tag but, from 1916, this improved pattern was introduced. The use of two fibre tags meant that, when a soldier was killed, one of them (the red one) could be removed to ensure that his death was recorded. The other was left on his body so that it could be identified regardless of whether it was buried in a marked grave or not.

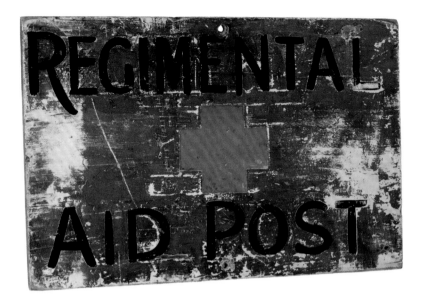

Officers had to cope with different claims upon their time out of the line. Mostly this consisted of paperwork – form filling or keeping up to date with the welter of tactical and technical instructions issued from above and printed at the front by the Army Stationery Service. Officers were also required to attend residential training courses at specialised training centres. It was the officer who had to bear the burdens both of the war's increasingly technical nature and of the ever-expanding bureaucracy which accompanied the rapid growth of the Army.

One of an officer's primary responsibilities was the maintenance of discipline. An officer could punish a minor offence, like failing to salute properly, with extra work duties. However he might have to request a court martial for a more serious offence like drunkenness. If found guilty, an offender could lose leave or pay, be sent to military prison, or receive a term of 'field punishment'. The latter involved making an example of the offender by tying his hands, or tying him by his hands and feet to a post or gun-wheel. When not tied up, he would have to carry out hard labour. For the most serious offences, the death sentence could be applied, although this required the authorisation of the Commander-in-Chief. Between 1914 and 1920, over 3,000 British and Empire soldiers were sentenced to death; the majority for desertion, but also for such offences as mutiny, rape and murder, as well as a more subjectively assessed offence: cowardice. Most of these sentences were commuted to hard-labour or prison, but over 300 men were executed.

Recreation

Despite their arduous life, soldiers at the front did manage to snatch the opportunity to indulge in such pleasures as were available to them. Chief among these was smoking, which could be enjoyed in almost any circumstance. Soldiers lived in a fug of cigarette smoke. Between 1900 and 1913, the use of tobacco had increased four times and the war spread the habit further. Brands from home, like Woodbines, were far more popular than Army-issue tobacco. At the front, smoking helped counter the obnoxious odours of the trenches, relieved boredom and soothed frayed nerves. Lieutenant Theodore Cameron Wilson wrote that tobacco 'fills the place in a man's life, out here, which the snuff box held with the old French aristocrat. It helps a man to go to his death with a brave hypocrisy of carelessness, just as it helped the aristocrat to go daintily to the guillotine.'

The second most popular recreation was football, with officers frequently remarking on the fact that even exhausted men would start kicking a ball about given the opportunity. Sports could also be played on a more organised level, with units and formations holding their own competitions featuring team sports, boxing or tests of horsemanship. Some of these competitions aimed to improve a unit's spirit and togetherness, others to sharpen military skills. Canadian machine-gunners competed with each other in the speed with which they could ready their guns for action after running 600 yards with them. The Tank Corps even held tank races.

Often forgotten, although its results are still to be seen in homes and museums all over the country, is another form of recreation: souvenir collecting. Hunting for mementoes of the war to take home became something of a mania in the British Army – all the more so because the war was seen as a once in a lifetime experience by most of its soldiers. The most prized souvenirs were trophies taken in action from the enemy, especially helmets. But battlefield debris such as shell fragments and shell nose-caps were also collected. Officers had an advantage in having a baggage allowance – the Tommy could only keep souvenirs which he was prepared to carry around in his pack. Composer and poet Ivor Gurney, who served in the ranks, expressed strong views on this issue:

Above: Souvenir hunting was acknowledged – even at the time – to have become a 'mania' among British soldiers. Their problem was that, although everyone would have liked to capture a German helmet or similar trophy, such an opportunity only fell to those involved in successful attacks. Ordinary soldiers were also limited to collecting souvenirs which they could carry with their kit. This unusual souvenir is a piece of **wallpaper torn from the wall of a German dugout**. Because the Germans adopted a largely defensive strategy on the Western Front, they dug deep shelters, which were frequently equipped with facilities such as electric light. Officers might equip their quarters with looted bedsteads and even add such homely touches as this wallpaper.

Above: Officers and men of the 26th Division Ammunition Train join in a game of **football** at Salonika on Christmas Day 1915. With minimal equipment necessary, football was the British soldier's most popular pastime. It could be played in alarming circumstances. Captain Charles May recorded a game played between the Border Regiment and his own Battalion of the Manchester Regiment prior to the Battle of the Somme: 'It was a good game and was rendered a trifle more exciting than some other matches I have been to by the fact that Fritz commenced shelling [...] whilst the game was in progress, the shells passing over our heads and exploding on the slopes above.'

'There is too much sniping for the fighters to get souvenirs, the salvage and burial parties get them. [. . .] People unfitted for the line, lunatics, funks, bosseyed idiots and such like, from whom an officer with 50 francs may make himself rich with booty – and reputation, the ASC do well, for they have room to store [. . .] Only the poor fool who goes over the top – and under the bottom – seems to be without anything at all.'

Some soldiers found an outlet for creative talents by re-working battlefield debris into homemade souvenirs – 'trench art'. Shell cases (which, officially speaking, should have been re-cycled) were turned into flower vases or tobacco jars. Copper driving-bands – which ensured that a shell fitted tightly into a gun's barrel – became paper knives. Men created art from the very weapons which had been intended to kill them. This sort of work required tools however, so the more ambitious examples were generally made by men of the Royal Engineers or the ASC, who had access to workshop facilities. For those who could not make their own souvenirs, there was the option of purchasing them. Trophies of the enemy frequently changed hands for money. Local craftspeople turned traditional skills in metal-working or lace making to the production of souvenirs for sale to soldiers.

One thing completely lacking in the front line was the presence of the opposite sex, although this was not the case when soldiers were at 'rest'. In 1914 Kitchener had warned the BEF that 'while treating women with perfect courtesy, you should avoid any intimacy'. Yet as the Army grew, the presence of vast numbers of young men prompted the growth of a considerable sex industry in towns behind the lines. The Army could not afford to ignore this aspect of its soldiers' lives; venereal disease could add hugely to the numbers of men going sick if allowed to spread unchecked. Over 150,000 British soldiers serving in France and Flanders were admitted to hospital with sexually transmitted diseases. Furthermore, and perhaps surprisingly, those in charge held the opinion that it was healthier for married men who enjoyed a sex life at home to be able to continue to do so at the front. The Army therefore accepted the existence of brothels and even supervised its own. Different establishments were made available for different ranks, and naturally it was not only married men who took advantage of their existence. Alongside the dirt and danger of the front line, it was perhaps in this respect above all others that life at the front divorced itself from the kind of existence which soldiers would have expected to live at home.

Opposite: War tested men's religious faith to the extreme, and the Army provided formal religious worship and pastoral care through the Army Chaplain's Department. But in the midst of danger, superstitious belief in charms and behavioural rituals assumed great importance for many soldiers.

These **lucky charms**, carried by British soldiers, were collected during the war by the English folklorist Edward Lovett. Londoner Lovett was already well known as a collector of charms and amulets in 1914 and, during the war, extended his collecting to soldiers' and sailors' charms.

Top row from left: Brass horseshoe charm made from a fragment of German shell, Ypres, by a wounded Belgian soldier; coal fragment sent to a soldier at the front for luck; Connemara marble boot charm, carried by an Irish soldier.

Second row from left: Lucky black cat brooch worn by a London soldier; marble four-leaf clover lucky charm belonging to an unknown soldier; lucky pig charm carved out of Irish bog-oak.

Third row from left: White stone arrow charm worn by a US soldier; chinese soapstone monkey, which was a charm carried by both British and Japanese soldiers; doll brooch representing a wounded soldier.

Bottom row: A small heart-shaped Connemara marble charm; carried by an Irish soldier

FAMILIAR
FRENCH.

An indispensable pocket
guide showing the correct
use of Idioms, Colloquial
Expressions and Apt
Proverbs commonly used in
French conversation, the
Slang of the French and
British Armies, etc.

WITH PHONETIC PRONUNCIATION.

An invaluable supplement to any English - French Phrase Book. 4ᵈ

Left: Most soldiers had never left England and spoke no French. They used **phrase books** like this, or loud 'franglais', to communicate. Failure to understand each other worsened disagreements between soldiers and civilians. British soldiers accused local tradespeople of watering-down beer and inflating prices. French civilians resented soldiers stealing their crops and animals and damaging property. Nevertheless relations with local people were an important aspect of most soldiers' experience of life at the front. Off duty visits to the local community gave soldiers the opportunity to relax in a non-military environment. Food and drink could be bought to supplement dreary rations and the presence of women and children gave men a glimpse of the family life which they had left behind.

4/

One of the most characteristic sights in the British Army & one of the most habitual is the following —

Other armies have them, but it does not seem to bother them in the same way. But it is pathetic to see our lads attempts at personal cleanliness. Yousee they have been used to an all over (but the middle & the back) wash every

3/ S. P.

his ferocious offspring emerging from the Egg bites the back that bred him. Does this horrible subject make you feel "itchy all over"? It does me! But then yours is all imagination, and mine probably has a vestige of truth in it.

When the men leave their packs at the transport lines in order to go up into the firing line, the season of rest & refreshment is used by the lodgers to the uttermost. Of course I cannot vouch for the truth of the following having only heard it from the transport & you cannot always believe what they say — but our packs were many & heavy. So some bright youth put the best part of a pot of jam on the tail board of a limber, and all the packs trotted along the road after it snapping for it.

Left: **Correspondence** was of huge importance to many soldiers, as letters from friends and family kept them in touch with life at home. In four years of war, the Army Postal Service despatched two billion letters and 114 million parcels to serving soldiers. Soldiers' own letters – usually subject to censorship – were written for a variety of reasons. Men sought to reassure their wives, amuse their children, impress their friends or boast to girls. The Reverend Cyril Lomax, an Army Chaplain, added sketches to his letters to his friend Doris Steinberg; bringing his experiences to life for her. This one depicts a perennial front line chore, **hunting for lice** in the seams of a shirt. In one letter, Lomax wrote, 'One is so utterly glad to receive a letter [. . .] You can have no idea how one looks for the post, and how disappointed one feels if there is nothing for one.'

Chapter Ten

MACHINES AGAINST MEN

'We feel the ground tremble and six mines go up, the machine gun barrage commences'

In 1917, the Allies looked increasingly to machines to win the war. They were now plentifully supplied with heavy guns, shells and machine guns. New tactics had been developed to make this immense firepower even more effective. Warfare had become more technological. Aircraft were now central to fighting battles. Tanks were available in large numbers. A wave of offensives in 1917 would exploit these developments. These Allied attacks were not to be a mere repeat of the previous year, but would apply lessons learned on the Western Front during 1915 and 1916.

New Technology, New Tactics

In the eyes of the public one new weapon stood out above all others – the tank. Following its first appearance in support of British troops on the Somme, the tank had been regarded as a wonder weapon. German soldiers were certainly terrified of it when they first faced it. Even when they became more accustomed to its appearance on the battlefield, less motivated men used its presence as an excuse to surrender. As one tank commander, Gordon Hassell, noted in 1917 'the Germans were only too ready to hold "hands up" and came in almost without being invited'.

Yet despite its impact the tank was never capable of being a war-winning weapon, as the technology of the day did not allow it to be. The chief problem was its slow speed. The standard British tank of 1917 could only manage four miles per hour on good ground. In action, a tank soon consumed its limited supplies of fuel, making it a short range – 'one-shot' – weapon. In creating the tank, the available technology had been pushed to its limits. As a result these 'landships' were plagued with mechanical problems.

Tank crews themselves faced terrible challenges in action. The eight man crew of a British tank shared a single fighting-compartment with the engine, which leaked poisonous carbon monoxide fumes. Fumes caused by firing the tank's guns added to the problem. In facing these threats the

Above: The **Vickers Gun** was the standard machine gun of the British and empire armies. From late 1915 all Vickers Guns came under the control of the Machine Gun Corps. This formation concentrated all the expertise in machine-gunnery in one place, and allowed the British and empire forces to take the lead in the development of sophisticated machine gun tactics. They learnt how to fire safely over the heads of friendly troops and to hit targets hidden to the gunners themselves – effectively turning their guns into miniature artillery pieces. From 1916 onwards British soldiers became accustomed to the rushing sound of machine gun bullets passing overhead to strike at the enemy.

tank men had surprisingly little in the way of protection. While immune to shrapnel, shell fragments and normal bullets, the tank's armour could be penetrated by newly introduced German armour-piercing bullets, and a direct hit from an artillery shell meant certain destruction. In the words of infantry officer Rowland Feilding 'for a tank to be of much use you want a superman inside it [. . .] Nevertheless, tanks are a good thing to have with you, so long as you do not count too much on them.'

Despite these drawbacks, Britain pushed ahead with tank development and the Mark IV of 1917 was a significant improvement upon the Mark I of 1916, being faster and better armoured. By the spring of 1917 the French too had tanks in service. Both armies intended to use them to spearhead new attacks on the Germans. However tanks did not lie at the heart of the Allied plans, which were instead founded on the weapon-system which had always dominated the Western Front – artillery.

Left: Life inside a tank was scorching, deafening and filled with poisonous engine fumes. Crewmen were issued with leather helmets fitted with anti-splinter masks to protect their faces from the showers of hot metal fragments caused by bullets striking the tank's armour. This **helmet** was worn **by a tank commander, Second Lieutenant Gordon Hassell, at the Battle of Cambrai**. Hassell's tank 'Harrier' was knocked out by shellfire but he survived to write home of his lucky escape. 'I had 8 men inside with a large black German dog, which had refused to run away with retreating Bosch soldiers. Apart from scratches we had no casualties.'

Not only did the Allies now have plentiful shells and guns – especially the essential heavy guns – but they had learnt to use them in more effective ways. Before 1916 the French had led the way in developing new methods of artillery fire, the most important of which was the creeping barrage. In this tactic the lighter artillery pieces were used to lay down a curtain of fire in front of advancing infantry, either killing the defenders or forcing them to keep under cover. The British began to use this technique during the Somme battles. 1917 witnessed further advances, including the widespread use of smoke shells to mask advancing troops from enemy observation and new and sensitive fuzes which allowed high explosive shells to destroy barbed wire entanglements.

The chief threat faced by attacking troops came, as always, from enemy artillery. However the Allies now had plenty of guns to devote to destroying it with 'counter-battery' fire. To achieve the best results they had developed improved methods of pinpointing the enemy's guns. Survey teams located them by observing the muzzle flashes of firing guns – flash-spotting – while the British and French co-operated to develop advanced acoustic equipment that enabled enemy artillery to be found by sound-ranging.

The enemy defenders would also be facing a new threat – the machine gun barrage. This technique was developed by the Machine Gun Corps which, since late 1915, had formed part of the British and empire forces. In essence it involved the use of machine guns like miniature pieces of artillery, firing over the heads of friendly troops; frequently at targets which the gunners could not directly observe. The machine gun barrage could be used to 'thicken' the creeping artillery barrage which accompanied an attack, but was even more effective when fired as an 'SOS' barrage in response to flares sent up by infantry units facing counter-attacks. Before the battle the machine-gunners would have registered their guns on any fold in the ground in which the enemy were likely to mass troops for counter-attack.

The tactics of the men who actually fought the enemy face to face had also undergone huge changes since 1915. Once again the Battle of the Somme had spurred the British Army to pick up on and further develop tactics pioneered by their French ally. The most important change was made possible by the widespread issue of light automatic weapons. The French CSRG automatic rifle and the Lewis Gun (a pre-war American design manufactured in Birmingham, England) transformed the way in which

Above: The artillery had struggled with the problem of destroying enemy barbed wire entanglements, which could be several metres deep and anchored to stout metal rods or picquets. Shrapnel shells provided a literally hit and miss method of cutting the wire, while high-explosive shells buried themselves before exploding and merely jumbled the wire up. This situation changed with the development of the **Fuze Number 106**. It was so sensitive and quick-acting that it detonated any shell to which it was fitted at very first contact. High-explosive shells could now blast wire to shreds. Infantry officer Rowland Feilding was sufficiently impressed to explain this innovation to his wife, writing 'such shells burst instantaneously – as the nose touches the ground, and the pieces fly horizontally to a great distance. They make scarcely any crater at all.'

the infantry fought. In 1914 the standard fighting unit had been the infantry company, consisting of around 200 riflemen. By 1917 the primary unit was the platoon, of which there were four in each company. Their method of fighting was to use specialised teams of 'bombers' and men armed with rifle-grenades in conjunction with the firepower of a Lewis Gun. Theoretically an infantry platoon was now equipped to overcome any small enemy strongpoint unaided.

To the frustration of all armies however, these advances were balanced by a technological bottleneck in another crucial area – that of communications. It was not possible at the time to build a wireless radio capable of being carried into an attack. Field telephones were reliant upon cables which were vulnerable to artillery fire, and needed constant repair. These problems meant that all sides continued to employ more primitive forms of communication such as signalling lamps and flags, carrier pigeons and messenger dogs. The communication problem hampered the generals in directing their troops in battle. They were often forced to rely upon outdated reports of what was happening. This caused particular problems when conducting attacks, as the commander waiting to commit his reserve troops to action had no real-time picture of how the battle was developing.

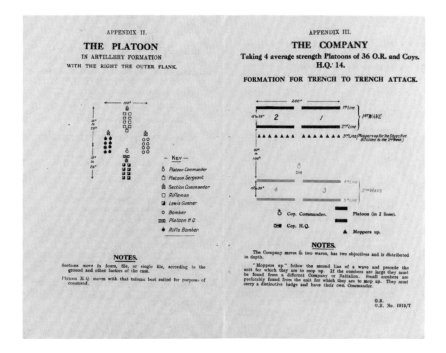

Left: The diagram in this **set of instructions for British platoon commanders** makes clear how infantry tactics had developed by 1917. Instead of consisting purely of riflemen as it had in 1914, the platoon was now composed of separate sections of specialists who acted in co-operation with each other. When an enemy strongpoint was identified, the Lewis Gun section fired at it to keep the defenders' heads down. Rifle grenadiers would fire their grenades from a distance, while 'bombers' with hand grenades would work around it to a position from which they could launch an attack. While the position was being 'bombed' the Lewis Gunners would re-position themselves to shoot down any of the enemy seen retreating.

The Cavalry of the Clouds

During 1916 aircraft had established themselves as an indispensable tool of warfare. Since the early days of the war they had superseded the cavalry as the chief means of reconnaissance. Now Lloyd George publicly referred to them as 'the cavalry of the clouds.' Britain's airpower was furnished by the Army's Royal Flying Corps, and the Navy's Royal Naval Air Service. Their primary duty was to observe for the artillery. Without their eyes in the sky, the guns could not find and attack their targets. In addition to this techniques had also been developed for low-level bombing, enabling flyers to strike at the enemy's troop concentrations and transport infrastructure. During 1917 aircraft were integrated into plans of attack; being directed to carry out dangerous low-level strikes against enemy troops on the battlefield itself. Fighter aircraft – generally known at the time as 'Scouts' – were tasked with shooting down enemy reconnaissance aircraft and protecting their own. Fighter pilots expressed pity for the observers who 'float at about 6,000 feet [. . .] all day while they are doing artillery work or photography – and who can be attacked by anybody [. . .] on account of their slow speed'. In fact fighter pilots, tasked with aggressively seeking combat in high-performance aircraft which were frequently challenging to fly, were to account for over half of the casualties of the British flying services. Each side strove to introduce fighter planes which had a higher performance than those of the enemy. From late 1916 until the summer of 1917 Germany was able to dominate the skies with advanced fighter aircraft, but the British and French wrested the advantage back with the introduction of new types such as the Sopwith Camel, SE5a and Spad S XIII.

Above and below: Major **James McCudden** was a leading British air ace, credited with 57 'kills'. Once a Royal Flying Corps mechanic, McCudden had risen through the ranks. His success lay not in reckless bravery, but in professionalism and a thorough knowledge of his machine. His achievements earned him the Victoria Cross. McCudden was killed in July 1918, aged 23, when his engine stalled shortly after take-off. This **shattered windscreen** was recovered from the SE5a plane in which he met his death. Flying accidents were an all too common cause of death and injury in early air combat.

The struggle for command of the air also gave rise to a new phenomenon: the air ace. An ace was an airman who had shot down more than five enemy aircraft. The leading air aces had many more 'kills' than that to their name, and became huge heroes in their home countries. The Frenchman René Fonck boasted 75 victories; the top ace in the Royal Flying Corps was Canadian Billy Bishop, with 72; but the greatest ace of all was a German, Manfred von Richthofen. With 80 kills to his name the 'Red Baron' – so called due to the red paint he favoured on his aircraft – became a celebrity on both sides of the line.

The ever-growing importance of airpower was to be recognised in Britain by the formation, in April 1918, of the Royal Air Force as a third arm of service alongside the Royal Navy and the Army. It brought together the existing Royal Naval Air Service and Royal Flying Corps.

Right: The final eighteen months of the war witnessed the increasing use of fighter aircraft to attack enemy ground troops on the battlefield. This **painting** is part of a series produced to instruct British pilots in various flying techniques. Ground attacks were particularly demoralising for their targets, and highly dangerous for the attackers. Royal Flying Corps Lieutenant Arthur Gould Lee described attacking German artillery at Cambrai in his Sopwith Camel: 'So there we are, the three of us, whirling blindly around at 50 to 100 feet, all but colliding, being shot at from below, and trying to bomb places accurately.'

Far left: German **Baron Manfred von Richthofen** became the most famous airman of the war. A brilliant tactician, cool-headed pilot and inspirational leader, the 'Red Baron' commanded a squadron of brightly-painted aircraft; known to his enemies as the 'Flying Circus'. After shooting down 80 Allied aircraft, he met his death aged 25 on 21 April 1918; hit by ground fire from Australian troops while engaged in a low-level dogfight. Such was his fame, even among the Allies, that he was buried with full military honours by the Australian Flying Corps. A less chivalrous response came from British ace Edward 'Mick' Mannock, who is reported to have said 'I hope the bastard burned the whole way down'. Richthofen took his victories seriously, having silver 'honour cups' made to celebrate them and **decorating his apartment** with trophies taken from their wreckage.

Left: **Richthofen's trophy room** in the family home at Schweidnitz, Lower Silesia.

WHEN OUT GROUND STRAFING :—

(1) FLY AS LOW AS POSSIBLE.

(2) DODGE ROUND HOUSES, TREES, WOODS, ETC., AND NEVER FLY STRAIGHT WHEN IT CAN BE AVOIDED.

BY SO DOING YOU WILL MAKE THE MOST OF THE CHIEF FACTORS IN YOUR FAVOUR, MORAL EFFECT AND SURPRISE, EXPOSE YOURSELF FOR THE BRIEFEST PERIODS TO EFFFCTIVE FIRE, AND OFFER THE ENEMY A MOST DIFFICULT TARGET.

Left: A sergeant of the Royal Flying Corps demonstrates a C type aerial reconnaissance camera fixed to the fuselage of a BE2c aircraft, 1916

Bite and Hold

The first great Allied attack of 1917 was launched by the British at Arras on Easter Sunday. The new tactics and technology, combined with meticulous planning, brought early success with major advances almost everywhere. This initial victory was crowned by the sensational capture of the commanding position of Vimy Ridge, in an operation spearheaded by the Canadian Corps. But the battle degenerated into a grinding struggle reminiscent of the Somme, and no decisive result was achieved.

The Battle of Arras had only been intended to draw German reserves away from an even bigger attack planned by the French. General Robert Nivelle had replaced Joffre as commander of the French Army on the Western Front. He had won spectacular victories at Verdun with aggressive tactics based on artillery fire. He boasted that, by employing these tactics on a grand scale, he could win decisive victory on the Western Front within 48 hours. In the event his great offensive, aimed at a strong German position on the heights above the River Aisne, failed to come anywhere near such a result. While not the bloodiest of battles, the contrast between what Nivelle had promised and what he achieved led to his dismissal and shattered the morale of the French Army.

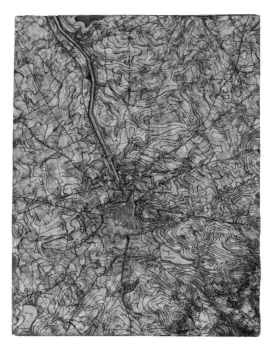

Left: This relief map of the area around the town of Ypres is part of a set covering the whole British sector of the Western Front, which was used at British General Headquarters in France.

With Russia also struggling to sustain the fight, and American troops yet to arrive in force, Field Marshal Haig now commanded the only effective Allied army. He wanted to keep the pressure up on the Germans, so turned to a long-cherished plan to beat them on the flat Flanders plain in Belgium. At Ypres British troops manned a line which bulged into German-held territory. An attack from this position offered the chance of seizing the vital German rail junction at Roulers. Its capture would undermine the northern section of Germany's defences in Belgium by cutting off supplies and reinforcements. Such a success might even allow British forces to threaten the German U-boat base at Bruges.

For the British offensive to take place at all, the high ground south of Ypres had to be seized. On 7 June British, Australian and New Zealand forces achieved a victory to match Vimy, with the capture of Messines ridge. The battle was notable for the detonation of huge mines placed under the German positions by British tunnellers, in what can claim to be the largest man-made explosion of the pre-atomic age. Once the mines had been blown the ridge and the surrounding area were drenched with artillery and machine gun fire co-ordinated by the most sophisticated fire-plan yet devised. Major Robert Blackadder of the Royal Garrison Artillery recorded the scene in his diary: 'At 3.10 sharp we feel the ground tremble and six mines go up, the machine gun barrage commences with a rattle and the guns open up, – the attack has commenced. We can see nothing in the dawn but clouds of smoke from the mines.'

On 31 July the British launched the Third Battle of Ypres. Advances were made but within hours the attackers were slowed by heavy rain. Artillery fire had destroyed the drainage system on the low-lying battlefield, which became waterlogged. Tanks could barely operate and all movement became slow and difficult. Improved conditions in August and September saw more successful attacks, directed by the victor of Messines, General Herbert Plumer. Plumer advocated a policy of 'bite and hold', a tactic well described by a man on the receiving end, Colonel Albrecht von Thaer:

'I just don't know what can be done to counter the English. They set themselves a fairly limited goal, an advance of only 500 to 1,000 metres, albeit on quite a lengthy frontage. In front of this space, deep into our own zone, such devastating British shellfire is laid down that in fact no being is left alive [. . .] they then simply advance without too many losses into this field of corpses, swiftly establish themselves, and our counter-attacks first have to cross the raging fire wave, only to find a solid phalanx of machine guns behind it, and they are smashed to pieces.'

Yet although Plumer's tactics might kill many Germans, they could not deliver the breakthrough which Haig desired. The rain and mud returned, turning the battlefield into a what a British artillery Captain Ernest Boon, described as 'a quagmire of mud and water, the whole area blown to pieces time after time and thousands of shell holes everywhere, splintered wood, barbed wire, dead horses and men [. . .] a desolate and soul destroying waste'. The battle now degenerated into a morale-sapping struggle against the conditions as much as the enemy. On 10 November the attacks were ended, after the capture, by Canadian troops, of the shattered village which gave the battle the name by which it is usually called: Passchendaele.

In a final effort to end the year on the offensive, Haig sanctioned an attack at Cambrai. The plan did not share the ambitious strategic goals of the Third Battle of Ypres, but it was a technical and tactical masterpiece. Massed tanks, supported by ground attack aircraft, punched a hole in the enemy defences. They were aided by a new technique, the silent registration of artillery. Instead of firing ranging shots to zero-in their guns – thereby warning the enemy – British artillery experts used accurate maps and mathematical calculation to bring down a barrage which came as a complete surprise to the Germans.

Church bells were rung in England to celebrate what appeared to be an almost miraculous success, but the Germans struck back. Sending their best infantry – men trained in new assault tactics – to the area, they showed that they had been making tactical advances of their own, as the British were thrown back. The year's campaigning, which had already caused more British casualties than that of 1916, ended on a sour note. While new technology and tactics meant that the Allies could break into the German defensive positions, they still lacked the recipe to break out of them. The artillery had proved capable of smashing anything in range, but the difficulties of bringing it forward in the wake of an advance meant that set-piece attacks were easier to mount than sustained advances.

The Most Frightful Nightmare of a Country...

Although far from being the most costly Western Front battle, the fighting at Ypres had a depressing impact on the soldiers who fought there. Once again, their efforts had failed to win a decisive victory, and this time they had been made in an appalling mud-soaked environment which magnified exhaustion and war-weariness. The British public too were to pick up on the dreary atmosphere which prevailed in Flanders. They were able to gain a realistic impression of the battlefield because of official efforts to record the war for their benefit.

Since 1916 official photographers had been sent to the front to record the Army's efforts. The waterlogged and open expanses of the Ypres battlefield in particular inspired them to raise record-photography into an art form. It was there that they photographed the scenes which have printed themselves indelibly on the minds of people all over the world as the defining images of Passchendaele, and even of the whole war on the Western Front, with men struggling and suffering in deep mud, surrounded by shattered trees and flooded craters.

The photographers were joined by official war artists, selected and employed by the government's Department of Information. The Department (which became a Ministry in 1918) took a surprisingly liberal attitude to the commissioning process. The artists chosen were generally young and were certainly not practitioners of the traditional style of art which might have been expected to form the basis of any government scheme. The chief organiser of the scheme, Charles Masterman, told artist Christopher Nevinson to 'paint anything you please'. The artists were simultaneously inspired and appalled by the scenes which they found to paint in what one of them, Paul Nash, described as 'the most frightful nightmare of a country'. The resulting works, most of which found their way into the collections of the Imperial War Museum, have made a major contribution to the way in which the First World War has been remembered across the world.

Overleaf: The low-lying land of Flanders relied upon man-made drainage systems which were smashed by the heavy artillery fire of repeated battles. During the Third Battle of Ypres, unseasonal rain in August, followed by more predictable downpours in October, turned the battlefield into a fearful quagmire. This **photograph** was taken on 29 October by Australian Official War Photographer Captain Frank Hurley. It shows Australian troops picking their way along wooden duckboards through the remains of Chateau Wood. This subsequently became one of the most abiding and frequently reproduced images of the Western Front.

Left: *After a Push*
CRW Nevinson, 1917
Christopher Nevinson had been prevented by bad health from joining up in 1914, but experienced the horrors of war as a driver for the Quaker Friends Ambulance Unit. He was later recruited as an Official War Artist. The scheme's co-ordinator described him as 'a desperate fellow, without fear [...] only anxious to crawl out into the front line and draw things full of violence and terror'. Nevinson had been a British adherent of the Futurist movement, but his experiences during the war induced him to start working in a more representational style. This painting shows to great effect the phenomenon of the 'empty battlefield' which was one of the most noticeable outcomes of industrial warfare. Across a sea of mud and craters, the only sign of human activity is some shells bursting in the distance.

Left: *The Menin Road*
Paul Nash, 1919

Artist Paul Nash was conscripted into the Army, but seconded to the Official War Artist scheme in October 1917. During the Third Battle of Ypres he began work on two paintings which would come to symbolise war on the Western Front for future generations; the ironically-titled *We Are Making a New World* and this huge canvas *The Menin Road*. The latter was intended for exhibition in a planned 'Hall of Remembrance', which was never to be built. Nash described the battlefield in a letter to his wife, 'the rain drives on, the stinking mud becomes more evilly yellow, the shell holes fill up with green-white water, the roads and tracks are covered in inches of slime, the black dying trees ooze and sweat and the shells never cease'.

Chapter Eleven

BREAKING DOWN

'Faces like masks, blue and cold and drawn by hunger'

By 1917 the war was straining both armies and home fronts to breaking point. The huge but indecisive battles of 1916 had marked a watershed. All sides were faced with the harsh reality that further heavy loss of life and the total commitment of national wealth would be required to have any hope of victory.

Most soldiers and civilians were willing to make these sacrifices, but some voices began to call for a negotiated peace. With no apparent end in sight on the fighting front and hardship afflicting the home front, these voices began to grow in number.

Peace?

In Britain, the left wing of the Labour Party and a minority of Liberals had always opposed the war. Many intellectuals also questioned its continuance. They found a voice in the Union of Democratic Control. The UDC was not a pacifist organisation, but it denounced 'secret diplomacy' and demanded openness about war aims. Its demands drew little support from the public. The press dismissed its members as 'peace prattlers'. A more surprising denunciation of the war came from former foreign minister Lord Lansdowne. He feared that no victory could compensate for the war's ever-spiralling cost, stating that 'generations will come and go before the country recovers from the loss it has sustained in human beings, and from the financial ruin and the destruction of the means of production which are taking place'.

Lansdowne's opinions ran counter to the determined mood of the politicians now striving to bring victory at almost any cost; nevertheless, the leaders of both sides did toy with the possibility of negotiating a peace settlement. Until early 1917 they were encouraged in this by the neutral USA, who's President, Woodrow Wilson, was eager to establish a 'just and lasting' peace in Europe. Most of the peace feelers were extended by members of the Central Powers. In Germany anti-war sentiment had a strong political base in the left wing of the large Socialist Party.

To appease their demands for an end to the war (and also to placate America), the German leadership issued a 'Peace Note' in December 1916. President Wilson knew that the Allies would not negotiate under conditions laid down by Germany, but asked both sides to state what peace terms they might be willing to accept. The Allies provided Wilson with a statement – albeit selectively worded – of their aims. This brought about the failure of the whole initiative, because Germany's leaders were unwilling to state their own war aims. These were ever-changing but generally very aggressive. To reveal them would have caused huge political problems at home, as the government had built support for the war by characterising it as a struggle for the defence of Germany.

A more realistic prospect would have been for the Allies to negotiate a separate peace with Austria-Hungary. In November 1916 Emperor Franz Josef, who had ruled since 1848, died, removing the principal focus for unity in the fragmented Hapsburg Empire. His young successor Karl was eager to take Austria-Hungary out of the war and put out secret peace feelers to the Allies. These failed due to the promises of Austrian territory the Allies had made to Italy to induce it to join them. News of these approaches leaked out, however, and Karl's German allies were enraged. Although trust was destroyed between them, the failure of their tentative peace negotiations meant that Germany and Austria-Hungary were bound even more closely together. The Germans resented the repeated need to prop-up Austria-Hungary's failing army and the Austro-Hungarians described their more powerful partner as 'our secret enemy'; but neither could continue the war without the other.

So while peace without victory was never impossible, it was always unlikely. Each combatant had aims which they felt had to be achieved to make worthwhile the terrible price that they had already paid in blood. Anything but outright victory would be seen as a defeat, which no government or regime would be able to survive. It was not only the governing elite who held such views. In Britain and its empire alone, by the end of 1917, 800,000 men had been killed. To most citizens of the British Empire, striking a bargain with Germany would have suggested that these men had died for nothing. Both sides found enough positives in the course of the war to sustain their belief in the possibility of victory. One way or another, the war would now be fought to a decisive conclusion.

Right: One soldier who became disenchanted with the war during this period is now better known for his poetry and memoirs. **Siegfried Sassoon** had served on the Western Front for 19 months and had won the Military Cross for his bravery. In the summer of 1917 however, he refused to return to duty from convalescent leave and published a 'declaration' against the continuation of the war. He claimed that the war had ceased to be one of 'defence and liberation' and was now one of 'aggression and conquest', which was being needlessly prolonged. Sassoon was aware that this action might result in severe punishment, but the Army and the War Office moved quickly to dampen any controversy. They had Sassoon treated for 'neurasthenia' – in other words, shell shock. He later returned voluntarily to the front.

The Breakdown of Armies

While politicians explored and ultimately dismissed the possibility of a negotiated peace, some soldiers at the front began to take more direct action.

After the failure of General Nivelle's spring offensive in 1917, of which so much had been promised, the French Army began to suffer serious disciplinary problems. In what has variously been called a mutiny or a 'military strike', large numbers of French infantrymen disobeyed orders and staged demonstrations. They stopped short of deserting their trenches, but refused to take part in further attacks, with many of them openly calling for peace. As one of them said, 'we are men and not beasts to be led to the abattoir to be slaughtered [. . .] we demand peace'.

General Pétain, the hero of Verdun, had been given command after the sacking of Nivelle and carefully restored order. Almost 700 of the mutineers were sentenced to death but less than 50 – arbitrarily chosen to make an example – were executed. Pétain began a step by step process to restore his army's morale. Amongst other measures he improved his soldiers' food and reformed the process by which they were sent on home leave. Pétain understood that his men were civilians in uniform who had rights as well as duties.

LES FOYERS DU SOLDAT
Y.M.C.A
UNION FRANCO-AMERICAINE

Left: General Philippe Pétain was tasked with restoring morale after the French Army mutinies of mid-1917. He understood his soldiers and introduced improved leave and conditions of service. "Soldiers' Homes" like the one depicted in this **poster** were established to offer somewhere for men to relax when out of the line. They were staffed by American volunteers. He also improved the food given to soldiers, which had long been a cause of complaint. At the same time Pétain cleverly rebuilt the offensive spirit of the Army by mounting a series of carefully planned, but limited, attacks backed by massive artillery support.

While the French Army recovered itself, those of Austria-Hungary, Italy and Turkey began to crumble. The Austro-Hungarian Army had never recovered from its defeats by the Russians in 1914 and 1916. Its leaders had performed poorly and some of its troops had proved only too ready to surrender, or even to desert, to the Russians. The one struggle which unified it was the defence of imperial territory against the Italians. Italy, a supposed friend in 1914, was despised as a 'snake' for joining Austria-Hungary's enemies in 1915. Germany was desperate to keep its main ally fighting into 1918, so it sent troops to the Italian front to help Austria-Hungary win a morale-boosting victory.

In October 1917, the Germans and Austro-Hungarians attacked at Caporetto. The Italian 2nd Army broke. Thousands of men surrendered or deserted and the Central Powers advanced for over 60 miles. With Italy on the brink of ruin, its Army finally established a new defensive line, but not before British and French troops had been rushed to Italy. The sought-after new ally of 1915 had become a liability.

For Turkey the victories of early 1916 seemed long in the past. Turkey did not have the industrial power or transport infrastructure to fight a prolonged war. Britain's response to its defeats had been to pour more resources into the Middle-East. By early 1917 British and empire forces were once more advancing in Mesopotamia. They captured Baghdad in March. Another army invaded the Turkish province of Palestine. It faced determined Turkish resistance at Gaza but, in early November achieved a breakthrough which resulted, shortly before Christmas, in the capture of Jerusalem. This provided a seasonal boost to British morale, but was a mortal blow to Turkish prestige. A Turkish writer, Falih Rifki, recorded that 'the words "Jerusalem has fallen" spread like news of a death in the family'. Turkey's soldiers had endured poor conditions and harsh discipline. By 1917 it was estimated that 300,000 Turkish Army deserters were living as fugitives or brigands in the countryside – by 1918 this figure would top half a million.

Despite these crises, all of these armies would keep fighting for now. Soldiers were inspired by a sense of duty, patriotism, comradeship or hatred of the enemy and coerced by the threat of punishment – including execution. Above all, most could simply see no alternative to carrying on. And wise commanders realised that soldiers who had proper food, rest and leave, and the hope of victory, were far more likely to keep fighting.

Left: This photograph shows troops of a **Hungarian regiment trudging through a Russian village**. The war on the Eastern Front had been hideously costly for Austria-Hungary's multi-ethnic Army. The great defeats of 1914 and 1916 had resulted in the loss of most of its best troops and had sapped the empire's resources of manpower. But the defence of its south-western border against the Italians united the Austro-Hungarian Empire. Here Germans, Hungarians, Czechs, Slovaks, Romanians, Slovenes, Croats, and Bosnian Muslims fought hard side by side.

Left: Italian soldiers had endured huge losses in the harshest of conditions. They also suffered under a disciplinary system which allowed for the execution of randomly selected soldiers from units which had 'failed' in battle. In October 1917, when a joint Austro-Hungarian and German offensive crashed upon it at Caporetto, the army on the Isonzo front broke. This extraordinary photograph shows **Italian prisoners running into the Austro-Hungarian lines during the battle**. One Italian soldier reported the mood among his comrades, 'We were all happy, all saying "it's home or prison, but no more war"'.

Hunger

By 1917 the warring nations were faced with threats to their ability to keep their people fed. The Central Powers were the first to suffer. Germany had been feeling the effects of the British naval blockade since 1916; Austria even earlier. Now Germany's U-boats were attempting to starve Britain. Admiral David Beatty was of the opinion that 'our armies might advance a mile a day and slay the Hun in thousands, but the real crux lies in whether we blockade the enemy to his knees, or whether he does the same to us'.

Britain appeared to be most vulnerable to blockade, as it had imported 60 per cent of its food prior to the war. Although counter-measures were successfully implemented to lessen the impact of the U-boats, Britain's capacity to ship food was inevitably diminished. So throughout 1917 and 1918 British people were forced to cope with shortages. The greatest threat to the nation's food was posed by a shortage of wheat, most of which Britain imported. Efforts were made to increase domestic production, and also to grow and use alternative crops. The government encouraged people to plough up all available land and to use their own gardens to grow potatoes. They brought agriculture under state supervision to maximise output. Voluntary rationing schemes were set up, encouraging people to reduce their food consumption or, if they were wealthy, to avoid buying cheap foods which provided nutrition for the poor.

Scottish War Savings Committee
25 Palmerston Place, Edinburgh

THE FIGHT IS NOW

THE WOMEN

VERSUS

THE SUBMARINE

SEMEZ DU BLÉ

C'EST DE L'OR POUR LA

FRANCE

VILLE
DE PARIS
ÉCOLE COM.ᴸᴱ
221 B.ᴰ PEREIRE

Imprimerie de Montrouge (Montrouge)

Opposite and above: These **posters** address a key threat faced by Britain and its allies in 1917–1918: a shortage of wheat. Bread and other foods made from wheat flour formed an important part of people's diets – especially those of the poor – and much of the grain was imported. U-boat attacks and pressure on shipping space meant that these supplies were reduced. The Allies all launched domestic campaigns to sow more wheat at home, and to encourage care in its use. Farmers and housewives were now in the front line. The consumption of alternative sources of nourishment such as potatoes or rice from India was promoted.

Left: **Ration cards** were issued to British citizens from January 1918 onwards. They were later superseded by ration books. They entitled the holder to purchase a set quantity of meat, lard, sugar and butter or margarine per week. Everyone had to register with a supplier, who was only permitted to stock enough of these basic foodstuffs to feed the customers who had registered with him. Like many other people responsible for feeding a household, Kent woman Ethel Bilbrough was surprised and delighted at the impact of the scheme, writing 'in years to come people will hardly believe that such things really were [. . .] the whole scheme has succeeded wonderfully well, in spite of the stupendous difficulties that had to be overcome'.

Left: 'What a number of cards we now have: bread cards, meat cards, soup cards, butter cards, rice cards, oil cards etc, etc.' So wrote one German woman to her husband in 1916. This **egg card**, from the city of Frankfurt an der Oder, relates to one of the myriad local rationing schemes introduced in Germany, alongside a system of maximum prices. These controls left plenty of opportunity for profiteering and corruption, so only the wealthy could afford a sufficient food intake. Ethel Cooper, an Australian living in Leipzig, wrote 'You have no idea of the general corruption here – everybody who can bribes his trades people[. . .] those who will not or cannot bribe, are told that the meat is sold out, and the others get four times the proper amount.'

Yet this was not enough. Food prices rose and food queues became a daily annoyance. 'We have to line up for everything, tea, sugar, marg, and a joint of meat is a thing of the past' wrote a Walthamstow housewife to her husband at the front. Public discontent grew until, in the early months of 1918, the government took the plunge and reluctantly introduced rationing. The German decision to unleash the U-boats had been based on the expectation that British civilians would not put up with such restrictions. However, rationing was an immediate success. The system introduced proved very efficient and, because it was fair and reduced the food queues, it was surprisingly popular.

In Germany and Austria-Hungary the situation was very different. Theoretically both empires were self-sufficient in food, but the war had deprived the land of men and horses, and agricultural output was hit by a succession of poor harvests. The blockade prevented the Central Powers from making good the shortfall by importing food. Germany had been forced to grapple with this problem from late 1915, by which time Austrian cities had already witnessed food riots. German civilians endured morale-sapping hunger during the winter of 1916–1917. A poor harvest and a failure of the potato crop led to the so-called 'turnip winter', with Germans forced to survive on a type of coarse swede normally fed to cattle. In early 1917 diarist Princess Blücher noted seeing 'faces like masks, blue and cold and drawn by hunger, with the harassed expression common to all those who are continually speculating as to the possibility of another meal'. Hungary, with rich agricultural land, was the least affected, but it refused to send grain to its Imperial partner Austria; preferring to sell it to the German Army.

The crisis was worsened by the counter-productive nature of the efforts made to control it. Attempts to manage food supplies were fragmentary, localised and open to abuse. If a maximum price was imposed on a vital foodstuff, farmers would stop producing it in favour of something more profitable. Ration cards were issued, but a lack of control over distribution enabled those with money to bribe their suppliers. The unfairness of the system, combined with steeply rising food prices, led to strikes and riots. As one woman wrote to her soldier-husband, 'yesterday it was war here also. Soldiers with bayonets were behind us [. . .] All the bread shops, as well as some of the greengrocer's and grocer's shops, were wrecked'.

Wollt Ihr Oel, dann sammelt Bucheckern!

Kriegsausschuß für Oele und Fette

Opposite page, top left: *Fishermen, Bring Train Oil! Catch Dolphins and Seals!*
Julius Gipkens, 1917, Germany

Top right: *Our Army needs Metals! Purchase of War Metals*
R Geyer, date unknown, Austria-Hungary

Bottom from left: Women and Girls! Collect Women's Hair!
Jupp Wiertz, date unknown, Germany

Collect Stinging Nettles!
Josef Geis, 1918, Germany

Exhibition of Substitute Products
Alfred Offner, 1918, Austria-Hungary

Left: *If You Want Oil, Collect Beechnuts!* Julius Gipkens, date unknown, Germany

These **posters** make plain the extraordinary lengths to which Germany and Austria-Hungary were forced to go in order to make good the shortages caused by the British blockade. It was not just food which was in short supply. Metals such as aluminium and copper were recycled for the war effort. Stinging nettle stalks were made into thread, women's hair was woven into drive-belts for factory machinery. Rabbit skins made felt for military kit, nuts and fruit stones were crushed to make oil. To keep the trains running, fishermen were exhorted to catch dolphins and seals, so that their fat could be made into lubricants. A whole industry was created to develop and manufacture substitute products.

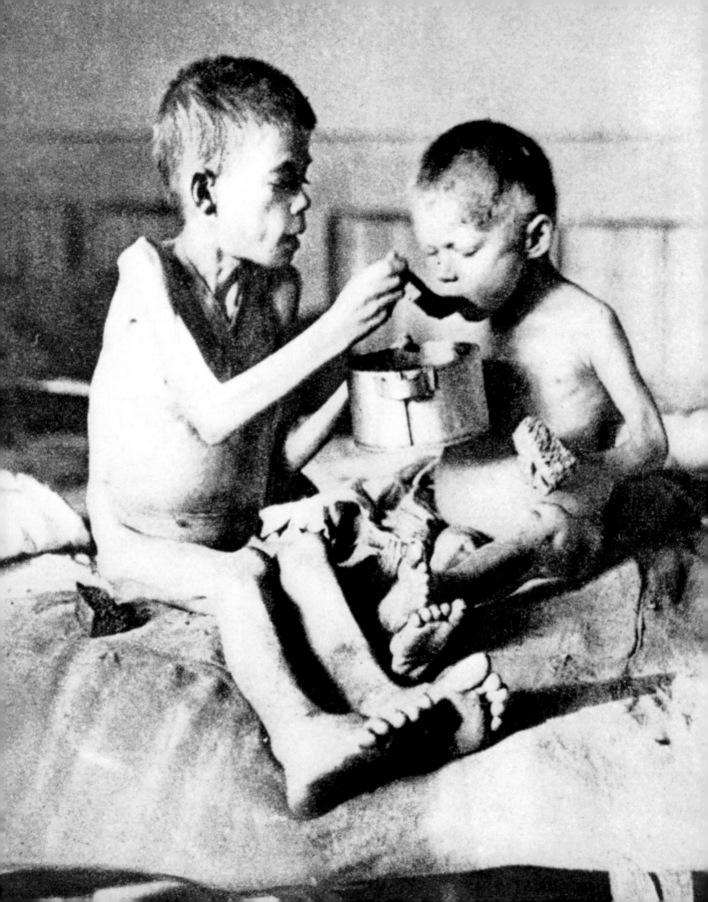

Germany attempted to make up shortages by importing food and goods through the Netherlands and Scandinavia, but the Allies exerted pressure on these neutrals to secure this produce for themselves. After the occupation of most of Romania, the Central Powers set about exploiting its resources. But the amount of grain they acquired was less than the quantity they had purchased there before the war. Another initiative was the introduction of substitute (*Ersatz*) products. 'War tobacco' contained tree bark. *Ersatz* coffee was made from roasted barley. Tea was made from raspberry or strawberry leaves. Hundreds of barely edible concoctions were promoted as substitutes for meat. The most hated food was war bread, the wheat flour content of which was increasingly replaced by oats, barley, potato starch and even pulverised straw. The health of German civilians suffered both from lack of food and from eating poor-quality substitutes. The elderly and those in care suffered most. In the worst example, patients in mental institutions, with their rations cut, simply starved to death.

Similarly, efforts were made to provide substitutes for the raw materials which the blockade was denying Germany and Austria-Hungary. The armies had first call on the dwindling supplies of cotton, wool, leather, and many metals. War industry consumed most of the available coal supplies. Civilians were reduced to wearing clothes made of woven paper and shoes soled with wood. In addition to malnourishment, they had to endure cold and dirt due to a lack of water and fuel to heat houses. The effects on an advanced nation like Germany could be startling. Ethel Cooper, an Australian who spent the war stranded in Leipzig, recorded that 'there is an outbreak of something here [. . .] an extremely infectious dysentery [. . .] One can't well go into details, but I assure you that we see the results everywhere on the pavements – especially in the poorer streets – it is horrible'. In Austria things were even worse – people in the cities began to starve.

Opposite: These **malnourished children** were photographed by an American relief organisation immediately after the end of the war. Startlingly, they were inhabitants of one of Europe's most sophisticated cities: Vienna. Food shortages struck Austria from 1915 onwards, and by 1917 the situation had become critical. An American reporter, Wolf von Schierbrand, witnessed a food riot and noted that 'many women forming part of it looked haggard, desperate and famished. Some had pallid babies clinging to their wasted bosoms'. But for Austria's leaders the need to fight the war took precedence. As one general put it, 'The Army must eat [. . .] it is a matter of indifference whether a few more old people in the hinterland die or not'.

DIE DEUTSCHE
KRIEGSPFANNE

DAS KRIEGSERINNERUNGSZEICHEN
DER DEUTSCHEN HAUSFRAU◆

DRUCK·GERSTUNG·OFFENBACH

Below and left: This iron 'war-frying pan' was used by German women who had patriotically given up their copper cookware for the war-effort. The British naval blockade cut Germany and its allies off from supplies of many essential metals. Foremost amongst these was copper – urgently needed for electrical wiring and to make brass for use in shell-cases and other military equipment. The public were urged to give up brass and copper items for recycling. The verse around the rim of the pan celebrates the fact that the 'German housewife offers up copper for iron'. The moulded figures on the handle make plain the close connection which the authorities wished to make between sacrifices on the home front and the ability of the soldiers to keep fighting.

Revolution

The hope of victory still encouraged whole nations to endure hunger and cold. When that hope failed, the outcome was dramatic. Russia, the least economically developed of the Allied powers, was the first to break. Russia's food distribution system was collapsing. Plenty of food was produced in the countryside, but the underdeveloped transport system was unable to deliver it to the cities; where growing numbers of industrial workers were toiling to supply the Army. And the Army was not winning the war. Brusilov's great triumph in 1916 had not brought victory any nearer.

The blame fell upon Tsar Nicholas II. Upon taking command of the Russian Army in 1915, he had said that 'perhaps a scapegoat is needed to save Russia. I mean to be the victim. May the will of God be done.' His words were prophetic. The Tsar and his German-born wife were held responsible for the failures at the front and the chaos at home. During the winter of 1916–1917, food riots broke out in the capital, Petrograd. The regime struggled to keep order. But the Tsar was not deposed by a people's revolution. Instead, on 15 March 1917, he was forced to abdicate by his own generals, who had lost confidence in his ability to lead the country.

Russia's allies welcomed its new democratic Provisional Government, which pledged to continue fighting whilst introducing reforms at home. But indiscipline and desertion undermined the Army and the new government struggled to keep order on both the home and fighting fronts. In the autumn the communist Bolshevik party mounted a second revolution – actually more of a political coup. Its supporters seized control of Petrograd and the party's leader, Vladimir Lenin offered the people 'Peace, Bread and Land'.

The Germans had helped Lenin to return from exile in neutral Switzerland in the hope that he would stir up revolution in Russia. He exceeded their expectations by taking Russia out of the war entirely. The Bolsheviks wanted to concentrate their efforts on securing their grip on power at home and approached the Central Powers for peace terms. Political manoeuvring delayed the signing of a treaty until March 1918. The Treaty of Brest Litovsk was immensely harsh, depriving Russia of huge tracts of territory and imposing financial reparations amounting to six billion German Marks. The collapse of Russia isolated Romania and forced it to sign the humiliating Treaty of Bucharest, which effectively made it a German client-state.

ПРОЛЕТАРІИ ВСЕХ СТРАН СОЕДИНЯЙТЕС"! В БОР'БЕ ОБРЕТЕШ ТЫ ПРАВО СВОЕ!

Although the peace treaty with Russia had taken months to negotiate, Germany knew from November 1917 that the war there was effectively over. It began to concentrate its military power in the West. Men of prime fitness, in their twenties, were transferred to units in France and Belgium. A million others – the old and the very young – were left in the East. The latter would attempt to exploit the resources of occupied areas and of Ukraine, whose independent existence was backed by Germany.

The Allies faced a crisis. They were deprived of Russia's manpower, and the American Army was not yet ready to make good the loss. Now, more than ever, it was clear that the Western Front would be where the decisive events of the war would take place. Early in 1918 the German novelist Herman Hesse wrote:

> 'With bated breath the world is looking eastwards, to the peace negotiations at Brest Litovsk. And at the same time, it is watching the Western Front in dire anguish, for everyone feels, everyone knows that, short of a miracle, the most dreadful disaster that has ever befallen men is there impending; the bitterest, bloodiest, most ruthless and appalling battle of all time.'

Opposite: This banner was paraded by Bolshevik activists at the time of the 'October Revolution', when Lenin's communist party seized power in the Russian capital Petrograd (St Petersburg). It bears the slogan 'Workers of all countries unite! In the struggle you will obtain your rights!' By the spring of 1918 the Bolsheviks had taken Russia out of the war, but a greater disaster was about to unfold. A civil war had to be fought before the Bolsheviks could assure their hold on power. It ravaged the whole of Russia, costing millions of lives. During 1918 and 1919 Allied forces attempted to intervene. This banner was captured by the British. It had been sent from Petrograd to stiffen the morale of 'Red' soldiers in fighting them in North Russia.

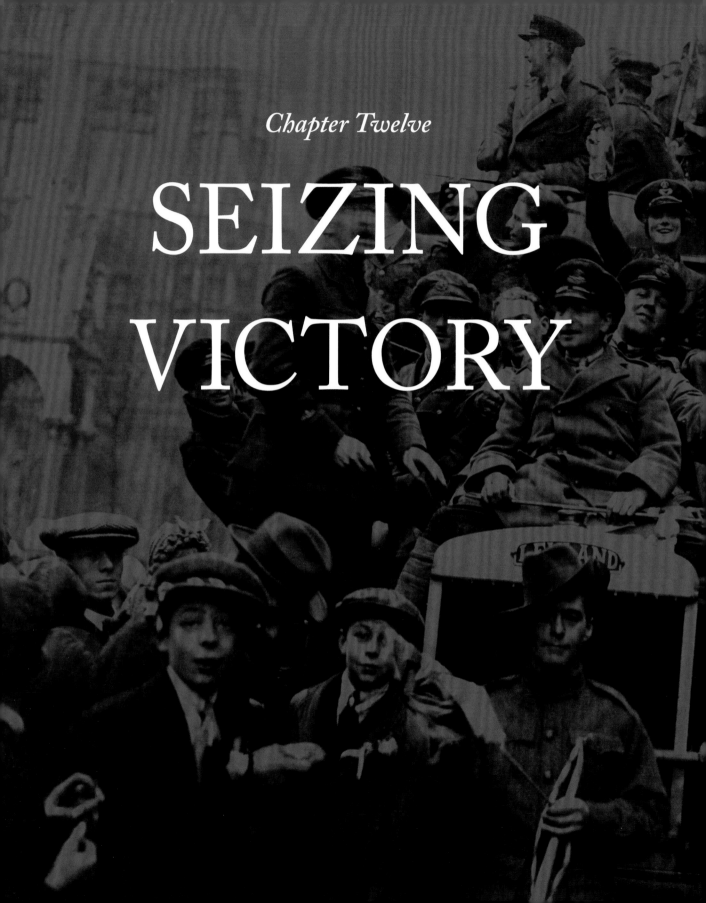

Chapter Twelve

SEIZING VICTORY

'Tomorrow there will be nothing to keep secret – for then hell breaks loose'

By the beginning of 1918 all eyes were focused on the Western Front. British forces were exhausted by their recent efforts, and the French Army had only just regained its fighting fitness. The political leaders of the two Allies resolved to wait until the American Army was ready to fight en masse before returning to the attack.

But the master of German strategy, General Erich Ludendorff, had very different ideas. The collapse of Russia allowed him to concentrate his best men on the Western Front. He resolved to attack and defeat Britain and France before the Americans could arrive in force. The Germans would be staking everything on one last roll of the dice. The decision would bring the war to a frightful crescendo of violence and destruction, and lead to the most dramatic and unexpected of outcomes.

Hell Breaks Loose

On 20 March 1918 a huge German force – over a third of those present on the Western Front – supported by almost half of Germany's artillery, stood ready opposite a thinly-held section of the Allied line, east of the old Somme battlefield. Cavalry officer Rudolf Binding confided to his diary, 'tomorrow there will be nothing to keep secret – for then hell breaks loose'. In the early hours of the following day another diarist, Lieutenant Edgar von le Suire wrote, 'All are impatiently standing in the trenches which we have come to despise; they do not fit in with German manliness.'

At 4.40 am on 21 March an artillery barrage of unprecedented ferocity was unleashed. In just four hours the Germans fired more shells than the British had in a full week of bombardment prior to the first attack on the Somme. Lieutenant Colonel Rowland Feilding described the experience to his wife, 'The forward areas were drenched with poison gas, and the back areas, to a distance of over five miles behind the front line, were shelled with the most savage fury.' Through an early spring fog the

Above: **Camouflaged helmets** were worn by many **German soldiers** in 1918, particularly by the elite assault troops. Beginning in 1915, the Germans had formed specialist assault units, who pioneered new methods of infantry attack based on speed, shock and infiltration of the enemy's defences. By 1917 these tactics had been rolled out to selected units throughout the Army. They were employed with success at Riga in Russia, at Caporetto against the Italians and during the counter-attack against the British at Cambrai. Assault-trained soldiers spearheaded the German offensives of 1918, but their numbers were worn down in repeated attacks, depriving Germany of many of its best soldiers by the middle of the year.

German infantry now launched itself upon the stunned survivors of the inferno. Within two days the Germans had achieved what every general on the Western Front had longed for – a breakthrough. The British Fifth Army had only recently taken over this long stretch of the front line and its defences were underdeveloped. Within a week it had been thrown back 40 miles. The British, and by extension the Allied cause, were facing disaster. An excited Kaiser Wilhelm shouted the news to an honour-guard of soldiers awaiting him at a station, 'The battle is won! The English have been utterly defeated!'

Lack of preparedness on the British side was not the only reason for German success. The Germans had learned from their combat experience just as the Allies had done over the preceding three years. They too had been honing their artillery techniques, but their main initiative was a reorganisation of their infantry to maximise the impact of new assault tactics, which they had been developing since 1915. Their best soldiers were concentrated in 'Mobile' and 'Attack' divisions. Mobile divisions were composed entirely of men trained in the new tactics; attack divisions contained specialist battalions trained in them. These formations were made mobile by giving them almost all of Germany's limited quantities of motor transport and draught-horses. However the creation of these elite units had an inherent weakness. Little could be expected of remainder of the troops, concentrated in 'Trench' divisions, who were starved of training, equipment and transport. And there were 136 of these on the Western Front, compared with 56 Attack and Mobile Divisions.

Left: German field sign for a 'Horse Collecting Point'. The German Army had far fewer motor vehicles than the Allies, still relying principally on horse power. It acquired 1.4 million horses during the war; 400,000 of these were lost to enemy action and a further 500,000 to disease and malnutrition. By mid-1918 the Germans were acutely short of horses, with 29,000 having been killed in the March offensive alone. And they were unable to properly feed the ones they had. On 27 June German officer Rudolf Binding wrote 'The shortage of horses is bad enough; but the shortage of fodder! [. . .] we shall [. . .] have to leave guns behind, ammunition-wagons and so on. This will reduce our artillery strength by about a quarter. It would not be safe to let the infantry know that.'

Nonetheless, this limitation did not impede the German advance in March 1918. By 26 March the situation had become critical for the Allies. Field Marshal Haig was, according to one witness, 'cowed. He said that unless the "Whole French Army" came up we were beaten and it would be better to make peace on any terms we could.' He had received French reinforcements in response to urgent pleas to General Pétain; but the latter feared that the German attack was just a prelude to an assault on his own sector of the front. At this point the Allied governments intervened. The French President and Prime Minister and Lloyd George's representative Lord Milner summoned their senior commanders to a meeting at the front. Together they agreed on a decisive move. General Ferdinand Foch, who had led the French on the Somme, was appointed to co-ordinate the Allied armies. Aggressive and optimistic, Foch was the man for the job. He immediately set about sending further reinforcements to stop the German advance.

Above: This photograph shows French and British infantry intermingled in a makeshift defensive position during the German offensive of March 1918. The availability of French reserves was vital to Allied chances of halting the initial German breakthroughs. Ludendorff had planned to destroy the British Army and then turn on the French. His plans did not take into account how efficiently the two armies were to co-operate – particularly after the appointment of Foch to direct operations.

In fact the German breakthrough had never entirely routed the British defenders and, with the aid of reinforcements, the latter began to recover from their hurried retreat. As the Germans advanced beyond the support of their artillery, their attack lost impetus. They were further slowed by their troops taking advantage of what they saw as a land of plenty. They marvelled at the quantities of food and clothing which they found in captured British supply dumps, but also stopped to loot alcohol. One of their commanders, Crown Prince Rupprecht of Bavaria, noted that 'The lack of discipline in the troops is serious. Almost every time they take a town the troops look for food and wine. Since they are exhausted and without food, they get drunk fast.' An attempt to widen the offensive with an attack at Arras had been a costly failure, and Ludendorff began to focus his attention further north. On 9 April he launched a new offensive, against the British line south of Ypres.

Below: German infantry out in the open, May 1918. 1918 witnessed a return to a more mobile form of warfare on the Western Front. This inevitably brought with it casualties on the horrific scale which had last been seen in 1914. Once again men were exposed to the deadly fire of modern weapons without the cover of trenches. Both sides suffered equally, although many of the Allied losses early in the year came in the form of prisoners – most of whom would at least survive the war. The Allies could also look to the growing American Army to tip the balance in their favour. Germany simply did not have enough manpower to make good its losses.

This attack might cut the British Army in two, and even reach the Channel ports. Like the March offensive, it was initially successful. Once again Haig began to fear defeat. On 11 April he issued an order of the day exhorting his men to fight to the last 'With our backs to the wall and believing in the justice of our cause each one of us must fight on to the end'. This time, however, there was no disorderly retreat, and Foch quickly sent French reinforcements. The newly-created RAF hurled itself at the attackers. On 12 April it dropped more bombs than on any other day of the war. Its pilots were told that 'very low flying is essential. All risks to be taken.' The German advance was halted and once again Ludendorff began to look elsewhere. Now, he reasoned, he should attack the French to prevent them from reinforcing the British, on whom he could turn later. Four consecutive offensives were launched against the French front. The first of these caused alarm among the Allies; bringing German troops closer to Paris than they had been since 1914.

Ludendorff-Spende für Kriegsbeschädigte

LUDENDORFF

Left: Apart from its appearance on this charity appeal poster, General Erich Ludendorff's face was less familiar to the German public than that of the senior partner in the German high command, General Hindenburg. Yet it was Ludendorff who made the strategic decisions – a task for which he proved ill-fitted during 1918. In fact he publicly shunned strategy when making his original plans, saying 'we will punch a hole, for the rest we will see'. Lacking focus, he switched too easily from one plan to another. During his attacks on the British in March and April the chance arose of capturing key rail junctions at Amiens and Hazebrouck. If either had fallen, the British forces north of them would have been virtually cut off from supply. But Ludendorff failed to seize the opportunity, sending his troops in different directions.

But the repeated attacks consumed German resources and also deprived their tactics of the element of surprise. The follow-up offensives gained little ground. Then, on 18 July, as the Germans pressed home their latest attack, they were thunderstruck when the French, supported by hundreds of mobile light tanks and eight divisions of American troops, launched a brutal counter-attack. This battle, which became known as the Second Battle of the Marne, transformed the strategic situation. There were no more German offensives. Ludendorff's plans had failed; his army was depleted and exhausted. The return to mobile warfare had raised casualties to terrible levels on both sides. German losses for the period from March to July approached 800,000 men. Their use of specialised assault units in repeated attacks meant that many of their best fighting-men had been killed or wounded.

Now is the Time to Act with Boldness

On 24 July 1918 Foch proclaimed that 'the moment has come to abandon the general defensive attitude [. . .] and to pass to the offensive'. He found an eager supporter for this view in Sir Douglas Haig, whose forces would play a dominant role in the next Allied move. On 8 August, at the Battle of Amiens, Haig's men, spearheaded by Canadian and Australian Divisions, inflicted a dramatic defeat upon the Germans. Sir Henry Rawlinson, who commanded the attacking force, wrote, 'I think we have given the Boche a pretty good bump this time – the Australians and Canadians fought magnificently'. For the first time German soldiers began to surrender in large groups. They were beginning to realise that their sacrifices of the past few months had been for nothing.

Under Foch's direction and exhortations to attack 'with the utmost violence', the Allies now mounted a series of offensives all along the German line, pushing the enemy back to the positions where they had begun the year. British and empire forces played the most prominent part in these attacks, with Haig stating that 'now is the time to act with boldness'. He told Rawlinson that 'risks which a month ago would have been criminal to incur ought now to be incurred as a duty'. To the south of Haig's armies the French pressed forwards and they were joined, significantly, by the Americans. The American Commander, General John Pershing, had resisted Allied attempts to use American soldiers to strengthen their own armies. During the crisis caused by the German spring offensives, he had sent some units to fight alongside the French

Above: The American Army had to prepare itself for the nature of warfare on the Western Front. This **tunic** was worn by Private Gilbert Wien, of the **1st US Gas Regiment**. This unit's chemical warfare specialists took part in every major US battle of 1918. American units were the strongest on the Western Front in terms of both manpower and firepower, but lacked experience. This led initially to high casualties among their infantry, and the breakdown of their supply and transport systems. Lessons were speedily learned. By the war's end the Germans were unable to stop the American Expeditionary Force's advance.

Left: These **caricature Toby jugs** depict Field Marshals **Haig** and **Foch**. They are from a set depicting Allied leaders, created between 1915 and 1919 by the political caricaturist Francis Carruthers Gould. The relationship between Foch, as supreme Allied Commander, and Haig, who commanded the most effective Allied army in 1918, was crucial to the unexpectedly swift victory on the Western Front. The two men met to confer on over sixty occasions between March and November 1918. Haig was reported as looking 'ten years younger' once Foch took control, and proved both willing and able to put the latter's attacking strategy into effect.

and British. But now the American Expeditionary Force – with over half a million troops in the front line, and more on the way – was ready to fight under his leadership as an independent army.

The Allies could now deploy more men than their enemy, and also had more guns, aircraft and tanks. Yet the most crucial advantage held by the Allies was in transport – particularly motor-transport – which enabled them to move their troops around the front. In action the Allied soldier could expect lavish artillery and machine gun support. Corporal Talbot Mohan of the Wiltshire Regiment recorded an attack in his diary, 'Before us was this immense wall of fire and smoke, bursting and rending shells [. . .] Together with this went the crackle of hundreds of machine guns, which reminded me of sticks crackling in a fire.' On the other side of the line, German soldiers were faltering. General Max von Boehm made the following diary entry on 20 September: 'Day of terror [. . .] The troops no longer have the old firm hold, efficient officers are missing above all, and the resources of the men are tried to the utmost.'

On 28 September Sir Henry Rawlinson wrote:

> 'under Foch's tuition and the lessons of over four years of war, we are really learning [. . .] if the Americans are inexperienced, they are as keen as mustard and splendid men [. . .] DH came to see me [. . .] He thinks we will finish the war this year, and I hope he may be right, but it is no certainty.'

In holding this belief Sir Douglas Haig was in a small minority of optimists among the Allies. Most believed that, although victory now looked assured, it would not come until 1919. Haig was to play a leading part in making his own vision come true during the next phase of Foch's 'grand offensive'. The time had come for the Allies to assault the complex system of defensive positions which they called the 'Hindenburg Line'. Attacks were mounted at multiple points. In the south the Americans and French ground their way forward through difficult terrain. In the north the Belgian Army, supported by a British force, advanced to begin the liberation of its homeland. The most dramatic events, however, took place in the centre when, between 29 September and 5 October, British and empire forces broke through the strongest part of the German line along a 19 mile front. It was one of the clearest victories of the war. Australian Corporal Oswald Blows surveyed the captured defences and wrote 'there is no end of barbed wire and the trenches are very wide, & many deep dug outs [. . .] absolutely impregnable it was once thought – & would have been still if his men had fought as of old, but they're breaking, thank the Lord.'

Peace at Any Price

The inability of his exhausted army to halt the Allied advance was now becoming obvious to Ludendorff, subjecting him to extreme psychological pressure. Doctors prescribed for him a regime of morning walks and folk song singing. But, on 28 September, he suffered a mental collapse when he received news that the Bulgarians, bereft of German aid, starving and with revolution brewing, intended to give up the fight on the following day. They had been containing the Allied army in Macedonia, which was now free to advance against Germany's remaining allies, Austria-Hungary and Turkey. The architect of Germany's strategy lost his belief in victory. He informed the government that they would have to seek an armistice – a cessation of hostilities which would allow Germany to draw breath and consider peace negotiations. The German government approached President Wilson to request an armistice based on the 'Fourteen Points' which Wilson had laid down in January as his basis for peace in Europe. Wilson's ideas were of a liberal nature and focused on self-determination for national and ethnic groups in Europe. They had been publicised in a vain attempt to keep Russia in the war, but were also a message to the political left of both sides – an encouragement to German socialists to seek peace, and a reassurance to Allied socialists that their cause was just.

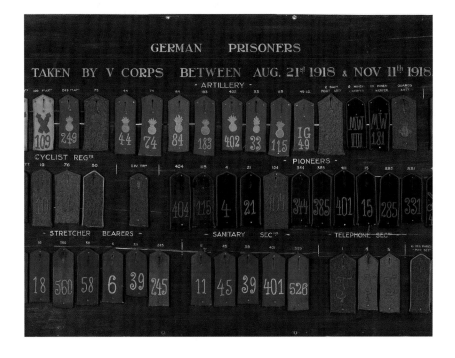

Left and overleaf: By the autumn of 1918 the German Army was beginning to crumble. A French analysis of interrogations of prisoners reported that 'officers in particular inform us of the weakness of their forces, the youth of their recruits, and the influence of the American entry. They are depressed by their heavy losses, by the poor quality of their food, and by the crisis inside Germany.' The clearest sign of this came in the number of prisoners taken by the Allies. Whole German units were beginning to surrender – frequently with their officers. These **German shoulder straps** were **taken from prisoners** to create a record of all the German units faced by British V Corps in the autumn of 1918. They were mounted on three boards to commemorate the Corps' part in the Allied victory.

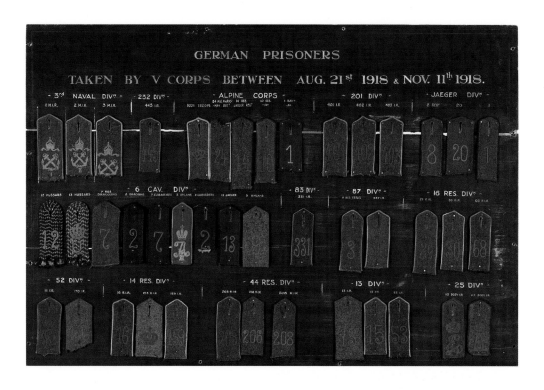

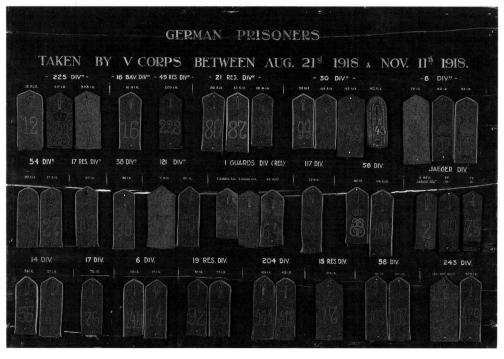

But Wilson and his advisors had been alarmed by the near success of Germany's latest attempt to crush its enemies with military might. Now they were horrified by the deliberate and widespread acts of destruction carried out by the German Army as it withdrew, not to mention the continued sinking of neutral shipping by German submarines. This left Wilson in no mood to treat Germany gently. He was happy for the Allies to draw up the terms of the armistice with military advice. When Ludendorff became aware of these developments he reversed his policy and advised continuation of the war. He was too late. News of the armistice request had raised the tantalising prospect of peace. Many Germans, at home and at the front, had fixed their thoughts on that prospect. As the Allies commenced a new series of advances, the German Army began to collapse.

Crown Prince Rupprecht of Bavaria wrote in despair, 'the morale of the troops has suffered seriously and their power of resistance diminishes daily. They surrender in hordes whenever the enemy attacks, and thousands of plunderers infest the districts around the bases. We have no more prepared lines and no more can be dug.' This failure of fighting spirit was equally noticeable to ordinary Allied soldiers. Corporal James Murrell of the 2/4th York and Lancaster Regiment wrote home:

> 'Jerry is now beginning to realise that we are the master, and before many more weeks he will cry out for mercy, just now it is hell upon earth for him, and it's a wonder he is sticking it so long, the prisoners we take are a very dejected lot and are absolutely fed up with it, they say down with the Kaiser.'

In Germany the mood was similar. A local military administrator, General August Isbert, lamented that 'the broad masses want only peace, even if it is peace at any price'.

Germany's allies continued to collapse. By the end of October Turkey had conceded defeat. Its main army had been destroyed in September at the Battle of Megiddo in Palestine. The victory was won by an unlikely mixture of empire forces under General Edmund Allenby. Many of his troops were young Indian recruits who had only completed their training during the preceding summer. Turkey's leadership had been concealing the seriousness of the military situation, but when Bulgaria's surrender opened a land route to Constantinople to the Allied armies, they fell from power. A new Turkish government hurried to sign an armistice. On 4 November Austria-Hungary too left the war. By this time it was no longer

an empire. Hungary had broken its political union with Austria and the Slav citizens of the empire had declared themselves to be independent nations. An Italian offensive had finally broken the starving Austro-Hungarian Army and its soldiers began to head for home.

Meanwhile, in Germany, events had begun to move at breakneck pace. On 26 October Ludendorff had been forced to resign. On 3 November mutiny had broken out in the High Seas Fleet after the sailors got wind of a plan by their commanders to lead them on a suicidal attack against the Royal Navy – which had been reinforced since 1917 with American battleships. Revolutionary outbreaks now began to spread across German towns. On 9 November Berlin was paralysed by a general strike. Germany's generals and political leaders were terrified that the country would fall prey to a communist revolution. If the Army could be extricated from the war, it might be used to restore order, but its leaders knew that the men no longer supported their 'supreme warlord' the Kaiser. Acting on military advice, Wilhelm II abdicated on 9 November and went into exile in the Netherlands.

By the time German negotiators met with Allied delegates to arrange the armistice, Germany no longer occupied a military or political position from which it could negotiate. The Allied military leaders would only permit an armistice under conditions which made it impossible for

ACHTUNG !!!!

OESTERREICH UNGARN erklærte sich am 28 Oktober bereit, Einzelverhandlungen mit der Entente zu führen zum Abschluss sofortigen Waffenstillstandes auf allen austrungarischen Fronten.

Left: This **aerial propaganda leaflet** was released over the German lines in October 1918. It carries news of the armistice signed with Austria. Millions of leaflets like this were dropped during the autumn of 1918, largely by unmanned balloons. The programme reached a climax in October when Britain alone dropped over five million. The collapse of Germany's allies was strongly emphasised in the hope of demoralising German soldiers. The final straw came when Austria made a separate peace on 4 November. Artillery officer Herbert Sulzbach wrote 'now Germany faces the world alone, deserted by all her allies'.

Left: News of the signing of the **armistice** lead to scenes of wild rejoicing in Allied cities. This photograph shows an ecstatic **crowd in Birmingham**. From London, Laura Borton wrote to tell her father, a Kent landowner, that 'London has gone completely mad. I don't think I have ever seen such wild enthusiasm in my life. It was horribly sad too, as among all the roaring singing crowds one saw many women sobbing like children.' At the front, relief and even disbelief were the dominant emotions. Lieutenant Colonel Rowland Feilding wrote home describing the mood amongst his men:

'One of awe and inability to appreciate the great relief that had so suddenly come to them [. . .] I do not think many – if any – felt much inclined for jubilation, though I will not do them the injustice of saying that had they had the opportunity they would have failed to take advantage of it.'

Germany to return to the fight. The turmoil in Germany had now brought the Socialist Party to power. They were desperate to stave off a 'Bolshevik' revolution and ordered the armistice delegation to sign on any conditions. The terms of the Armistice signed on 11 November 1918 included the withdrawal of all German troops to the east of the River Rhine, with an Allied occupation zone created to its west; the handing over of virtually all the Army's artillery and machine guns, and the internment of the German fleet in British ports. It was far from the breathing space which Ludendorff had envisaged: it was a surrender.

Germany had begun the year of 1918 prepared to seize victory, only to find it torn from its grasp in the most dramatic reversal of fortune. The German people had been prepared to endure terrible hardships when victory seemed possible, but military defeat on all fronts destroyed their support for the war. Germany's armistice request had set in motion a series of events that led to an unexpectedly swift and complete Allied victory. German artilleryman Herbert Sulzbach summed up his country's fate: 'The war is over [. . .] How we looked forward to this moment [. . .] and here we are now, humbled, our souls torn and bleeding, and [we] know that we've surrendered.'

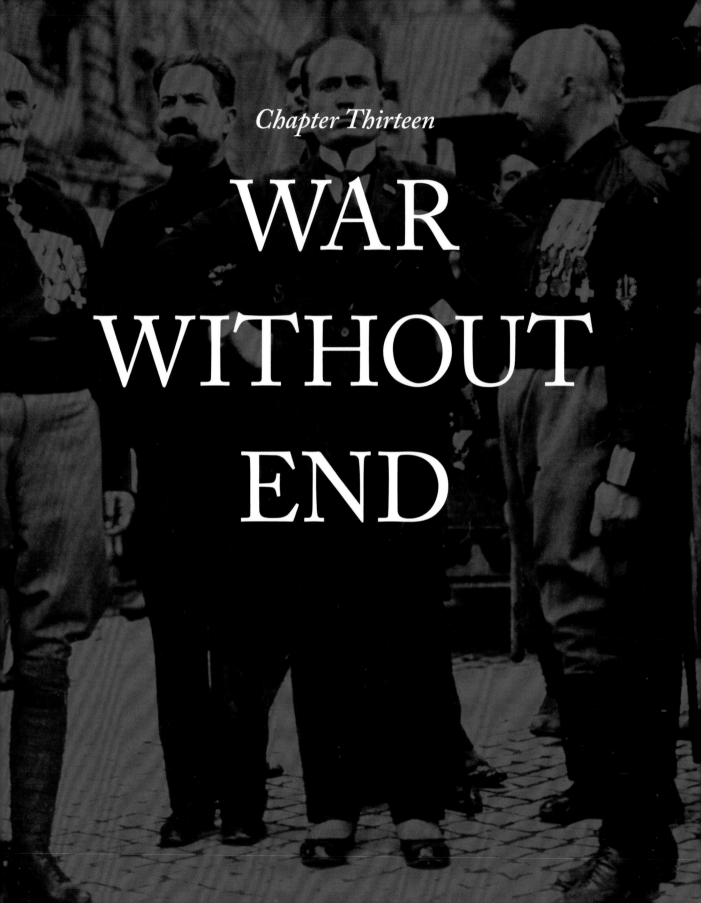

Chapter Thirteen

WAR
WITHOUT
END

'You hold in your hands the future of the world'

In 1919 the leaders of the victorious powers met in Paris to settle the peace. Britain and its empire were prominent among the triumphant peacemakers. People had high hopes that the victors would create a new, safer and better world. The war had swept away the old political and social order. Old empires had fallen; new nations had been born – creating new ambitions, rivalries and tensions. Revolutionary ideologies and extreme nationalism were on the march. And for many outside Western Europe, war had not ended.

The Restoration of Peace and the Treaty of Versailles

Many of the countries who had gone to war between 1914 and 1918 had paid a terrible price. Over ten million servicemen and women lost their lives. The number of civilian deaths is harder to assess, but certainly appears to have exceeded five million. Millions more received wounds, both physical and psychological, which would afflict them for the rest of their lives. To this burden of grief and suffering must be added the cost of physical destruction and the immense expense of fighting the war. Some countries paid a particularly high price. Serbia lost over 16 per cent of its population. In Belgium and France the 250-mile-long scar of the Western Front destroyed half a million homes in 1,659 different towns and villages. Russia was in the throes of a vicious civil war, which would cost it at least five times more lives than the world war had.

It was against this grim background that the victorious powers met to set the terms of the peace. President Poincaré of France told them 'You hold in your hands the future of the world.' The Paris Peace Conference gathered together delegates from over 30 countries. They included representatives from Britain's Dominions and from countries like China and Brazil, who had joined the Allied cause late in the war. Most of these delegations nursed secret and sometimes conflicting ambitions over what they hoped to gain from the conference; but all agreed that a lasting peace was necessary to prevent such a terrible slaughter from

happening again. The most fervent proponent of this view was President Wilson of the United States. He wanted to create a 'League of Nations', whose members could co-operate to maintain peace in the world and to resolve international disputes. Like the British campaigners of the Union of Democratic Control, he dreamed of a new type of diplomacy, without secret treaties and alliances. The first two months of the discussions at Paris were dominated by the creation of this organisation.

The conference then turned to setting the terms of the peace. The defeated Central Powers did not have a voice; any decisions would be imposed upon them. Germany was forced to sign the Treaty of Versailles, which stripped it of its colonies; gave parts of its territory to Poland, France, Denmark and Belgium, and installed Allied occupation forces along the Rhine. These measures did not weaken Germany in the long term, but caused great resentment. Even more hated by Germans were the financial reparations that they were compelled to pay to the Allies. To provide a legal basis for their imposition, Germany was forced to admit guilt for causing the war. Germans, who had for four years been told that they were fighting an essentially defensive war, were outraged. War guilt was perceived as a matter of such significance that the German foreign office set up a special department devoted to disproving it.

Few of the participants in the peace process were entirely satisfied by its outcomes. The French feared that the Treaty of Versailles was not sufficiently harsh to destroy Germany's potential to become a military threat to them again in the future. They were forced to place hope in an alliance with Britain and the USA, but this never came to pass. Despite the efforts of President Wilson before he succumbed to a stroke in October 1919, the United States turned away from involvement in European affairs, not joining the League of Nations, or even ratifying the Treaty of Versailles. The Italians had not received all the territories which they had been promised in 1915 and complained of a 'mutilated victory'. Japan was infuriated by the refusal to make racial equality part of the covenant by which the League of Nations was founded. China refused to ratify the treaty because Japan had been handed Germany's former possessions in China. Arab nationalists were denied the self-rule for which they had fought.

The peacemakers had faced an almost impossible task in resolving the conflicting requirements of the delegates in a way which allowed for the reconstruction of Europe. There was idealism in their creation of the League of Nations: the first body ever created to oversee international

Opposite: The Signing of Peace in the Hall of Mirrors, Versailles, 28th June 1919
William Orpen, 1919, France
William Orpen was commissioned by the Imperial War Museum to paint a record of the signing of the Treaty of Versailles. The artist's confidence in the peace process faded as the diplomatic wrangling dragged on over six months. The distorted reflections in the mirrored palace wall convey his reservations. Orpen's wartime associations with Sir Douglas Haig and his army had left him with a disdain for politicians or 'frocks' (after their frock coats) as they were known to Army officers. He wrote of the scene, 'It was all over. The "frocks" had won the war. The "frocks" had signed the Peace! The Army was forgotten. Some dead and forgotten, others maimed and forgotten, others alive and well – but equally forgotten.'

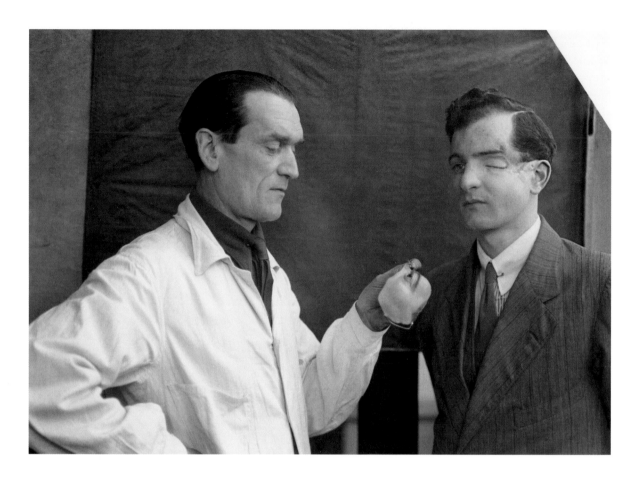

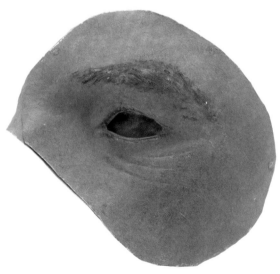

Above and left: Over 60,000 British soldiers suffered head or eye injuries during the war. Some of these wounds caused lasting disfigurement. New Zealander Harold Gillies pioneered modern plastic surgery techniques in an effort to repair such damage. Some men were given painted metal prostheses to cover facial scars. The sculptor **Francis Derwent Wood** (above with patient), who first made them, sought 'to make a man's face as near as possible to what it looked like before'. The masks were produced in a hospital department in Wandsworth, London, known as the 'tin noses shop'. Each was fitted individually and painted to match the wearer's skin tone.

relations. Furthermore, new nations had been created or re-created, with Poland, Czechoslovakia, Yugoslavia, Finland and the Baltic states giving self-rule to former subjects of the Austro-Hungarian and Russian empires. The new world which came out of the Paris conference was far from perfect, but it did appear to offer every chance of a peaceful future. President Wilson summed up his own feelings in a letter to his wife: 'Well, little girl, it is finished, and, as no one is satisfied, it makes me hope we have made a just peace; but it is all in the lap of the gods.'

A Changing Empire

The British people took pride in their victory and what they had achieved between 1914 and 1918, but the British Empire had paid a heavy price. Britain itself lost three quarters of a million servicemen and women, and almost 250,000 soldiers from the empire also perished. Terrible as the losses were, there was in fact no 'Lost Generation' of young British men. Almost ninety per cent of those who served returned alive, although some communities and families paid a disproportionately high price. Among those who came home were thousands who were damaged, physically or mentally, some irreparably. Ten years later nearly 2.5 million men were receiving a disability pension for injuries suffered during the war.

The war had brought tragedy and hardship, but also new opportunities and fresh experiences for many men and women all over the empire. Society was changing. Government intervention in industry and in everyday life was now accepted – even expected – on a scale which would have been unimaginable in 1914. Long-established moral, political, social and religious values were now questioned. Social deference – respect for one's 'betters' – was less in evidence. Politically the war led to Britain becoming more democratic. In February 1918 Parliament had given its overwhelming support to a new 'Representation of the People Act'. This extended the vote from just 8 million men in 1914 to over 21 million people. The right to vote was now enjoyed by virtually all men of 21 years or more and, for the first time, women (although only those over 30 – younger women would not gain electoral equality until 1929). Introducing the bill, the Home Secretary stated that 'the spirit manifested in this war by all classes of our countrymen has brought us nearer together, has opened men's eyes, and removed misunderstandings on all sides'. In reality, the move was inspired as much by fear as by goodwill. Politicians were keen to dampen any revolutionary fervour which might spread to Britain from Bolshevik Russia.

Far left: The first **poppy** appeal took place in 1921. The poppy had become a symbol of remembrance during the war. Anna Guérin, a French woman, originally had the idea of selling artificial poppies for charity. The idea was taken up by Field Marshal Earl Haig's British Legion and veterans' organisations throughout the British Empire. The poppies were made then, as they still are today, by disabled ex-service personnel at the Legion's factory in Richmond, Surrey. The First World War prompted the creation of a uniquely British language of remembrance, focused upon the ceremonies now held on Remembrance Sunday and the two-minute silence at 11am each 11 November.

Above right: The immediate post-war period witnessed the creation of veterans' associations, of which the **Comrades of the Great War**, represented by this **badge**, was one. Officers and men had formed close bonds in the trenches and looked to maintain a memory of them in peacetime. In 1921, the British Legion was formed by amalgamating the four largest veterans' associations; including the Comrades of the Great War. The most prominent of the Legion's founders was Field Marshal Earl Haig. The British Legion was a politically neutral organisation, open to all ex-servicemen. By contrast, Germany had several politically-aligned veterans' associations; adding to the troubled political scene in that country. In France veterans' associations found a growing anti-war voice as the immediate glow of victory faded.

The first election fought under the extended franchise took place in December 1918. It was won by the coalition of Liberals and Conservatives forged during the war under the leadership of David Lloyd George, who promised to create a country 'fit for heroes to live in'. But the new government's first priority was to speed the return of four million servicemen to civilian life. The initial slowness of the process of demobilisation caused widespread frustration and anger. In the short term the reintegration of ex-servicemen was aided by a brief economic boom, but this was followed by a depression and growing unemployment. The industrial unrest which had plagued pre-war Britain returned. National finances were also damaged by the Bolshevik government's refusal to repay Russia's huge wartime debt to Britain.

Victory had secured the British Empire from foreign threats. But for the people of the Dominions – especially Australia and Canada – who had sacrificed much to achieve that security, the war had fostered a heightened sense of national identity. Their citizens expected a greater measure of independence, and equality with Britain in an evolving empire. As one Canadian, Alexander Young Jackson, put it 'we are no longer humble colonials, we've made armies'. In the non-white empire, especially India, demands for self-rule became more vocal. Indian Nationalists were disappointed to find that India's wartime efforts had brought them no nearer their goal. Between 1919 and 1922 Britain faced civil disturbances in India, inspired by the Nationalist leader Mohandas Gandhi. The use of force, of which the worst example was the shooting of hundreds of rioters in Amritsar in 1919, caused more problems than it solved. It became clear that concessions would need to be made to keep India within the empire. Another Nationalist, Madan Mohan Malaviya, suggested, with some justification, that 'the war has put the clock of time fifty years forward'.

A new and unstable element was added to this changing Imperial scene due to Britain's wartime intervention in the Middle East. Britain and France had secretly planned to carve up the Ottoman Empire. At Versailles the two countries were awarded League of Nations 'Mandates' to govern parts of formerly Turkish territory. Britain was given control of Palestine, Transjordan (now Jordan) and Mesopotamia (Iraq). The French were awarded control of Syria and Lebanon. During the war important Arab leaders had supported the Allies, believing that this would win them control of their own destinies. Now most Arabs felt that they had merely exchanged one colonial master for another. The writer and traveller Gertrude Bell, who became hugely influential in the creation of Iraq, was filled with misgivings:

> 'they are making such a horrible muddle of the Near East, I confidently anticipate that it will be much worse than it was before the war [. . .] It's like a nightmare in which you foresee all the horrible things which are going to happen and can't stretch out your hand to prevent them.'

PARLIAMENTARY ELECTION
1918
ROMFORD DIVISION

VOTE FOR

MARTIN

MAKE GERMANY PAY FOR THE WAR
AND
HANG THE KAISER

Printed & Published by A. HARVEY, (L.S.C.) 20. Sunningdale Avenue, Barking and New Road, E.

Left: In December 1918, Lloyd George – hailed as 'The Man Who Won the War' – called and won a general election. This **campaign poster** is for Liberal candidate Albert Martin who won the seat of Romford in Essex. The election was known as the 'Coupon Election' due to the coupons issued by Lloyd George's coalition to identify candidates, like Martin, who represented it. Calls to punish the Kaiser in person were loud at the time. His own cousin, King George V, regarded him as the 'greatest criminal known for having plunged the world into this ghastly war'. But this would have presented so many difficulties that most Allied leaders were privately relieved that the Netherlands granted him right of asylum. Not least President Wilson, who had pleaded 'Please don't send him to Bermuda. I want to go there myself!'

British colonial rule did not pass unchallenged. In 1919 a rebellion in Egypt was suppressed, but it persuaded Britain to grant a limited measure of independence. Iraq – important because of its reserves of oil – proved particularly troublesome. It suffered from being composed of three former Turkish provinces, populated by a volatile mix of religious and ethnic groups. Between 1919 and 1923 Britain found itself facing three major revolts there. Palestine caused Britain fewer immediate problems, but

began to store them up for the future. The Balfour Declaration of 1917 had announced British support for the creation of a Jewish homeland in Palestine. The establishment of the British Mandate encouraged a rise in Jewish immigration, which triggered anti-Jewish riots and Arab violence against Jewish settlers during the 1920s.

But the greatest change to the British Empire was the loss of one of its oldest constituent parts – Ireland. The second half of the war had witnessed a huge growth of republican sentiment there. Revulsion at the harsh government response to the 1916 Easter Rising combined with anger at the ever-present, though never enacted, threat that conscription would be introduced in Ireland. In the 1918 general election Republicans made a clean sweep of parliamentary seats outside Ulster. Refusing to attend Parliament in London, they set up an independent assembly in Dublin. The police in Ireland lacked the strength to re-impose government control and British troops and paramilitary auxiliaries were sent to support them. This signalled the start of a vicious guerrilla war between British forces and the Irish Republican Army (IRA). War veterans were prominent among the combatants on both sides.

By the spring of 1921, it was clear that the use of force had not only alienated the Irish population but was also deeply unpopular in England. At government request, the king made a speech in Belfast, calling for a truce. This was agreed in July. In October two months of negotiations began in London, resulting in the Anglo-Irish Treaty. Ireland was reconstituted as the Irish Free State: a Dominion of the British Empire. One of the Irish authors of the treaty, Michael Collins, described it as the 'freedom to achieve freedom'. But the six predominately Protestant counties of Ulster exercised an opt-out clause meaning that the island was divided. The 'Free State' also failed to satisfy the more militant Republicans, who could not accept Dominion status. In April 1922 a civil war erupted between the Provisional Government and the 'Anti-Treaty' Republicans. A further year of violence followed before an uneasy peace was established.

Opposite: Baghdad, 1919
Richard Carline, 1919
Richard Carline's painting offers an aerial view of Baghdad, the capital of the newly-created British Mandate of Iraq. In 1920, British forces crushed an Arab insurgency there. To head off further disorder, Britain installed their leading wartime Arab ally, Feisal, as king. The aerial perspective of Carline's painting prefigured a novel development in Britain's new middle-eastern Mandates. The suppression of the 1920 revolt had cost more money than Britain's entire wartime campaign in the region. In an attempt to reduce the cost of maintaining 'order' in this troublesome new possession, Britain adopted a policy known as 'Air Control'. At any sign of unrest, Royal Air Force planes would drop warning leaflets before bombing property and livestock. The need to introduce this cost-saving method of imperial policing was evidence of the strain which Britain was experiencing in holding its expanded empire together.

Fighting Continues

The Armistice of 1918 had brought peace to the Western Front, but fighting was to continue in the Middle East, Eastern Europe and Russia into the early 1920s.

In Eastern Europe, most of the new nations created by the peace conference, along with defeated Germany and Hungary, fought local wars to establish their borders. This extended the misery of war for their inhabitants. The many Jewish citizens of the former Hapsburg Empire also suffered; finding themselves effectively stateless in countries founded upon ethnic identity.

An ethnically based state also arose from the wreckage of the Ottoman Empire. Under the command of Mustapha Kemal, a hero of the Turkish victory at Gallipoli, the Turks drove occupying Greek forces from their territory, faced down Britain, and effectively overturned the peace treaty imposed upon them. A new treaty, signed at Lausanne in 1923, gave Turkey complete sovereignty over its territory. In its aftermath a ruthless forced transfer of ethnic minority populations between Greece and Turkey took place; adding to the horror of massacres had which had occurred during the expulsion of the Greek Army.

In Germany, irregular military units – the *Freikorps* – were used to fight for control of disputed sections of the border with Poland. These right wing paramilitary formations also played a violent role within Germany itself. During the immediate post-war period the Social Democrat government colluded with the Army and the *Freikorps* to suppress revolutionary disorder. Its Minister of Defence, Gustav Noske took on this task with zeal: 'Someone must be the bloodhound. I won't shirk the responsibility.' Significantly, the bulk of the German public accepted the extreme violence with which accompanied the process as the price of the return to 'normality'.

Worse still was the situation in Russia, where a bloody civil war raged. The Bolsheviks were threatened on many sides by the forces of their political enemies. Their regime survived because they controlled the industrial and communications hubs of Moscow and Petrograd and because their enemies lacked co-ordination. Russia's wartime allies sent forces to support the so-called 'White' counter-revolutionary armies, yet lacked the political will to intervene decisively. The Bolsheviks had to beat off internal threats to their rule from both the Right and the Left,

Right: This **poster** calls for support in the Russian Bolshevik government's fight for survival, asking 'What have you done for the Front?' By 1920 the Bolshevik Red Army, marshalled by Leon Trotsky, had defeated all of the Bolsheviks' powerful but disunited enemies. The main threat to communist rule came from the armies of 'White' counter-revolutionaries. But the Bolsheviks also had to crush left wing opposition from the Social Revolutionary 'Greens' who enjoyed strong support in rural areas, and from an Anarchist army in Ukraine. During 1920–1921, a Polish invasion was repulsed, and a short-lived Ukrainian People's Republic was brought under control, along with breakaway states in the Caucasus and Central Asia.

Left: This **poster** calls for recruits for Freikorps Hülsen; one of the many right wing militias which played a violent role in immediate post-war Germany. Both the government and a majority of the German people proved willing to turn a blind eye to the brutality of such paramilitary formations. They believed that the alternative was the 'Bolshevism' seen in Russia. The poster calls upon the potential recruit to 'Protect your Homeland. Enrol in the Hülsen Freikorps'. This unit took part in the suppression of left wing uprisings in Berlin in early 1919. Many *Freikorps* recruits were actually youngsters who had 'missed out' on fighting in the war itself and now belatedly sought its excitement. One Freikorps member was heard to say 'People told us that the war was over. That made us laugh. We ourselves are the war.'

and then repulse a Polish invasion. However by 1922 they had brought breakaway states in Ukraine, the Caucasus and Central Asia under their control and the Union of Soviet Socialist Republics (USSR) was created. The Russian civil war cost between nine and fourteen million lives. Only a minority of these perished in battle, most died in massacres, of disease, or from starvation caused by government requisitioning of food from the countryside to feed the cities.

The establishment of communist rule in Russia raised fears of revolution in the West. Both Hungary and, briefly, Bavaria in Germany became Soviet Republics during 1919. These succumbed to violent counter-revolutions from the Right in both countries, but communism posed a more difficult challenge for Democratic governments. Lenin's calls for workers' control of production and land for peasants had a potentially wide appeal and many in the West sympathised with the ideals promoted by the new regime in Russia. The leaders of democratic nations, including Britain, found themselves caught in a dilemma; being unable either to overthrow or to befriend the new Russia. But they took care to forestall revolution at home by making reforms to working conditions and social security payments.

Into the Future

The 1920s saw a partial end to the political instability brought about by the war, yet also a worrying portent for the future – the installation of a fascist government in Italy, led by Benito Mussolini. The Italian Fascist movement grew out of anger at the perceived lack of reward for Italy's costly participation in the war, and also reflected fears of the increasing power of the Left amongst Italy's industrial workers and peasants. Mussolini took advantage of the situation, promoting policies which the Italian establishment and business community found reassuring, while using his paramilitary 'Blackshirts' to launch violent attacks on his political opponents. Following the grandly-titled 'March on Rome' by his supporters in October 1922, Mussolini was handed leadership of the Italian government by the king. By 1924 he had established himself as dictator.

Little international concern was expressed at this development, which many hoped would bring stability to Italy. Overall the decade appeared to be witnessing improvements in this regard. Russia was too preoccupied

Right: The frozen corpses of victims of a Bolshevik massacre, displayed at Omsk in Siberia. Massacres and other atrocities were carried out by both sides in the Russian Civil War, as the Bolsheviks and their enemies attempted to purge the country of their political or class-enemies. Some anti-Bolshevik units also took the opportunity to commit atrocities against Western Russia's large Jewish population. British and US soldiers were sent to both Siberia and North Russia; the Japanese intervened in the far-east of Russia, while the French established a presence in Ukraine. However, the most important foreign force turned out to be the Czech Legion, formed of over 50,000 former Austro-Hungarian prisoners of war of the Russians, who seized control of much of Siberia during 1918.

Right: **Benito Mussolini** is pictured here, incongruously attired in spats, alongside some of his 'Blackshirt' supporters at the time of the Fascist **'March on Rome'** in October 1922. The Blackshirts, or Squadristi, were composed of a mixture of war veterans and young men who wished they had been old enough to fight. They had cut their teeth in strike-breaking and violence against the left wing press and politicians. Now they sought to seize power. The march was undertaken by only 30,000 of Mussolini's followers, but the king – fearing civil war – would not permit the Army to intervene. Mussolini himself did not take part in the march, but waited anxiously at his headquarters in Milan until a telegram sent on behalf of the king called him to Rome to form a government.

NOTGELD DER STADT DUISBURG

50 Billionen Mark 50

zahlen gegen diesen Schein dem Einlieferer die städtische Sparkasse, die Stadthauptkasse und die Zw...len dieser Kassen in Duisburg

Der Aufruf des Duisburger Staatnotgeldes erfolgt unter Angabe der Einlieferungsfrist in den Duisburger Tageszeitungen. Mit dem Ablauf der Einlösungsfrist verliert dieser Schein seine Gültigkeit

DUISBURG, den 15. September 1923

Der Oberbürgermeister I.V.

A 190 010

Left: This **German note** is an example of a type of emergency currency known as *Notgeld*, issued by local councils or savings banks when supplies of money from the central bank were interrupted. During the war *Notgeld* had taken the place of metal coinage, which was in short supply. In 1923 it came into use again when the massive inflation sparked by the Ruhr crisis meant that banknotes could not be printed quickly enough to meet demand. The denomination of this note – 50 billion marks – is a testament to the runaway nature of the inflation. The hyperinflation added to the financial suffering which ordinary people had already endured due to wartime inflation. Small savings were wiped out and Germany's young democracy was discredited in the eyes of many.

with rebuilding to pay much attention to spreading revolution. Following the death of Lenin in 1924, Josef Stalin established himself as Soviet leader – embarking on a policy of 'Communism in one country'. His ambitious programmes for the development of industry and agriculture, brutally pursued with no consideration for the suffering of those involved, were to begin the transformation of the USSR into a great power.

Germany had snuffed out revolution within its borders, but had difficulties in maintaining a vigorous democratic government. A series of short-lived governments left the country badly placed to cope with long-term challenges. However, all German politicians agreed on one issue: opposition to the reparation payments imposed by the Treaty of Versailles. Failure to maintain adequate payments provoked a Franco-Belgian occupation of the Ruhr industrial region in 1923, which looked to take steel and coal as a substitute for unpaid reparations. Miners in the Ruhr reacted by striking, and were supported by government subsidies. The strain on the economy caused hyperinflation in Germany.

This crisis brought a new and forceful German politician to prominence. Gustav Stresemann set about restoring Germany's international position; calling off the Ruhr strike and confirming Germany's adherence to the Versailles treaty. This enabled him to negotiate a new reparations deal, under which Germany would be assisted by loans raised in the USA. By the time of his death in 1929 Germany was enjoying stability and rapid economic growth. But his work was about to be undone by the worldwide economic slump which spread in the wake of the Wall Street Crash.

Waiting in the wings to take advantage of this new crisis was the National Socialist German Workers' Party, a Fascist organisation with a paramilitary wing. It was led by an Austrian-born veteran of the Western Front, Adolf Hitler. Hitler had built his party on the basis of extreme nationalism, antisemitism, resentment at Germany's defeat, and repudiation of the Treaty of Versailles. It had begun as a party of outsiders, and Hitler's 1923 attempt to seize power in Bavaria had been suppressed with ease. Following a prison sentence, Hitler turned to seeking power by electoral means; although still with the violent assistance of his 'Brownshirt' paramilitary supporters. The prosperity of the late 1920s brought a downturn in his party's fortunes and it was the economic catastrophe of the Great Depression that revived Hitler's push for power, culminating in his election as Chancellor of Germany in 1933.

But in 1929 – ten years after the Paris Peace Conference – these developments lay in the future. Europe was at peace, and its people could legitimately hope that, as far as they were concerned, this situation would continue indefinitely. A decade of reflection was by this time resulting in much public soul-searching as to the meaning and worth of the what was then known as 'The Great War' or 'The World War'. Novels, memoirs, poetry and films all contributed to the debate over the next few years. In Britain in particular, the validity of the whole war came into question – even in the pages of newspapers that had been amongst its most fervent supporters.

Yet the British people were in a unique position. Unlike their wartime allies, they had never endured enemy occupation. Unlike several of Europe's nations, they did not owe their independent existence to the war. Unlike the Germans, they did not smart from the humiliation of defeat. This allowed them to view the war with more detachment than their neighbours. There was an upsurge in pacifism and anti-war sentiment; although this was not entirely at odds with the predominant mood that the sacrifices made would prove worthwhile if the Great War did prove to be the 'war to end all wars'. The people of Britain were united in their determination to hold on to the peace which their victory had won. They shared the hopes of their king, expressed at the opening of the Imperial War Museum in June 1920, that it was now possible to 'look back upon war, its instruments, and its organisation, as belonging to a dead past'.

Overleaf: In the years immediately following the war, balls, such as the fancy-dress one for 1925 publicised by this **poster**, were held to celebrate the victory of 1918. At this time formal remembrance of the war dead in state or religious ceremonies was not the only way in which British people engaged with the war's legacy. Church attendance actually declined – people's faith had been shaken by the war. Increasing numbers turned to spiritualism, attempting to contact lost loved ones in séances. By contrast many veterans used Armistice Day as an opportunity to meet up and talk over their wartime experiences. The accompanying drinks frequently helped to turn these meetings into riotous occasions. Such jollification increasingly met with public disapproval and attracted criticism from the press. A more sombre approach to Armistice Day had become the norm by the late 1920s.

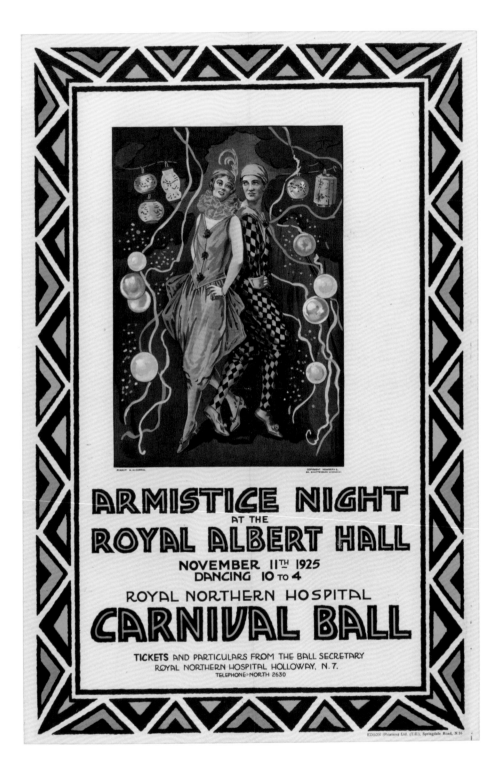

FURTHER READING

1914–1918: The History of the First World War
David Stevenson (Penguin, 2012)

Forgotten Victory: The First World War, Myth and Realities
Gary Sheffield (Headline Book Publishing, 2001)

The First World War: A Very Short Introduction
Michael Howard (OUP Oxford, 2007)

The First World War
Hew Strachan (Simon & Schuster, 2003)

The Great War
Ian FW Beckett (Routledge, 2007)

The Great War: Myth and Memory
Dan Todman (London: Hambledon Continuum, 2007)

The Imperial War Museum Book of the First World War
Malcolm Brown (London: Sidgwick & Jackson, 1991)

The Imperial War Museum Book of the Western Front
Malcolm Brown (London: Sidgwick & Jackson, 1993).
Republished in paperback by Pan in 2001.

The Myriad Faces of War: Britain and the Great War, 1914–1918
Trevor Wilson (Cambridge: Polity Press, 1986).
Republished by Faber & Faber in 2010.

Tommy: the British Soldier on the Western Front, 1914–1918
Richard Holmes (London: HarperCollins, 2004)

ACKNOWLEDGEMENTS

This book is based on the content of IWM London's First World War Galleries, and on the research conducted in the course of their creation by the following team:

Matt Brosnan, Laura Clouting, Paul Cornish, Ian Kikuchi, Louise Macfarlane, Sophie Piggott, James Taylor.

The historical content of the galleries, and by extension this book, has been created in consultation with the following advisory board:

Sir Hew Strachan, All Souls College, Oxford (Chair)

Professor David Reynolds, Christ's College, Cambridge

Professor David Stevenson, London School of Economics

Dr Deborah Thom, Robinson College, Cambridge

Dr Dan Todman, Queen Mary University of London

Further thanks are due to Terry Charman, Nigel Steel, Rebecca Wakeford, the late Rod Suddaby and the curators of the museum's Collections and Research Division.

Thanks also to Madeleine James, Caitlin Flynn and Elizabeth Bowers in the Publishing team, Naomi Korn for advice on intellectual property, and the IWM Design team.

PICTURE CREDITS

All images © IWM unless otherwise stated. Every effort has been made to contact all copyright holders, the publishers will be glad to make good in future editions any error or omissions brought to their attention.

8 (Q9509), 13 (UNI 12422), 14 (MOD 49), 15 (Q81819), 16 (Q81771), 17 (Q81486), 19 (EPH 2937), 21 (Q81831), 23 (IWM PST 5755), 24 (IWM PST 6962), 27 (EPH 6284), 28 top (IWM PST 9324) © Artist's Estate, 28 bottom (IWM PST 9323) © Artist's Estate, 30 top (Access_003114_2), 30 bottom (ORD 125), 31 (MUN 397), 32 (UNI 14089), 33 (FLA 426), 34 (HU 57551), 35 (FLA 5433), 36¬–37 (Q51489), 38 (UNI 12214), 39 top (Q65817), 39 bottom (Q45995), 40 top (Q56325)© Artist's Estate, 40 bottom (Documents_021924_A_1) © Estate of Eric E Rowden, 41 (Q 11718), 43 left (Q53271), 43 right (IWM ART 6158) © Estate of Grace Digby, 45 (EPH 4083), 46 (FIR 10668), 48 top (IWM PST 0318), 48 bottom left (IWM PST 5111), 48 bottom centre (IWM PST 0408), 48 bottom right (IWM PST 2666), 49 top left (IWM PST 0950), 49 top centre (IWM PST 13657), 49 top right (IWM PST 5096), 49 bottom (IWM PST 13601), 50 top left (IWM PST 12437), 50 top centre (IWM PST 0355), 50 top right (IWM PST 12541), 50 bottom (IWM PST 2727), 51 (UNI 12205), 52 (Q111826), 53 top left (INS 7635), 53 top centre (INS 7638), 53 top right (INS 7629), 53 centre left (INS 7631), 53 centre right (INS 7265), 53 bottom left (INS 7359), 53 bottom right (INS 7641), 54 (84/2687), 56 (EPH 9387), 57 (EX.872), 58 (Q 2969), 59 (EPH 2171), 60 (EPH 5245), 61 (Documents.13978/A) © Estate of Alfie Knight, 64 (FEQ 366), 65 (EQU 3926), 66 left (ORD 32), 66 right (ORD 27), 67 (WEA 2157), 68 left (MUN 3222), 68 right (WEA 685), 69 (UNI 6105), 71 (Q50687), 72 (FEQ 874), 74–75 (Q 29001), 76 (EQU 3812), 77 (Q17390), 79 (FLA 174), 80 (Q82506 © Artist's Estate), 81 (EPH 9031), 82 (PST 2756) © Artist's Estate, 83 (FIR 9269), 84–85 (Q98441) © Artist's Estate, 86 far left (Art Ephem 516), 86 top left (Art Ephem 505), 86 top centre left (Art Ephem 504), 86 top centre right (Art Ephem 503) © Estate of Hans Pollack, 86 top right (Art Ephem 510) © Estate of Erich Heermann, 86 bottom left (Art Ephem 512) © Estate of Erich Heermann, 86 bottom centre (Art Ephem 508), 86 bottom right (Art Ephem 507)© Estate of Karl Holleck-Weithman, 87 (Q15625), 89 (EPH 951), 90 (HU 50622), 91 (HU 95127) © Sergeant Percy Elgey, 93 (PST 0501) © Estate of L A R, 94–95 (Q52297), 98 (SP2036), 99 (UNI 11978), 100 (Q114833) © Artist's Estate, 105 (IWM PST 8365), 107 top left (INS 8381), 107 top right (INS 8386), 107 centre left (INS 8377), 107 centre right (INS 8370), 107 bottom left (INS 7811), 107 bottom right (INS 7809), 109 (Documents.17742/A) © Martin Catford, 110 (Q 103334), 111 (IWM PST 5112), 112–113 (Q30018), 115 (EPH 3255), 116 (UNI 10345), 117 (HU 70114), 120 (IWM PST 12772), 121 (Q 54534), 123 (ORD 108), 124 (FIR 9151), 125 top left (HU 112461), 125 top right (UNI 8199), 125 bottom (HU 112462), 126–127 (Q79501), 129 top (CO 827), 129 bottom (UNI 10830), 130–131 (Q823), 132 (UNI 288), 135 (IWM ART 2121), 136 (Q 27637), 137 (Q 27639), 138 (IWM ART 2378), 143 (IWM PST 0435), 144 (EPH 4126), 145 (UNI 12729), 146 top (Q 19640), 146 bottom (INS 8391), 147 (93/242), 148 (IWM PST 10244), 150 (EPH 2212), 151 left (EPH 907), 151 right (Q 58470), 152 (Documents.9614), 154 (MOD 2005) (MOD 2037) (MOD 2205) (MOD 2164), 155 (MOD 2009) (MOD 2093) (MOD 2098) (MOD 2022), 156 (IWM PST 0515), 159 (IWM PST 3284), 162 (FIR 55), 164 left (EQU 714), 164 right (EPH 4379), 165 top (Q 1617), 165 bottom (EPH 8524), 166 (EQU 3904), 167 (FEQ 384), 168 (EPH 8262), 169 (Q 31576), 170 (EPH

INDEX

Page numbers in *italics* refer to illustration captions

A

aerial photography *137*
Afghanistan 88
Africa 14, 87–88 *see also* South Africa
air raids 149–150, *150*, *151*
aircraft *151*, 179–180, *180*, *181*, 217
   Zeppelins 149, *150*, *151*
Alsatian, HMS 97
America *see* USA
Amiens, Battle of (1918) *222*
ammunition 177, *177*
   advances in 29, *31*, *39*
   gas shells 76
   shell shortage 111–116
Amritsar riots (1919) 234
Anglo-Irish Treaty (1921) 237
Annunzio, Gabriele d' *92*
anti-British feeling 60
anti-German feeling 59, *60*, *104*
antisemitism 42, 237
Arabic (liner) 98
Armenians 81–82
armistice 221–227, 229–231, *243*
armour 69–70
Arras, Battle of (1917) 182
artillery *39*, *123*, 177–178
   advances in 29, *30*
   trench artillery 66, *66*
artists 185
   CRW Nevinson *189*
   Muirhead Bone *134*
   Norman Wilkinson *155*
   Paul Nash 185, *191*
   Richard Carline *237*
   William Orpen *139*, *231*
Asquith, Prime Minister Herbert 25, 142
   forms an all-party coalition 114
   on potential allies 91
Australia 14, 47
   Battle of the Somme (1916) 128
   conscription 111
   Gallipoli 88–89, *89*, 90
   national identity 234

Austria-Hungary 13, 18
   assassination of Archduke Franz Ferdinand *20*, 20–22
   the breakdown of the Army 197, *198*
   early failures 33
   the effect of war on civilians 42
   in Galicia 121–122
   life on the home front 203–207, *207*
   secret peace talks 194
   silk ribbons *86*
   surrender of 223–226
   the Triple Alliance 91
   troop numbers 27
   war plans 31

B

badges 53
Bahadur, Kalander Khan *91*
Balfour Declaration (1917) 237
Balkan Wars (1912–1913) 22, 79
barbed wire 65, 177, *177*
Barham, HMS *101*
battles
   Amiens (1918) *222*
   Arras (1917) 182
   Cambrai (1917) 184
   Caporetto (1917) 197
   Gallipoli 88–89, *89*, *90*
   Jutland (1916) 99–101
   Le Cateau (1914) 35
   Loos (1915) 73, *73*, 76
   the Marne, First Battle of (1914) 33, *33*, 35, *35*
   the Marne, Second Battle of (1918) 218
   Masurian Lakes (1914) 34
   Megiddo (1918) 223
   Messines Ridge (1917) 183
   Mons (1914) 35
   Romani (1916) *79*
   the Somme (1916) 122–132, *123*, *124*, *125*, *127*, *129*, 133, 134, *137*, *139*, 177
   Tannenberg (1914) 34

Verdun (1916) 119–121, *120*, 133, 182
Ypres, First Battle of (1914) 35, *35*, *38*, *40*
Ypres, Second Battle of (1915) 73
Ypres, Third Battle of (1917) 183–185, *185*, *189*, *191*
Bavaria 240
Beatty, Admiral David 99, 199
Beddington-Behrens, Lieutenant Edward 128
Bedford, Madeline Ida 114–115
Belgium 23, 35
   German atrocities 42–43, *43*, 59
   and the Treaty of Versailles (1919) 231
Bell, Gertrude 235
Best, Lieutenant Jack *132*
Bilbrough, Ethel 104, 108
Binding, Rudolf 213
Bishop, Billy 180
'Black Hand, The' 22
Blackadder, Major Robert 183
Blows, Corporal Oswald 128, 220
Board, Vyvyan 64
Boehm, General Max von 219
Bolshevik Party, Russia 209, *211*, *238*, 238–240, *240*
Bone, Muirhead *134*
Boon, Captain Ernest 184
Borton, Laura *227*
Bosnia 20, *20*, 33
Bottomley, Horatio 59, *104*
Bradley, Thomas 99–100
Brazil 229
Breslau (German ship) 80
Brest Litovsk, Treaty of (1918) 209
Brice, Private John *129*
Britain 13
   anti-German feeling 59, *60*, *104*
   anti-war sentiment 193
   armistice *227*
   badges *53*
   the British Empire 14–18, 233–237

casualty rates 38, 124, *124*, 157, 194
conscription 108, 110–111
the counter to Germany's global
    strategy 87–90
Defence of the Realm Act (DORA)
    103–104
enters the war 23–25
industry and production 15, 16,
    106–108, 114–116, 145, 149, 233
leadership changes 142–144
life on the home front 45–61,
    103–104, *144*, 144–157, *145*, *147*,
    148, 199–203, *201*
the Morocco crisis 20
patriotism 16, 45, *45*, 46–47, *48*, *49*,
    50, 51
post-war changes in 233–237, 243
propaganda 59, *226*
recruitment 106–108
religion in 16, *243*
reserved occupations 106, *106*
shell shortage 111–116
taxation and its effects 55, 104, 148
uniforms and equipment 38, *51*, *53*,
    65, *69*, *76*, *129*, 163, *164*, *176*
the war at sea 96–101
war winning plans 119
British Legion, the *234*
British Red Cross, the 55, 56
Brittain, Vera 68, 145
Brodie, John *69*
Brooks, Albert 104
Brooks, Mr E *108*
brothels 171
Brusilov, General Alexei 121, *121*, 122
Bucharest, Treaty of (1918) 209
Bulgaria 91, 92, 221
    surrender of 223

C
Cadorna, Luigi 91–92
Cambrai, Battle of (1917) 184
camouflage 70–72
Canada 14, 47
    Battle of the Somme (1916) 128, *129*
    casualty rates 128
    conscription 111
    national identity 234
Caporetto, Battle of (1917) 197
Carline, Richard *237*
casualty rates 38, 121, 124, *124*, 128,
    133, 157, 194, 229

Caucasus, the 81, *238*, 240
Cavell, Edith 57, *57*
Cendrars, Blaise 68
Chair, Rear Admiral Sir Dudley de 96,
    97
Chandler, Doctor Frederick 55, *167*
Changuinola, HMS 98
charities, for war relief 55–56
Childers, Erskine 14
children, and the war effort 146
China, and the Treaty of Versailles
    (1919) 231
Chinese Labour Corps 166
Chisholm, Mairi 57
chlorine gas *73*, *76*
Christmas Gift Boxes 55, *56*
Christmas Truce (1914) *40*, *41*
Churchill, Winston 59, 88
Clark, Andrew *54*
class distinction, in Britain 16
clubs 67, *67*
Collins, Michael 237
communication trenches 64
communications 178
Comrades of the Great War *234*
Conan Doyle, Sir Arthur 59, 69, *127*
Congreve, General Sir Walter *125*
Connolly, James 151, *152*
conscientious objectors *110*, 111
conscription 27, 108, 110–111, *158*
Consett-Stephen, Lieutenant Adrian
    123, 128
convoy system, the 157, 158
Cooke, Private Stanley *79*
Cooper, Ethel 207
Cope, Second Lieutenant Harold *129*
correspondence, importance of *173*
Cosens, Monica 115
Cotton, Elmer 73
CSRG automatic rifles 177–178
Curzon, Lord 14
Czechoslovakia 233

D
Daily Express 108
Daily Mail 19, 111
Daily Mirror 142–144
Dale, Bombadier George 89
Dane, Edmund 65
Daphne de Marie 47
Dardanelles campaign, the 88, *89*, *90*

Defence of the Realm Act (DORA)
    103–104
demobilisation 234
Denmark 231
Derwent Wood, Francis *232*
Desagneaux, Lieutenant Henri 120
desertion 167
Dillon, Captain Harry 38
discipline, at the front 167
Donaldson, Captain Geoffrey *76*
Dreadnought, HMS 19
Dunn, James *33*

E
Egypt 81, 236
    Native Labour Battalions 166
Emden (German ship) *81*
'enemy aliens' *104*

F
Fairfax, Lieutenant Colonel Bryan *125*
Falkenhayn, Erich von 34, 35, 83, 119,
    121, 134, 141
Falkland Islands 82
Fayolle, General Émile 65
Feilding, Captain Rowland *64*, 128,
    176, *177*, 213
Feisal, King of Iraq *237*
Ferdinand, Archduke Franz,
    assassination of (1914) *20*, 20–22
Finland 233
fire trenches 64
Fisher, Herbert 146
Foch, General Ferdinand 215, 217,
    218, *219*
Fonck, René 180
food shortages 199–207, *201*, *202*
Four Feathers, The (Mason) 108
France 13, 18
    casualty rates 121
    conscription 27
    early German victories in 33
    the effect of war on civilians 42
    enters the war 23
    the Morocco crisis 20
    mutiny in the Army 196
    and the Treaty of Versailles (1919)
        231
    uniforms and equipment 27, *27*, *32*,
        125
    war plans 31, 32, 119
    weapon advances 29, *30*

Franz Josef, Emperor of Austria-
    Hungary 13, 194
Freikorps, the 238, *239*
French, Sir John 35, 111, 122
Fryatt, Charles 57
Furse, General William *132*

G
Gallipoli 88–89, *89*, *90*
Gandhi, Mohandas 234
Garry, Private Kenneth *70*
gas *73*, 73–76, *76*
George V, King of England 56, *235*
Germany 13, 20
    anti-British feeling 60
    anti-war sentiment 193–194
    armistice 221–227
    atrocities 42–43
    backs Austria-Hungary in war 22
    casualty rates 121, 133
    early victories 33
    the effect of war on civilians 42
    the *Freikorps* 238, *239*
    the German Empire 18–20
    global strategy 79–83
    hyperinflation in 242, *242*
    industry and production 15, *19*
    leadership changes 141–142
    life on the home front 142, *202*,
        203–207, *205*, *208*
    medals 59
    naval race 19
    patriotism 60
    propaganda *28*
    silk ribbons *86*
    and the Treaty of Versailles (1919)
        231, 242, 243
    the Triple Alliance 91
    uniforms and equipment *40*, *132*, *213*
    the war at sea 96–101
    war plans 31, 32, 34, 119–122
Gift Boxes 55, *56*
Gillies, Harold *232*
Goeben (German ship) 80
Gotha bombers *151*
Gould Lee, Arthur *180*
Great Britain *see* Britain
'Great Retreat, the,' Russia 83, *83*
Greece 91, 92, 238
Greenwell, Captain Graham 163
grenades 67, *68*, *76*

Gurney, Ivor 168–171
Gwyer, Margaret *99*

H
Haig, General Sir Douglas *219*
    Battle of Amiens (1918) 218
    Battle of Cambrai (1917) 184
    Battle of the Somme (1916) 123
    becomes commander of the British
        Army 122
    believes that the Allies are beaten
        215, 217
    and the British Legion *234*
    First Battle of Ypres (1914) *35*
    predicts the end of the war 220
    Third Battle of Ypres (1917) 183
hairbrush grenades *68*
Hammond, Barbara 144
Hampshire, HMS 116
Hapsburg dynasty, the 13
Hassell, Second Lieutenant Gordon
    175, *176*
helmets 69, *69*, *76*, *125*, *132*, *176*, *213*
Henson, Herbert Hensley *127*
Hercules, HMS *14*
Hesse, Herman 211
Hindenburg, Paul von 34, *34*, 134,
    141–142, *142*, 153
'Hindenburg Line,' the 134, 142, 220,
    220
Hitler, Adolf 243
Hollister, Joe *145*
Holy War *80*, 80–81
home front, life on the
    in Britain 45–61, 103–104, *144*,
        144–157, *145*, *147*, *148*, 199–203,
        200, *201*
    in Germany 142, *202*, 203–207, *205*,
        208
Hötzendorf, General Franz Conrad
    von 31
Hungary 240 *see also* Austria-Hungary
Hurley, Captain Frank 185
hygiene, at the front 163–164

I
India 14
    the Indian Army 38, *40*, 47, *91*, *132*
    nationalism in 234
    Native Labour Battalions 166
Inglis, Dr Elsie 57
Iran 88

Iraq 88, 89, *91*, 197, 235, 236, *237*
Ireland 111
    Easter Rising 150–151, *152*
    Irish Home Rule 16, 18, 237
    Irish Republican Army (IRA) 237
    Ulster Volunteer Force 16
Isbert, General August 223
Italy 13, 18, 23
    the breakdown of the Army 197, *198*
    enters the war 91–92, *92*
    fascism in 240, *240*
    occupation of Libya 81
    and the Treaty of Versailles (1919)
        231

J
Jack, Captain James 25, 66, *124*, 163
Jackson, Alexander Young 234
Japan 82
    and the League of Nations 231
Jellicoe, Admiral John 100–101, 153
jihad 80, 80–81
Joffre, Joseph 31, 33, 119, 182
John Bull 104, *110*
Jones, Private Charles 51
Jordan 235
Jutland, Battle of (1916) 99–101

K
Kemal, Mustapha 238
Kipling, Rudyard 59
Kitchener, Lord Horatio Herbert 45,
    45, 106, 111, 114, 116, 171
Knight, Alfie 60
knitting, for the war effort 54, 55
knives, as weapons 68, *68*
Knocker, Elsie *57*

L
Lansdowne, Lord 193
Lausanne, Treaty of (1923) 238
Lawrence, T. E. 'Lawrence of Arabia'
    199
Le Cateau, Battle of (1914) 35
League of Nations 231–233
Lebanon 235
Leefe-Robinson, William 149
Leighton, Roland 68
Lenin, Vladimir 209, *211*, 240, 242
letters from home, importance of *173*
Lewis Guns 177–178, *178*
Libya 81

Lissauer, Ernst 60
Livens Projector 76
Lloyd George, David
    on aircraft 179
    becomes Prime Minister 142–144
    on Britain's drinking culture 104
    on British trade at the onset of war
        45
    and the Morocco crisis 20
    munitions production 114, *115*, 116
    and the unions 115, 149
    wins the 1918 election *235*
    and women's war work 108
Lomax, Reverend Cyril *173*
London, Treaty of (1915) 91
Loos, Battle of (1915) 73, *73, 76*
Lovett, Edward *171*
Loyd, Lieutenant Geoffrey 38
Ludendorff, Erich 34, *34*
    advises continuation of the war 223
    mental collapse of 221
    orders construction of the
        'Hindenburg Line' 134
    resignation of 226
    strategy in 1918 213, *217*, 218
    the U-boat blockade 153, 213
    and the war effort 141–142
Lusitania (liner), the sinking of 97, *99*

M
MacDonagh, Thomas *152*
Macedonian Front, the 92
machine guns *124, 175*, 177
Malaviya, Madan Mohan 234
Malaya, HMS *101*
Manchester Guardian, the *89*
Marne, First Battle of the (1914) 33,
    33, 35, *35*
Marne, Second Battle of the (1918) 218
Martin, Albert *235*
Martin, Vincent 31
Masterman, Charles 185
Masurian Lakes, Battle of the (1914) 34
Mathy, Kapitän-Leutnant Heinrich *150*
Matthews, Lady Annette 55
Maxim machine guns *83*
May, Captain Charles *169*
McCudden, Major James *179*
McNeal, Reverend George 46
medals, German *59*
Megiddo, Battle of (1918) 223

Mesopotamia (Iraq) 88, 89, *91*, 197,
    235, 236, *237*
Messines Ridge, Battle of (1917) 183
Mexico 157
MG 08 machine gun *124*
Military Service Act (1917) 110
Mills Bomb, the *76*
Minnie, Elsie 47
Mohan, Corporal Talbot 219
Moltke, General Helmuth von 22, 32
    and the Battle of the Marne (1914)
        33
    suffers a mental breakdown 34
Mons, Battle of (1914) 35
Montagu, Edwin 133, 144
Morocco 20
mortars 66, *66*
Mountford, Lance Corporal Roland
    163
Mrizah, Shah *132*
Müller, Karl von *81*
Munitions of War Act (1915) 115
'Munitions Wages' (poem) 114–115
music hall singers 47
Mussolini, Benito 240, *240*
mustard gas 76
mutinies 196–197

N
Nash, Paul 185, *191*
Native Labour Battalions 166
naval blockade, the 96–97
Nevinson, CRW *189*
New Zealand 14, 47
    Battle of the Somme (1916) 128
    conscription 111
    Gallipoli 88–89, *89, 90*
Nicholas II, Tsar of Russia *13*, 209
    prepares for war 22–23
Nikolai, Grand Duke 31
Nivelle, General Robert 182, 196
Noske, Gustav 238
nursing, women and 57, *57, 144*,
    144–145

O
officers 161–164, *162*, 167
Orpen, William *139, 231*
Ottoman Empire, the 79–82, 88–89,
    235–236

P
Palestine 197, 223, 235, 236–237
Palmers and Jarrow *14*
Pankhurst, Christabel 106
Pankhurst, Emmeline *16*, 106
Paris Peace Conference 229–233
Parliamentary Recruiting Committee
    (PRC) 49
Passchendaele, Battle of (1917)
    183–185, *185, 189, 191*
Paterson, John *54*
patriotism
    Britain 16, 45, *45*, 46–47, *48, 49, 50*,
        51
    Germany 60
peace 221–227, 229–231, *243*
Pearse, Patrick *152*
periscopes *70*
Pershing, General John 218
Persia (Iran) 88
Pétain, General Philippe 120, 121,
    196, 215
phosgene gas 76
pistols *162*
Plumer, General Herbert 183
Poincaré, President of France 229
Poland 231, 233
poppy appeals *234*
posters
    armistice *243*
    the Battle of Verdun (1916) *120*
    enlistment *23, 47, 49, 50*
    food shortages *201, 205*
    German propaganda *25, 28*
    knitting for the troops *54*
    the manpower problem *111*
    political campaigns *235, 239*
    resource shortages *204*
    the Russian civil war *238*
    the U-boat blockade *157*
    the war effort *208*
PRC (Parliamentary Recruiting
    Committee) 49
Princip, Gavrilo 20, *20*
prisoners of war (POWs) *220, 221, 222*
propaganda
    British 59, *226*
    German *28*
Prussia 13

Q

Quinn, Major Hugh *90*

R

RAF (Royal Air Force) 217
RAPs (Regimental Aid Posts) *167*
rations, at the front *164*
Rawlinson, Sir Henry 218, 220
recreation, at the front *168*, 168–172,
   169, *172*, *173*
Red Cross, the 55, 56
Regimental Aid Posts (RAPs) *167*
religion
   antisemitism 42
   in Britain 16, *243*
   at the front *171*
Remembrance Sunday *234*
Repington, Charles 111
reserved occupations 106, *106*
RFC (Royal Flying Corps) 179–180
Richthofen, Baron Manfred von 180,
   180
Riddle of the Sands, The (Childers) 14,
   20
Rifki, Falih 197
rifles 177–178
RN (Royal Navy) 14, 19, 96–98,
   99–101, 226
RNAS (Royal Naval Air Service)
   179–180
Robertson, General Sir William 89
Romani, Battle of (1916) *79*
Romania 91, 134, 142, 209
Rowden, Corporal Eric *40*
Royal Air Force (RAF) 217
Royal Flying Corps (RFC) 179–180,
   181
Royal Naval Air Service (RNAS)
   179–180
Royal Navy (RN) 14, 19, 96–98,
   99–101, 226
Rupprecht of Bavaria, Crown Prince
   216, 223
Russia *13*, 18, 80, *198*
   in the Caucasus 81
   civil war in 238–240, *240*
   conscription 27
   creation of the Union of Soviet
      Socialist Republics (USSR) 240
   Josef Stalin becomes leader 242
   mobilisation for war 22–23
   offensive in Galicia *121*, 121–122

revolution in 209–211, *211*
'the Great Retreat' 83, *83*
uniforms *13*
war plans 31

S

Sassoon, Siegfried *194*
Schierbrand, Wolf von *207*
Schlieffen Plan, the 31
Schneller, Karl 122
Scottish Women's Hospitals (SWH) 57
Scrimgeour, Alexander 97
Senussi sect, the 81
Serbia 20, 20–22, 33, *92*
   casualty rates 229
   the effect of war on civilians 42
   the occupation of 92
Seymour, Bruce 46
Shaw, James 96–97
shells *see* ammunition
ships
   Arabic (liner) 98
   Breslau (German) 80
   Emden (German) *81*
   Goeben (German) 80
   HMAS *Sydney 81*
   HMS *Alsatian* 97
   HMS *Barham 101*
   HMS *Changuinola 98*
   HMS *Dreadnought* 19
   HMS *Hampshire* 116
   HMS *Hercules* 14
   HMS *Malaya 101*
   HMS *Tiger* 99
   HMS *Valiant 101*
   HMS *Warspite 101*
   Lusitania (liner) 97, *99*
Siberia *240*
Siegfried Position, the 142
Singapore *80*
Snell, Lieutenant Francis 162
snipers 70
Somme, Battle of the (1916) 122–132,
   123, *124*, *125*, *127*, *129*, 133, 134, *137*,
   139, 177
Sopwith Camel aircraft *180*
South Africa 20, 47, *50*, 87–88
   Battle of the Somme (1916) 128
   Native Labour Battalions 166
souvenir hunting *168*, 168–171
Soviet Union *see* Russia
Spee, Admiral Maximilian von 82

Spies of the Kaiser (le Queux) 20
St John Ambulance 56
Stalin, Josef 242
Stresemann, Gustav 242
submarines 153–157, *157*, 158
Suez Canal, the *79*, 80
suffragettes *16*, 18
Suire, Lieutenant Edgar von le 213
Sulzbach, Herbert 227
SWH (Scottish Women's Hospitals) 57
Sydney, HMAS *81*
Syria 235

T

tanks *134*, 175–176, *220*
Tannenberg, Battle of (1914) 34
Tattersall, Lance Corporal Norman
   123, 124
Taylor, Bernard *108*
technology, advances in 29, *30*, *31*, *39*,
   175–178
Tempest, Lieutenant Wulfstan *150*
Thaer, Lieutenant Colonel Albrecht von
   133–134, 183–184
Tiger, HMS 99
Times, The 55, 69–70, 111, *127*
Transjordan (Jordan) 235
treaties
   Anglo-Irish Treaty (1921) 237
   Treaty of Brest Litovsk (1918) 209
   Treaty of Bucharest (1918) 209
   Treaty of Lausanne (1923) 238
   Treaty of London (1915) 91
   Treaty of Versailles (1919) 231, *231*
trench signs *64*
trench warfare 63–77
Triple Alliance, the 91
Trotsky, Leon *238*
tunnels 72, *72*
Turkey 79–82, 238
   the breakdown of the Army 197
   surrender of 223

U

U-boat blockade 153–157, *157*, 158
UDC (Union of Democratic Council)
   193
Ukraine 238, 240
Ulster Volunteer Force *16*
uniforms and equipment
   British *38*, *51*, *53*, *65*, *69*, *76*, *129*,
      163, *164*, *176*

French 27, 27, 32, 125
German 40, 132, 213
Russian 13
USA 218
Union of Democratic Council (UDC) 193
United Kingdom see Britain
USA 13
  conscription 158
  enters the war 157–158
  industry and production 15
  protests against the British naval blockade 97
  and the sinking of the Lusitania 97–98
  uniforms and equipment 218
USSR see Russia

V
Valiant, HMS 101
venereal disease 171
Verdun, Battle of (1916) 119–121, 120, 133, 182
Versailles, Treaty of (1919) 231, 231
veterans' associations 234, 243
Vickers Guns 175
Vimy Ridge 182
Voluntary Aid Detachments (VADs) 144, 145
voluntary organisations, popularity of 56
voting rights, Britain 16, 18, 233

W
Wakefield, Private George 46
Walwyn, Commander Humphrey 101
war bonds 148, 148–149
Warspite, HMS 101
weapons
  advances in 29, 30, 31
  artillery 29, 30, 39, 66, 66, 123, 177–178
  for close combat 67, 67–68
  grenades 67, 68, 76
  machine guns 83, 124, 175, 177
  mortars 66, 66

pistols 162
rifles 177–178
Webley Mark VI revolvers 162
Wells, H G 59
Werner, Grace 117
white feather, as a symbol of cowardice 108
Wien, Private Gilbert 218
Wilhelm II, Kaiser of Germany 13
  abdication of 226
  approves a U-boat blockade 153
  asylum in the Netherlands 235
  believes the war has been won 214
  and the naval race 19, 20
  uniform 13
  war plans 31
  on war with the British 79
Wilkinson, Norman 155
Williams, Company Sergeant-Major William 38
Wilson, General Sir Henry 133
WIlson, Lieutenant Theodore Cameron 168
Wilson, President Woodrow 97, 157–158, 193–194, 221–223, 231, 233
women
  voting rights 16–18, 233
  and the war effort 54, 55, 57, 57, 144–145
  war work 106–108, 114–116, 116, 117, 144, 145, 145, 146
Women's Social and Political Union (WSPU) 16
writers and poets
  Erskine Childers 14
  Falih Rifki 197
  Gertrude Bell 235
  H G Wells 59
  Herman Hesse 211
  Madeline Ida Bedford 114–115
  Rudyard Kipling 59
  Siegfried Sassoon 194
  Sir Arthur Conan Doyle 59, 69, 127
  William le Queux 20
WSPU (Women's Social and Political Union) 16

Y
Young Men's Christian Association (YMCA) 56
Ypres, First Battle of (1914) 35, 35, 38, 40
Ypres, Second Battle of (1915) 73
Ypres, Third Battle of (1917) 183–185, 185, 189, 191
Yugoslavia 233

Z
Zeppelins 149, 150, 151
Zimmermann, Arthur 157
Zouave regiments 27